T0360440

ROUTLEDGE LIBRARY EDITIONS:
PUBLIC ENTERPRISE AND
PRIVATIZATION

Volume 10

PRIVATISATION IN THE UK

PRIVATISATION IN THE UK

Edited by
V.V. RAMANADHAM

Routledge
Taylor & Francis Group

LONDON AND NEW YORK

First published in 1988 by Routledge

This edition first published in 2019
by Routledge
2 Park Square, Milton Park, Abingdon, Oxon OX14 4RN

and by Routledge
52 Vanderbilt Avenue, New York, NY 10017

Routledge is an imprint of the Taylor & Francis Group, an informa business

British Library Cataloguing in Publication Data
A catalogue record for this book is available from the British Library

ISBN: 978-0-367-14233-9 (Set)
ISBN: 978-0-429-25929-6 (Set) (ebk)
ISBN: 978-0-367-18984-6 (Volume 10) (hbk)
ISBN: 978-0-429-19973-8 (Volume 10) (ebk)

Publisher's Note
The publisher has gone to great lengths to ensure the quality of this reprint but points out that some imperfections in the original copies may be apparent.

Disclaimer
The publisher has made every effort to trace copyright holders and would welcome correspondence from those they have been unable to trace.

PRIVATISATION IN THE UK

The Conservatives' privatisation programme is one of the most ambitious aspects of their attempt to redraft the political and economic map of the United Kingdom. This book explores the processes of privatisation from a variety of standpoints. Its contributors include academics, enterprise executives and government officials, many of whom had been closely involved in the programme. Fiscal, legal and social aspects of privatisation are explored but the book treats the subject as more than an immediate political issue and takes the opportunity to discuss the success — or otherwise — of public enterprise and to explore the implication of the UK experience for other countries which have an interest in privatisation.

Privatisation in the UK

♦

Edited by
V.V. RAMANADHAM

ROUTLEDGE
London and New York

First published in 1988 by
Routledge
a division of Routledge, Chapman and Hall
11 New Fetter Lane, London EC4P 4EE

Published in the USA by
Routledge
a division of Routledge, Chapman and Hall, Inc.
29 West 35th Street, New York NY 10001

© 1988 V.V. Ramanadham

Printed and bound in Great Britain by Mackays of Chatham Ltd, Kent

British Library Cataloguing in Publication Data

Privatisation in the UK.
  1. Great Britain. Public sector.
  Privatisation
  I. Ramanadham, V.V.
  354.4107′2
  ISBN 0-415-00150-1

Library of Congress Cataloging-in-Publication Data

ISBN 0-415-00150-1

Contents

Contents

Tables

Figures

Abbreviations

ATM	Air Transport Movement
BA	British Airways
BAe	British Aerospace
BAA	British Airports Authority
BASL	British Airports Services Ltd
BG	British Gas
BL	British Leyland
BP	British Petroleum
BR	British Rail
BT	British Telecom
CAA	Civil Aviation Authority
CCA	Current-cost accounting
C & W	Cable and Wireless
DHSS	Department of Health and Social Security
DLO	Direct Labour Organisation
DSO	Direct Service Organisation
ESI	Electricity Supply Industry
GCC	Gas Consumers' Council
GMB	General Municipal and Boilermakers' Union
IFS	Institute of Fiscal Studies
LDCs	Less developed countries
MMC	Monopolies and Mergers Commission
NAO	National Audit Office
NBC	National Bus Company
NEDO	National Economic Development Office
NHS	National Health Service
NRA	National River Authority
NUPE	National Union of Public Employees
OFGAS	Office of Gas Supply
OFT	Office of Fair Trading
OFTEL	Office of Telecommunications
PAC	Public Accounts Committee
PBX	Private branch exchange
PE	Public enterprise
PLC	Public Limited Company
PSBR	Public Sector Borrowing Requirement
PTA	Passenger Transport Authority
PTE	Passenger Transport Executive
R & D	Research and development
RPI	Retail Price Index
RR	Rolls Royce
T&GWU	Transport and General Workers' Union

Abbreviations

TRRL	Transport and Road Research Laboratory
TUC	Trades Union Congress
WSPLC	Water service public limited company

Preface

This volume contains the papers presented at the Seminar on Privatisation conducted at Templeton College, Oxford, from 22 September to 15 December 1987. The contributors included academics, enterprise executives and government officials. Many of them have been closely involved in the privatisation measures undertaken by the British Government. The topics cover the issues, sectors and processes of privatisation. It is hoped that the wide spectrum of views presented by the papers and the discussions (highlighted in my 'Concluding Review') will convey the essence of the UK experience in privatisation and that the volume will also be of use to other countries which have an interest in privatisation.

I record with grateful thanks the co-operation of the writers of the papers and the discussants and the facilities offered by Templeton College for the conduct of the seminar. I must make special mention of my friend Nick Woodward whose constant help contributed to the successful conclusion of the seminar activity.

Professor V.V. Ramanadham
Editor
Oxford

Part I

The Approach

1

The Concept and Rationale of Privatisation

V.V. Ramanadham*

This is in the nature of an introductory paper for the Seminar on Privatisation. It is in four parts. The first contains a review of the concept of privatisation; the second aims at an analysis of the rationale of privatisation; the third is a brief statement of conclusions; and the fourth outlines the broad range of issues that merit detailed discussion as the seminar progresses. The approach of the paper is analytical; and the occasional empirical references are not limited to the UK experience alone.

THE CONCEPT OF PRIVATISATION

Analytically, if the essence of public enterprise is that it rests on some kind and degree of de-marketisation of enterprise operations, privatisation implies some kind and degree of re-marketisation.[1] The connotation of public enterprise is wide indeed, in terms of both government or public ownership and government or public control. Correspondingly privatisation comprehends a continuum of measures that erase certain or all elements of publicness characterising an enterprise or an economy.

Before looking at the continuum, we may note that there are two levels, not mutually exclusive, at which the concept can be understood: privatisation of the economy, and privatisation of an enterprise.

*   Templeton College, Oxford

The Concept and Rationale of Privatisation

Privatisation of the economy

This represents a policy dimension going beyond the privatisation of an individual enterprise, and involves a decline in the relative extent of public enterprise in the national economy. It can result from

(a) no expansion of public enterprise as private enterprise expands;

(b) an expansion of public enterprise at a lower rate than that at which private enterprise expands; and/or

(c) some reductions in public enterprise such that, irrespective of the rate of new private investments, the private share in the economy tends to be higher than before.

Categories (a) and (b) go along with category (c) in many countries. The relative significance of the third category varies among countries: for example, it is high in the UK, whereas countries like Kenya[2] or India fall within the second category. It is hard to find an exact case under the first category, not even the USA, for it is likely that some expansion, even if very limited, takes place in the public enterprise segment of every country, in some sector or other, though, on the whole, it comes within the description of category three.

There are two directions of privatisation which do not automatically reduce the (absolute) extent of public enterprise in the economy, though, thanks to its own growth, private enterprise tends to occupy a relatively larger share of it. The first is where some public enterprises are privatised - let us say, because they are mature enough not to need continuance in the public sector, e.g. electricity and gas enterprises. At the same time, in certain sectors like chemicals and heavy-machine building, the technological and investment characteristics may - even currently - call for public enterprise initiative. Thus, the two processes of privatisation of certain enterprises, which are of age, and of new public enterprise inceptions in nascent fields, may go on hand in hand. There are elements of national investment planning here, in that certain resources which are available in private hands for investment as they wish are syphoned off into the public exchequer for investment in directions that, by hypothesis, private investors do not take up but are

4

considered important on macro grounds. It is likely that the investment rotation in the public enterprise sector operates in a spiral fashion, such that as the economy matures and progressively marketises itself, the new public investments would be lower than the divestments. Just how much lower is a function of the development status of the country in question: they will be lower, the more advanced the economy and the more buoyant the entrepreneurship.

It is useful to recognise this facet of privatisation; for it can go some way in softening the emotional antipathy that exists in some developing countries to the idea of disbanding public enterprises. It helps to promote pragmatism in the formulation of policies which, far from denying the relevance of public enterprise, underscores the desirability of a change in its sectoral composition over time.

The other aspect of privatisation, which calls for more serious attention than it seems to have attracted, is that a public policy of privatising the economy, i.e. of reducing the relative share of public enterprise in the economy, has the implication, in certain countries, of reducing public investments in non-financial enterprises - such as manufacturing, trading and transport - while increasing public investments in financial enterprises. The latter essentially result from the fact that the aim of promoting private enterprise (and the policy of increasing the private share in the economy) predicates the supply of capital through public sector agencies in some measure. The degree of dependence of private investors on a public financial enterprise varies from country to country; but it is fairly high in countries where investible savings from private enterprise activities are not large and industrial risk taking is still underdeveloped. Thus, the extent to which divestments from non-financial public enterprises transform themselves into additions to public investments in financial enterprises depends upon the effectiveness of capital markets, given the public preferences, if any, as regards the organisational, sectoral, locational, and scale characteristics of the private enterprises. Where the government strongly favours the evolution of small-sized and new entrepreneurs, investments in the backward regions of the country, and a developmental focus on the rural and informal sectors, a substantial part of the moneys available to the government as a result of privatisation measures is likely to end up as its fresh investments through the medium of financial enterprises.

The latter may either lend to, or hold shares in, enterprises.

A similar result may occur through another route. A government not interested in direct involvement as investor may find itself in a situation of being the direct recipient of foreign aid - a situation brought about by economic, administrative or political considerations; then it lends the funds on to private entrepreneurs. In this way public involvement in non-financial enterprise arises, often as an owner.

Whether a growth in financial public enterprise under a policy of privatisation is an acceptable proposition, and what problems it raises, are questions that are not examined here. Undoubtedly they are important, even as the results of many existing public financial institutions in several countries suggest.

Privatisation of an enterprise

The reasons why this may be distinguished from the overall economy level are that:

(a) the government may not have an overall policy of privatisation; yet it is willing to privatise a given enterprise on specific grounds; and

(b) even where the government has a general policy of privatisation, its implementation proceeds through individual measures of privatisation; and the selection of candidates for privatisation and the precise shape and process of the privatisation measures can only be determined with due consideration for the circumstances of individual enterprises.

Thus, what privatisation signifies with reference to a given enterprise becomes important. This may be examined under three headings: (1) ownership structures, (2) organisational devices, and (3) operational modalities.

Ownership structures

The most obvious of these is the denationalisation of a public enterprise or parts of it. This implies a transfer of ownership rights and benefits, along with which go management rights, to private parties.

Another possibility is that of reducing the proportion of

public ownership, so that a wholly publicly owned enterprise becomes partially publicly owned, or a partially owned public enterprise becomes more partially publicly owned. The underlying theme here is that a joint venture between public and private owners offers ownership and management/control rights to the two sides in some proportion linked to the respective slices of ownership. (A recent illustration of linkage between the ownership proportion and governmental rights of directoral appointment comes from Britoil.)[3] There is one qualification to the principle of proportionalism. However logical, it may not necessarily be observed in every case. A recent uranium contract between the government of Guyana and foreign investors, for example, provided for the Government's rights of majority directorships despite its minority ownership.[4] Another version comes from China where joint venture agreements stipulate the condition of unanimity for decisions even in cases of minority equity investment by the government.[5]

The convenience that joint-venture participation by the government offers in the context of privatisation has long been recognised in many countries,[6] though it has not been fully availed of. Even as early as in 1954 it was recognised by the UN Seminar on Public Enterprises held in Rangoon that a 'mixed-ownership corporation' could be a 'useful device' for the eventual transfer of the industry to private enterprise.[7]

The substance of privatisation through the medium of a joint venture depends on the actual fairness characterising the government's exercise of ownership rights in management. The ownership proportion is not a conclusive index of privatisation. The joint-venture method of privatisation provides an inherent convenience to the government in the actual process of sale. Assuming that the shares are quoted on the Stock Exchange, the government can go by that barometer in determining the prices at which its shares may be transferred in appropriate instalments to private investors.

The ultimate subhead under ownership changes consists of liquidation, where a public enterprise has done too poorly to merit continuance in its present shape. This can also be treated as one kind of disposal (of assets) obviously at a distress price. It is interesting to refer at this point to the statutory specification of liquidation as the final one among the measures laid down for dealing with the self-managed enterprises that are in chronic difficulty in Yugoslavia (The

The Concept and Rationale of Privatisation

Associated Labour Act, Article 342).

Organisational devices

One can construe elements of privatisation in certain distinctive features of organisation marking a public enterprise. One of these refers to the holding-company form of organisation under which, while invariably not so in every case, only the apex may be brought under the purview of direct government control, and the operating companies as well as any intermediate sub-holding companies are left to operate under direct market discipline within the general supervision of the apex level. IRI of Italy is a good example. It is interesting to note at this point that the case frequently made for introducing the holding-company system[8] in public enteprise, and for its distant cousin, the Policy Councils,[9] rests in part on the possibility of substantially insulating the operating companies from the de-marketisation that direct government control might exert over their working. There are two severe qualifications, however. Firstly, if the holding company complex so works as to breed the subsidisation of the weak constituent units by the others, in whatever obvious or subtle manner, the element of market discipline correspondingly thins out, and so does the essence of privatisation that the system could, in theory, contain. Secondly, if the apex functions as a tier that compounds rather than minimises the impacts of government control on the operating companies, the latter correspondingly lose the opportunities of being guided by market disciplines.

The monolithic enterprise is an organisational form prevalent in many developed and developing countries: eg., the British Steel Corporation, the Central Electricity Generating Board, British Coal, Electricité de France, the Ghana Industrial Holding Corporation, the Steel Authority of India Ltd and Bharat Heavy Electricals Ltd. What is needed in such cases is a meticulous review of how far the economies claimed for the monolithic structure on technical and other grounds are outweighed by a loss of benefits that autonomous managerial units might offer as an alternative. Where totally independent units cannot be created at once, the technique of forming reasonably independent subsidiaries can be adopted. To the extent that this introduces or reinforces proxies for market forces in the operations of the giant organisation, one can find in it clear traces of privatisation in substance.

Some of the monolithic enterprises claim that, for internal purposes, they do treat their plants as different units in essence and adopt rigorous techniques of scrutiny over inter-unit transfer transactions. Such proxies can be made more powerful as well as real by reconstituting them as independent subsidiaries, as a first step, and eventually as independent enterprises wherever their interrelationships can be handled across the market without a net loss in the conduct of operations.

There are two other organisational innovations which a government interested in privatisation can adopt without disturbing the ownership structure. The first relates to an arrangement of lease of the assets of a public enterprise to the best bidder or to a party determined as the most appropriate in given circumstances. The benefits of ownership are retained in the public sector, but the operations are, in effect, privatised. The lease may incorporate, if necessary, certain terms that guarantee to preserve any desired elements of publicness in the operations. There are two favourable aspects of the lease method: it gives the government time to decide on (total) denationalisation; and in the mean time it helps establish the comparative advantage that the enterprise has in the public or private sector. (Management contracts are another substantive version of the lease technique.)

The other organisational device consists of a genuine declaration by the government that, irrespective of its bulk ownership of an enterprise, it undertakes not to interfere with the commercial decisions of the enterprise. It represents an act of self-denial in the matter of control, except in the normal corporate parlance of commercial management. (The prospectus of Associated British Ports Holdings PLC, which contained governmental declarations of such self-denial, is one of the early instances of this method in UK experience.) The effectiveness of the device as a vehicle of managerial privatisation depends on the actual weight that the big brother in practice exerts on the board. Where the intention is gradually to transfer its holding to private investors, it can be expected that the government will stick to its self-denying assertions.

Operational modalities

One of the ways in which elements of privatisation, in the sense of marketisation, can be introduced in the operations of a public enterprise is by encouraging the management to go in for acquiring certain inputs across the market rather than produce them internally. This would have two good results. Firstly, the input costs are likely to be favourable, reflecting the economies of scale in their supply; and in addition, there tends to develop a vertical and perhaps a horizontal disintegration of the enterprise in favour of promoting activity outside the public enterprise. The larger are the buying-out practices, the more the enterprise becomes confined to the benefits of ownership with carefully abridged operational functions. The persistent efforts made by Indian public enterprises to develop input-supply relationships with 'ancillary' enterprises illustrate the nature of the device.[10] Similar is the progressive search by the British Railways Board for areas in which contracting-out, as against in-house production, is economical enough to adopt.

Furthermore, this device can come in handy in the case of an enterprise operating with poor cost efficiency and can be a prelude to eventual ownership-privatisation: for, by hypothesis, purchases from across the market are likely to replace inside production activity on a substantial scale.

Let us turn next to an interesting development that incorporates elements of privatisation. It is possible to devise, without disturbing ownership and management structures, criteria of managerial behaviour that force a public enterprise to operate as if it were a private enterprise in the sense of being bound by market disciplines in investment, cost minimisation, pricing and production function. The criteria can, within the constraints of market insulation sought to be preserved in a given case, be so formulated as to operate as a surrogate for market forces. Required-rate-of-return specifications, targets of overall (as well as disaggregated) net returns, unit costs and productivity, and the obligation to resort to commercial markets for funds, are among the marketising instruments that governments have begun to wield in several countries. It is true that these instruments, as a cross-section, have not been very effective or genuine as of yet; but if governments effectively realise that the alternative consists of more drastic options, they might be impelled, as a first step, to inject force into those instruments.

One of the most powerful ways in which privatisation in operational terms can be visualised is to induce a public enterprise to go to the market for capital funds - a practice not adopted in the UK, by and large. Among the favourable results from the angle relevant to privatisation is the fact that the investments of the enterprise will be under market discipline. (Those that the government seeks to exclude from market criteria - on social considerations - will, of course, attract direct funding from it.) This element of privatisation applies to new investment decisions.

From a careful look at the varying circumstances of public enterprise and its performance around the world, it appears that the marketising instruments or control criteria, as suggested above, have an important place in the concept and processes of privatisation. They stand almost at one end of the conceptual continuum, with denationalisation standing at the other. They represent the minimal measures necessary if the government prefers efficiency of operations to sheer public ownership, and if it expects to realise ownership benefits in the shape of financial surpluses. Where ownership changes are not easy to implement at once, these measures can indeed act as a first step - in some cases the only step possible for a long while - in implementing the privatisation focus from the performance angle. It would be realistic for governments of developing countries to attach great significance to such measures.

At this point we may refer to the direction of public policy towards liberalisation and competition. This has relevance for both the organisational and the operational modalities of privatisation considered above. Conditions of competition or proxies for them can be created within a given monolithic or holding-company public enterprise. That would be an organisational modality. Alternatively, as more commonly understood, they can be created in a given sectoral activity by promoting entry and exit, so much so that private (or more public) units can compete with an existing public enterprise or contest for its markets. That would amount to inducing operational improvements on the part of the latter, so that it succeeds under market disciplines, if it can. The efficacy of the liberalisation policies is bound to vary from sector to sector and from country to country; and, correspondingly, so does its role as an instrument of privatisation.

THE RATIONALE OF PRIVATISATION

This discussion on 'Why privatisation?' essentially has a theoretical orientation, supported by some facts of experience, and excludes any ideological interest in the subject. Let us start at the overall level, and examine the macro-rationale of privatisation in an economy character-ised by a (relatively) large public enterprise sector - large in relation to the government budget (capital and/or revenue), gross domestic product, capital formation, and continuing investment magnitudes in major (non-agricultural) sectors. The UK (even today), France, Italy, India, Pakistan, Kenya, Tanzania, Nigeria, Senegal, Mexico and Peru are among the many such examples.

A number of arguments can be developed in favour of the principle of privatisation.

(1) A strong argument for privatisation is derived from the fact that the deficits sustained by public enterprise have an unwelcome impact on the public exchequer. The larger the deficits and the wider the ownership involvement of the government, the more serious the disadvantage. The budgets of certain countries such as Mali and Sierra Leone sharply illustrate the point.

An apparent truism, this argument calls for a serious probe into the origins of the deficits, which may be classified as illustrated in Figure 1.1. The 'planned' deficits, i.e. deficits attributable to extra-enterprise objectives injected into the operations of public enterprise, will remain, in whatever form, as a drain on the budget even after privatisation, if such objectives continue to be enforced, at a level that corresponds to box (i) in Figure 1.1. It is possible that a saving can be realised in box (ii), in that the scale of operations on deficit can be brought down to the planned or agreed level (i.e. box (i)) and leakages can be prevented in the eligibilities of markets and input sources to subsidy through appropriate streamlining of the operations. Since governmental pressures on privatised enterprises are unlikely to go beyond the realm of planned losses (to be reimbursed in some way), the budget burdens relevant to box (ii) can be controlled, if not eliminated. Its subdivision into (A) and (B) has a purpose. Box (A) notes deficits caused by an over-pursuit of a planned deficit involving input or output operations, e.g. concessional prices for students. Deficits could also result from a misinterpretation by managers, even if genuine, of the nature of social returns expected of their operations, e.g. while acting as 'model' employers or helping the 'poor' consumers. These are covered by box (B). This box also covers deficits which strictly belong to box (C)

Figure 1.1: The nature of public enterprise deficits

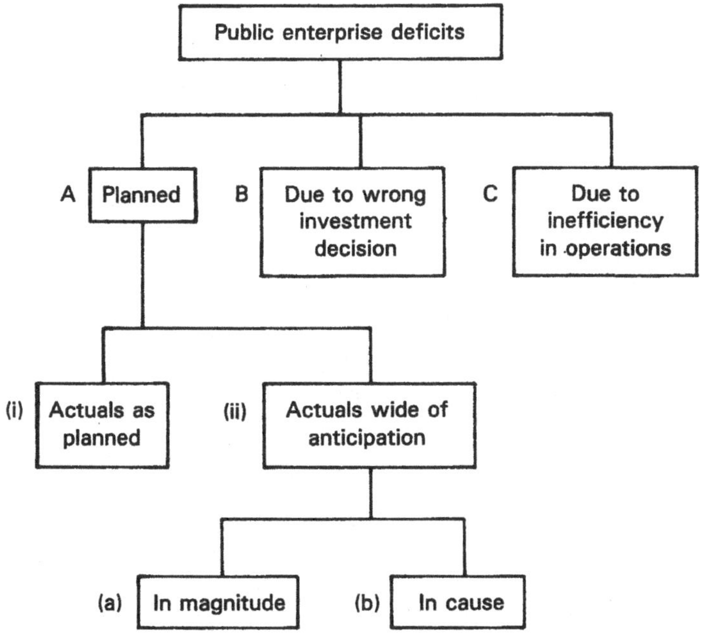

but are sought to be justified by managers on the pretext of social benefits.

The deficits traceable to what have turned out to be wrong investment decisions (box B), whoever may have taken them, devolve on the exchequer without choice, either through capital write-offs before privatisation or through low sales proceeds from privatisation.

It is in respect of the deficits caused by inefficiency (box C) that the exchequer can hope for benefit from privatisation. Here a word of annotation is called for. The box is composed of three elements:

(1) losses arising from managerial inefficiencies
(2) losses traceable to nontransparent externalities informally imposed on the enterprise; and
(3) cost-raising modalities of government control.

These also subsume the consequences of political pressures emerging from the self-interest of a group or a minister - for example, against a retrenchment of workers. Such 'induced' losses must be distinguished from the planned losses of box (A). Privatisation can relieve the government of the box (C) losses.

It is difficult to generalise on which of the three causes of deficits (A, B and C) is the greatest: the answer is specific to the country in question.

Three propositions merit notice. Firstly, the quantification of planned deficits is far from easy and can be subjective, since both the identity of extra-enterprise objectives and the instrumentality of a supportive price or input decision is inconclusive in most cases. Secondly, the most convincing answer on the wrongness of investment decisions taken can only come from a sale under privatisation. Thirdly, the inefficiency in operations is in no small measure traceable to the government's own role in the working of public enterprises.[11] Before rushing to privatisation in a situation of losses under box (C), the government ought to explore if a needed rationalisation of its role sufficiently alters the picture of deficits.

On the whole it was the poor financial condition of the cross-section of public enterprise that in many countries triggered serious rethinking on its place in the economy; and the influence of the World Bank and IMF has also been operating as a powerful spur to such rethinking.

2. Another exchequer-oriented argument for privatisation is that it subserves the 'public sector borrowing requirements' approach, reduces the potential needs of public enterprises for funds from government, and positively brings in cash resources to the government on the sale of assets. This line of thinking has been very prominent in the UK.[12] (Comments from the angle of individual enterprises will be presented later in the paper.) The argument is weaker than it sounds. The fundamental issue is whether a given investment proposal is justified and necessary. If it is assumed that certain investments are desirable, on whatever accepted criteria, privatisation simply shifts them from public sources (in the case of the UK, mainly from the government/National Loans Fund) to private investors. (It is a different matter if one were to argue that under government entrepreneurship the investment decision is frequently wrong and that privatisation therefore saves the economy from wrong investment choices.)

The arithmetical benefit in terms of budget balance no doubt follows privatisation which brings in cash through the sale of assets, and can be of value in situations where internal reasons of budget policy or any IMF compulsions necessitate such an improvement in the government's liquidity position. However, there can be long-term consequences from the angle of income (and wealth) distribution.

3. It can be argued that the distributional outcomes of public enterprise operations are not conclusively of the favourable kind, and that privatisation will constitute a right step in the direction of rectifying the position. Data in support of the argument (or otherwise) are not available in adequate quantity or quality, though several empirical findings broadly seem to lend support to the argument.[13] If the price benefits are enjoyed, disproportionately, by the relatively upper-income brackets and urban consumers, if the wage benefits go likewise to the better placed sections of the work-force, and if public enterprise deficits eventually lead to an increase in regressive taxation, privatisation that minimises these trends is, distributionally, a sound measure of policy.

There are two qualifications. Firstly, if public enterprise, on balance, has produced anti-distributional results, can they be amended through discreet revisions in investment and operational decisions? In other words, can the 'criteria' medium in the conceptual continuum of privatisation be adopted, with certain results? Secondly, if denationalisation proceeds are used by the government for tax reductions, for repayments of public debt, or for certain capital expenditure programmes, do these, on balance, tend to add in relative terms to the income benefits of the upper income brackets? If they do, the malady sought to be remedied creeps in again, perhaps more conspicuously in some cases. Statistics of share allotments on privatisation are no satisfactory evidence of deconcentration in the economy.

To conclude: if public enterprise runs profitably, if unintended distributional flows of benefit from its operations can be minimised, and if the government as the collector of its profits has an effective incomes policy in favour of the poorer people, public enterprise has merit on distributional grounds. Unfortunately these three 'ifs' are not satisfied in many countries. What is required, therefore, is a comparison between the distributional imperfections of public enterprise and those of privatisation, in the context of a given economy.

4. An interesting argument in support of privatisation is that it offers relief to the Civil Service, which is overburdened with involvements in public enterprise matters. It is true of several (developing) countries that senior officials in government departments are obliged to be distracted in this way from their essential tasks of administration and that, while their technical competence in enterprise matters is doubtful, their application to departmental work is in danger of being considerably weakened. The following are the major aspects of the uneconomical deployment of Civil Service talents:

(1) There is duplicatory and, in the end, often amateurish, application of Civil Servants' time and energy to approvals or disapprovals of investments in public enterprise. The parent ministry, the finance ministry, the planning ministry or agency, the Prime Minister's secretariat the central bank and any specific committees or commissions set up to process the project proposals at some stage - all concern themselves with the issues, often in a wasteful and unco-ordinated manner.

(2) Some senior Civil Servants sit on the boards of many enterprises: for example, 'About twenty top civil servants appear repeatedly on the boards of directors of public enterprises' in Singapore.[14] Moreover, it is standard practice in countries like Kenya[15] and Tanzania to have the permanent secretaries of the finance ministry and the parent ministry on every board; they can send 'alternates' - a system which is capable of causing its own problems.

(3) Several managerial controls, whose exercise should ideally rest with the enterprises, get externalised at the level of government departments. With probably little advantage to enterprise operations, they aggravate the workloads of Civil Servants and it is possible that they introduce into Civil Service behaviour (or intensify) temptations of nepotism and patronage.

(4) The generally inadequate resources of time and technical ability of the Auditor General, the Public Accounts Committee and Parliament in general would be pressed thinly into attention to public enterprise operations - at the cost of their more basic

responsibilities relating to the departments.

With few exceptions, governments have, on the whole, been unable effectively to scale down their interventions and involvements in public enterprise. It can therefore be claimed that privatisation eliminates this problem - assuming that any regulation that follows does not reintroduce it in some way.

One has to be circumspect in wielding this argument which presents a vicious circle. In the first place, by hypothesis, the nature of market forces or distrust of potential industrialists predestines direct governmental initiative in enterprise. However, this results in an overburden on the scarce administrative capability within the government. What is the trade-off? The answer is only clear where the diseconomy of the latter factor is found to be so heavy as to destroy or seriously condition the development strategy itself. In other cases it may be realistic to resort to the criteria-oriented modalities of privatisation, coupled with transparent public subsidisation of non-commercial operations.

5.   At least in theory the case for privatisation gains in strength if the instrumentality of public enterprise in a country's development strategy is perceived to have declined over time. If, in other words, market forces can be trusted - unlike in the earlier years when public enterprise emerged without a choice - to ensure national development, no inevitability attaches to the continuance of public enterprise on the existing scale.

It is difficult to assert that many countries in the developing world, in particular, have clearly reached such a stage. Though current development plans distinctly under-score the role of private investments and envisage a gradual investment strategy culminating in relative privatisation of the economy, wholesale denationalisation has not yet been the order of the day. (It may be recalled that ideological measures as in Chile after Allende, are kept out of the present discussion.) The pace of privatisation might have been impressive if foreign private capital could be freely let in; but that would not be appealing to most governments, and nor is their capability for effective control of foreign ownership and of transnationals high enough to encourage them to let them in. In fact, foreign capital has often been insisting on some government equity participation in the host country.

Furthermore, goals of social justice and softness for the low-income brackets or regions are becoming more, rather than less, pronounced in successive plans of most countries. This may act as a deterrent to quick privatisation measures, whatever their modality, unless governments genuinely realise that the track record of public enterprise in income distribution has not been impressive and that, on the whole, the budget can play a superior role as an instrument in this respect.

We shall now turn to the rationale for privatisation with reference to a given public enterprise. This part of the discussion has relevance to enterprise-specific policy.

The case for privatisation essentially rests on the loss in the comparative advantage of an enterprise operating in the public sector as against the private sector. (For a full discussion on this subject reference may be made to Chapter 14, 'The Concept of Comparative Advantage', in my book The nature of public enterprise.) It is not easy to produce statistical evidence of the comparative advantage in terms of cost and net revenue, which a public enterprise possesses or loses in sectors where private enterprises do not operate; nor to establish, with reasonable certainty, the exact trade-off to be imputed as between the financial and the social outcomes of a given public enterprise. It is in terms of this that the merits of its continuity, as against privatisation, must be evaluated, however difficult the exercise might be.

The need to make accounting adjustments in establishing the 'economic costs'[16] of the enterprises under comparison cannot be overemphasised; and nor can the importance of entrusting the evaluation of the comparative advantage to a technically competent non-government agency. One of the points not to be glossed over, in a situation of highly publicised inefficiency on the part of a given public enterprise, is the possibility of social wastes (and costs) that may be associated with the private enterprises that replace it; for it cannot be treated as axiomatic that competition, optimal organisation, operational efficiency and the full sway of market forces will follow in every case. Besides, the nature of the organisation(s) replacing a public enterprise - e.g. a workers' co-operative or a consumer co-operative - has its own influence in determining the actual degree of marketisation that can be achieved through privatisation and the kind of market imperfections that will be unleashed despite privatisation.

There are two other issues to be considered in the context of privatising a given public enterprise. Firstly, have its original objectives been achieved? These may cover sickness, structural reorganisation, industrial relations, gross mismanagement, and so on. If such objectives are achieved and if the original situation is unlikely to recur under privatisation, the decision can be easier than otherwise. Secondly, will the privatised operations contain a substantial 'social' segment; if they do, how easy (or cumbersome) will it be to ensure that it materialises as per public preference? Obviously the relevance of these questions is specific not only to the sector of activity (e.g. electricity, fertilisers, or small-industry promotion) but also to the country concerned.

A circumstance that substantially repeats itself in many countries is that a public enterprise needs investment injection - even for optimal operation within capacity - but that the government does not have the resources to provide it. Privatisation, at least in the sense of letting in private capital participation, would be purposeful; not to do so would amount to perpetuating the inefficiency of the enterprise and destroying its opportunities of (economical) expansion. It is the force of this logic that has persuaded some countries to formulate joint ventures or management contracts of some type with private, foreign capital.

At this point let us briefly look at a distinctive consequence of privatising a profit-making enterprise. If it can be assumed that the prices of a privatised enterprise - say, gas - will tend to be so regulated as to scale down self-financing, a possible result will be for millions of consumers each to enjoy a small amount of price benefit. It is likely that such income accretions will, in substantial proportion, go into consumption rather than investment, in contrast to the enterprise mopping up, for investment purposes, corresponding funds or even larger funds, if as a public enterprise, it could get off with the kind of pricing implicit in such a policy. This issue is, no doubt, very complex and, hopefully, will be picked up at some other point in the seminar.

To conclude: the rationale of privatisation needs to be established, enterprise-wise, in the interest of proper prioritisation in its implementation. Priorities are best worked out in the order of loss in comparative advantage on the part of individual public enterprises, from both the micro and macro standpoints. In many countries, unwinding public enterprise is bound to take far longer than in the UK and the planning of a time-frame is essential.

The deficits sustained by a public enterprise are an inferior basis, as earlier discussion suggests, though they powerfully trigger action towards privatisation.[17] They could approximate the comparative advantage criterion when proper allowance is made for planned losses and for possibilities of streamlining enterprise operations. Besides, even in a situation of profits the comparative advantage of a public enterprise over a private enterprise in a given sector could be shown to be low: hence, a plea for privatisation would be in order.

In evaluating the rationale for privatisation in a given case, it would be necessary to take cognisance of the 'unseen costs of privatisation'. These, broadly, are represented by

(a) the market imperfections that tend to prevail despite hopes of promoting competition,
(b) the social costs of private enterprise operations,
(c) the distribution implications of the privatisation processes and the long-term consequences in the context of ownership benefits, and
(d) the costs and inadequacies of the regulatory framework that accompanies privatisation.

Valid quantifications under these headings will only be possible after privatisation takes effect. However, thorough analyses of the likely consequences can be undertaken ex ante, and it is doubtful whether enough thought has been given to this matter in countries where privatisation is actively contemplated.

CONCLUSION

Privatisation in the sense of a mere change of public ownership into private hands represents a limited aspect of its broad connotation; and it is doubtful if, by itself, it is invariably the best policy option that the government can pursue in every case. The enterprises that stay in the public sector - and there would be some such in almost every country - can be exposed to several other modalities of privatisation, which will produce economical results.

The main case for privatisation ought to rest on the

evidence that a given segment of operations undertaken in the public sector has lost its comparative advantage and that the economy will therefore gain by privatising it, allowing for the continued public financing of 'planned losses' for social reasons, if any.

It is difficult to come to rapid conclusions as to the exact nature of the interface between the government and public regulation and privatised enterprises, and, therefore, as to the net benefits to society from privatisation, at least in the short run, in certain sectors of activity.

THE ISSUES

This chapter has concentrated on the concept and broad rationale of privatisation, though at certain points, brief references had to be made to issues that are likely to be picked up for full discussion in later sessions of the Seminar. It is perhaps useful to outline a comprehensive range of issues relevant to privatisation, which policy formulation and implementation have to reckon with.

A. Pre-privatisation

(1) A thorough analysis and quantification of the decline in comparative advantage of a public enterprise.[18]
(2) The effectiveness and favourable consequences of any withdrawals in government involvement in the working of a public enterprise.
(3) The accounting adjustments necessary before privatisation.
(4) The restructuring of the enterprise, financial and otherwise, before privatisation.
(5) The 'public' elements considered essential in the objectives of the enterprise in current context.
(6) The choice of enterprises for privatisation:

  (a) sectoral;

  (b) temporal; and

  (c) modality-wise.

B. Modality

(7) The most suitable modality of privatisation in the case of a given enterprise.
(8) The precise role of the government under the varying modalities of privatisation, in general, and, in particular, under the modality chosen in the case of a given enterprise.
(9) The role open to foreign capital in the context of a given modality of privatisation.
(10) The organisational nature of the enterprise(s) that will replace a given public enterprise.

C. Sale

(11) The pricing of the assets to be denationalised.
(12) The merits of sale to the enterprise workers.
(13) The taxpayer's interest under privatisation sales.
(14) The techniques of selling; and the choice in a given case.
(15) Sale in a multiracial environment.
(16) Restrictions on share allotments.

D. Macro aspects

(17) The exchequer options in the use of sales proceeds.
(18) The aggregate impacts of privatisation measures on budget balance year by year.
(19) Implications of privatisation in given cases for income and wealth distribution.
(20) Contingent compulsions of total or partial renationalisation in a given case - on non-ideological grounds.

E. Post-privatisation

(21) The assurance of efficiency in operations.
(22) The structure of regulation.
(23) Cultural changes implicit in privatisation.
(24) The preservation of social benefits expected to survive privatisation in a given case.

It is hoped that most of these issues will be discussed in varying depth in the course of the Seminar.

NOTES

1. One interpretation of privatisation is 'rolling back the activities of the state' in the context of 'provision, subsidy or regulation': Julian Le Grand and Ray Robinson (eds), Privatisation and the welfare state (London, 1984), p. 3. It reflects a 'political commitment to "roll back the public sector" and "to free market forces" ': David Steel and David Heald (eds), Privatizing public enterprises (London, 1984), p. 13.

2. In Kenya 'the structural adjustment strategy, which has been implemented progressively since 1980, is essentially a move away from direct government involvement in manufacturing and other sectors where the private sector can operate effectively': Economic management for renewed growth (Nairobi, 1986), p. 92.

3. The number of Government Directors which the Special Shareholder, i.e. the Secretary of State for Energy, may appoint shall be two when the shares registered in his name represent more than 35 per cent of the issued voting shares; it shall be one when his shares constitute 20 to 35 per cent; and none when the proportion is not more than 20 per cent: Seventeenth Report from the Committee of Public Accounts, session 1983-4, Sale of government shareholdings in publicly-owned companies (HMSO, London, 443, 1984) p. 15.

4. Transnational corporations in world development (Third Survey, UN Centre on Transnational Corporations, New York, 1983), p. 245.

5. Ibid.

6. For instance, the Investment Corporation of Papua New Guinea Ordinance, (1971) includes among its functions: 'to take up shares in overseas enterprises, and to hold them with a view to their future disposal to eligible persons' (Section 9).

7. Some problems in the organisation and administration of public enterprises in the industrial field (United Nations, New York, 1954), p. 30.

8. First Report from the Select Committee on Nationalised Industries, session 1967-8, Ministerial control of the nationalised industries, vol. I (London, 1969). See

The Concept and Rationale of Privatisation

Aubrey Jones's suggestion, p. 202.

9. National Economic Development Office, A study of the UK nationalised industries: their role in the economy and control in the future (HMSO, London, 1976), p. 46.

10. For an account of the recent developments in this regard, see Bureau of Public Enterprises, Public Enterprise Survey - annual volumes, New Delhi.

11. A recent illustration of the Government's admission of managerial involvement in public enterprises is provided by Privatisation of the water authorities in England and Wales (Cmnd 9734, London, 1986). The Government presented as one of the benefits of privatisation the fact that 'the authorities will be free of Government intervention in day to day management and protected from fluctuating political pressures' (p. 1).

12. Among several expressions linked to 'external financing limits', a recent one from a Report of the Committee on Public Accounts may be cited. 'The sale of IAL would assist BAB [i.e. the British Airways Board] to solve expected problems in meeting its 1982-83 external financing limit (EFL).' - Second Report from the Committee on Public Accounts, session 1985-6, Sale of subsidiary companies and other assets (HMSO, London, 1985), p. vi.

13. For example, in Brazil public enterprises in steel benefited 'large enterprises and upper-wealth groups' by supplying low-cost steel to the auto industry: Thomas J. Trebat, An evaluation of the economic performance of large public enterprises in Brazil, 1965-1975 (Austin, 1980), p. 20.

In the State Gold Mining Corporation in Ghana the average earnings per employee rose by 7 per cent a year while productivity fell by 8 per cent a year for five years: Second Development Plan, Accra.

In Argentina, public enterprises set up for the development of the Patagonic region sent to outside regions their 'material goods' or 'surpluses'. They 'increased the drain of basic resources towards more developed areas': Alejandro Rofman, 'Role of public enterprises in regional development in Latin America' (ICPE, Ljubljana, 1981), p. 29.

In the UK 'public sector trade unions have been extraordinarily successful in gaining advantages for themselves in the pay hierarchy by exploiting their monopoly collective bargaining position': J. Moore, Treasury Press Release 190/83.

14. Lee Sheng Yi, 'Public enterprise and economic

development in Singapore', Malayan Economic Review, vol. XXI, no. 2 (October 1976), p. 57. (Kuala Lumpur).

15. State Corporations Act, 1986 (Nairobi).

16. As defined, for example, in Accounting for economic costs and changing prices, Vol. I (HM Treasury, 1986), p. 5: 'The costs of resources used at the price they would be traded at in a highly competitive market, where entry to and exit from the market was easy.'

17. For instance, 'profitability crisis' and 'heavy indebtedness' 'weighed on the decisions taken by the managing bodies as to the companies to be re-privatised' by IRI, ENI, etc. in Italy: Emilio Lizza, 'The privatisation of state holdings in Italy up to 1984', Annals of Public and Co-operative Economy, September 1986, p. 320.

18. For some of the complications, see Richard Pryke, 'The comparative performance of public and private enterprise, Fiscal Studies, 1982; and Robert Millward, 'The comparative performance of public and private ownership', Lord Roll (ed.), The mixed economy (1982).

25

2

Has Public Enterprise Failed?

Maurice R. Garner*

My arguments in this chapter may well be controversial, for the thesis I shall present for examination is that, in so far as public enterprise has failed, it is a failure of government rather than of the institution of public enterprise itself.

DEFINITIONS AND A NECESSARY ASSUMPTION

I have referred to public enterprise as an institution. This vague expression conceals a multitude of difficulties of definition. It is useful, however, because the mere sound of the term registers the fact that public enterprise is not just a business. It should, indeed, pose the question whether it is a business at all. For a seminar of this kind, it is not possible to explore at all deeply the problems involved in defining the term 'public enterprise': they are surprisingly multifold and troublesome for an expression containing only two, seemingly straightforward, words. What, to start with, are we to understand by the word 'public'? It is common knowledge that there are three, virtually world-wide, forms in which public enterprise is constituted: as a government department, as a public corporation, and as a company under private law. In the case of enterprises constituted in this last form, at what percentage of ownership of shares by the state, municipal authorities, or other public institutions does an enterprise move from the public to the private sector?; and where shares are held by more than one type of public authority, are their shares to be calculated as a total or considered separately? Moreover, do the rules apply also to

* Formerly Visiting Professor at the London School

subsidiaries of the directly held companies and to the subsidiaries' subsidiaries? Public enterprise theory cannot shelter comfortably behind the British and Common Market convention that the cut-off comes at 50 per cent, firstly because it is not universally accepted, and secondly, because it is patently unrealistic as a test of control. Propagandists for privatisation have further muddied the waters by contending that the term 'public' properly applies only to enterprises open to control by members of the public through their holdings of shares in the enterprises. This is an entirely legitimate if paradoxical use of the term. Were I tempted to adopt it for the purpose of this chapter, we should then have no small number of public enterprises of the share-owned category that have unquestionably failed in their sole purpose, having incurred losses under categories B and C of Ramanadham's formulation (see Figure 1.1, p. 13), and these enterprises could be set alongside loss-making public enterprises of the conventional type. For illustrative purposes it will suffice to recall the performance of the British banks, with their enormous losses collectively on loans to the Third World, and with their individual losses in such cases as the Johnson Matthey Bank and the Midland Bank (through its investment in the Crocker Bank in the USA). However, I resist the temptation and merely make the point that the uncertainty of meaning attaching to the word 'public' in the expression 'public enterprise' tends to invalidate all generalisations about public enterprise made by those (I mean most economists) ignorant of public enterprise theory.

I shall leave aside for the present the difficulties of defining the word 'enterprise', merely registering the fact that they are substantial, and turn to the word 'failure', as used in this chapter's title. I think it is only possible to speak of success or failure when a perceived result is related to a pre-existing objective. In the case of private enterprise, there is no doubt about the nature of its objective, even though the precise quantum is often left unspecified. That objective is profit; it is the enterprise's raison d'être; and, in all but the most unusual circumstances, it is the enterprise's only real objective, other stated objectives, like market share, being ancillary and subordinate to it. This is very different from the case with public enterprise in which there is no necessary or invariable objective and where, instead, in the absence of a specific statement by government or enterprise, the objectives have to be looked for in legislation, or inferred from other authoritative pronouncements or from circumstances; and it is also different from the case with public enterprise in which it is normal for there to be several objectives, including adequacy of supply, maintenance of employment, low and stable prices, support for regional development, as well as avoidance of financial losses. Whereas, therefore, the success or failure of private enterprise can be measured against its single objective, profitability, by mere inspection of its accounts, the success or failure of public enterprise has to be measured against multiple objectives and this can only be done properly where the objectives have previously been quantified and a method agreed for weighting the importance of each individual objective in the overall result. Even in Britain, which is relatively advanced in the practice of specification and quantification of objectives, weighting is not practised, so a valid judgment as to the success or failure of individual public enterprises is not really possible.

In the effort to judge the success or failure of public enterprise as an institution, there is, intellectually, a further problem. Is the performance of public enterprise to be measured against the objectives of those who brought the enterprises into being or against the objectives of those responsible for their continuance today? Much of the pressure for the nationalisation of industries in Britain came from unions in those industries who were seeking better pay and conditions and greater security of employment. Today, however, for Mr John Moore, that 'public sector trade unions have been extraordinarily successful in gaining advantages for themselves in the pay hierarchy'[1] is a ground of criticism, not a recognition of achievement. Like the Common Agricultural Policy, it may be that public enterprise should be seen as an instrument for the achievement of sectoral advantage and its success or failure viewed from that angle: from that standpoint it might appear to have been not unsuccessful.

In the preparation of this discussion, I have not had either the time or the resources to make a systematic compilation - even one confined to the nationalised industries in Britain since, say, 1980 when sets of quantified objectives became increasingly common - that would relate the industries' agreed objectives to their eventual outturn, and so provide some kind of factual basis for a judgement as to the extent of success or failure of at least one part of public enterprise in one country. However, so that difficulties of definition and the absence of facts shall not deny us the opportunity of considering the thesis I have advanced as to the prime responsibility of government for any failure of public enterprise as an institution, I shall assume for current purposes that public enterprise is coterminous with the British nationalised industries and that, collectively, they have failed.

HOW GOVERNMENT CAUSED THIS FAILURE

In the search for the explanation of this (assumed) failure of public enterprise, it is natural that specialists tend to find the answers within the confines of their particular disciplines. Thus, economists attribute the failure to the absence of the disciplines and incentives of the market, whilst specialists on corporate structures point to the want of regard to property rights. Readers will accordingly not be surprised to learn that I locate the explanation within the field of political science and that, characteristically, I start by claiming that my 'medicine' is more powerful than the others' 'medicine', which I do by pointing out that the absence or limited extent of competition had not prevented some public enterprises from being profitable and innovative and generally successful as business organisations - the British Gas Corporation, for example. Whatever may be said about its servicing of domestic appliances, which would doubtless parallel what is being said about the servicing of domestic automobiles, there can be no doubt about the initiative, technical competence, and commercial drive with which the Corporation changed Britain from coalgas through oil-based gas, to natural gas, making large surpluses on the way. When British Airways, whilst still formally a public corporation, can be turned from a virtually bankrupt undertaking into 'the world's favourite airline', it is plain that factors other than status as a public enterprise or the forces of competition were operative. Indeed, it is natural that this should be so because, as Littlechild has sapiently observed, 'The whole purpose of public ownership is to make the allocation of resources subject to political rather than market forces.'[2] I turn now to government's three failings that brought about the failure of British public enterprise.

Has Public Enterprise Failed?

Failure to find the right organisational structure

It is now exactly 20 years since Sir Norman Chester pointed to what I believe to be a principal source of the difficulties with British nationalised industries.[3] As he noted:

> The public corporation in its simplest conception was a limited liability company without equity capital and therefore without shareholders. The London Passenger Transport Board was to Lord Ashfield, its first Chairman, the London General Omnibus Company much enlarged and given a monopoly, with a muted Minister of Transport in place of equity shareholders.

It was not inevitable that the public corporation should have been a simulacrum of the private law company - as Sir Norman crisply observed, 'the public corporation is a genus, not a species',[4] - but it was this kind of public corporation that became the British standard.

It was the adoption of this kind of public corporation that, in my opinion, gave powerful encouragement in Britain to the illusion that public and private enterprises are undertakings fundamentally identical in character and requiring only superficial modifications to reflect the difference in ownership. This is a fundamental misconception because:

(a) public enterprises do not usually have the single profit-making objective of private enterprises: they have multiple objectives, reflecting their role as an instrument of government. Multiple objectives are inconsistent with the normal decision-taking criteria and measures of performance;

(b) public enterprises, being part of government, cannot be subjected to the full disciplines of the market and it is difficult for the latter's incentives to be allowed to apply to them;

(c) the interests of the boards of public enterprises, unlike those of the boards of private enterprises, are not identified with the interests of their enterprises' 'residual risk bearers'.[5] To be the public enterprises' residual risk bearer is, however, a role which the state cannot normally avoid and which almost inevitably brings it into conflict with the boards' expectations of

autonomy;
(d) such expectations of autonomy are, contrariwise, justified in the case of private enterprises. This is because their directors usually have personal stakes in the enterprises sufficient to identify their interests with those of the enterprises' 'residual risk bearers', i.e. the general body of shareholders.

The form of organisation simulating the private law company adopted for public enterprises thus obscured the need for new measures of performance and decision-taking criteria, obscured the need for a new and distinctive pattern of disciplines and incentives, and obscured the difference in the relationship of the boards to their residual risk bearers. It was a fatal beginning.

Failure to make changes in response to experience

Failure to provide an appropriate organisational structure was followed by failure to provide any basic remedy for the consequential disorders that time brought to the notice of all concerned. The public enterprises' low rate of return on capital and undue dependence on the savings of the rest of society led in 1961 to the introduction of the policy of financial objectives - objectives, that is to say, to be agreed between government and individual public enterprises settling the rate of return on capital that the enterprise would seek to earn over a prescribed period, ideally five years.[6] This was certainly a belated assertion of the state's roles as residual risk bearer and macroeconomic manager but it was soon seen to be too tentative and too limited to have any significant impact on public enterprises' overall performance.
Relations between the state and public enterprises were thus still disordered when the Select Committee on the Nationalised Industries came, in 1967, to examine the question of 'ministerial control'.[7] The Committee diagnosed as the control system's fundamental weakness

an underlying confusion touching all the elements in the system, but centring on the sponsoring Departments. Sometimes this has revealed itself as a confusion about purposes... Sometimes it has been seen as a confusion about policies... Some-

> times it has been a confusion about methods ... But mainly it has been a confusion of responsibilities...[8]

The Committee's proposals for remedying this state of affairs focused primarily on the allocation of functions between departments and made no criticism of the enterprises' own organisational structure. The government of the day elected, however, to make no fundamental changes in either its own control system or the enterprises' structure,[9] so despite the unsatisfactory situation reported by the Committee, it received no attention for a further eight years or so, until dissatisfaction amongst all concerned led to the commissioning of a fresh and wider-ranging study, this time by the National Economic Development Office (NEDO).

In its report, the Office formulated the following searing conclusions:[10]

> there is a lack of trust and mutual understanding between those who run the nationalised industries and those in government (politicians and civil servants) who are concerned with their affairs;
>
> there is confusion about the respective roles of the boards of the nationalised industries, Ministers and Parliament, with the result that accountability is seriously blurred;
>
> there is no systematic framework for reaching agreement on long-term objectives and strategy, and no assurance of continuity when decisions are reached;
>
> there is no effective system for measuring the performance of nationalised industries and assessing managerial competence.

To remedy this situation, the Office, it is significant to record, for the first time in any official document, proposed far-reaching changes in the enterprises' organisational structure.[11] Once again, however, the government elected to make no major changes, leaving the situation as reported by the Office to continue into the current decade, 40 years after the initial, fundamental error.

Failure to administer consistently and effectively

Three White Papers issued between 1961 and 1978 have indicated the government's recognition of the need for its relationships with the public enterprises and their decision-taking to be based on published principles.[12] Amongst the principles proclaimed by these White Papers at different times were the settling of financial objectives, the determination of prices on the basis of marginal costs, loan capital to fund programmes of investments calculated to earn the prescribed test discount rate (later 'the required rate of return'), a central role for corporate planning, and publication of performance objectives. It is fair to say that these principles were, at best, implemented only partially and after considerable delay. Even in the heyday of the policy of financial objectives there were always some public enterprises with no objective or with an objective that had expired but was being extended pending a renegotiation that was considerably overdue. In 1976, when NEDO undertook its study, not one of a sample of four enterprises was basing its prices on marginal costs. Capital investment programmes, whenever it suited governments, were arbitrarily varied.[13] As late as 1983, the National Audit Office (NAO) was recording 'defects in the corporate planning and monitoring arrangements for the coal, telecommunications and railway industries'[14] defects in the case of railways dramatically enlarged upon in the report of the Serpell Committee.[15] In 1986, departments were shown by the NAO still to be equivocating in some instances over the fixing and publication of performance objectives.[16] Not only, therefore, did governments fail to make the reforms that were recommended to them by external agencies but they also failed to apply consistently and energetically the measures they themselves had declared to be necessary.

A lack of the relevant competence on the part of the sponsoring departments seems to have been an important factor in this non-enforcement of proclaimed principles. The Select Committee alluded to this in 1967, recording 'an urgent need to improve - in the direction of more specialisation, more continuity in experience and more use of specific expertise - the arrangements for staffing those divisions of the sponsoring Departments that deal with the nationalised industries'.[17] Almost a decade later, NEDO still found it necessary to report: 'The internal structure and staffing of sponsor departments and Treasury are not designed for the prime purpose of overseeing and developing relevant policy frameworks for massive public enterprises.[18] With exemplary patience, a further ten years later, the Public Accounts Committee noted:[19]

> We welcome the departments' recognition that there is scope for improvement and that in some areas they are already taking steps to achieve it although we find it disappointing that it has taken so long since the White Paper was published in 1978 to reach this stage.

Whether it is the consequence of shortage of personnel, impermanence of appointment, or want of appropriate education and training, and whether these are the result of ignorance or sheer lack of concern on the part of ministers and permanent secretaries, it can hardly be doubted that the departments' godlike attitude[20] to their task of overseeing the public enterprises has been an important factor in the enterprises' unsatisfactory performance.

CONCLUSION IN RESPECT OF BRITAIN

In the light of the foregoing considerations, I hope that every fair-minded reader will be ready to agree that my initial hypothesis has been established and that public enterprise in Britain has been so dominated by the actions and inactions of government that it is logically impossible to formulate any conclusion as to the inherent disposition of the institution towards either success or failure. In so far as there has been failure, it has been primarily a failure of government. In its dealings with public enterprise, government, it should be remembered, is not confronting a force of nature, such as the droughts recently afflicting Africa and India; it is dealing with institutions it has itself created and office-holders it has itself appointed, who are exercising powers it has itself defined and utilising resources it has itself provided. No doubt it is the case that, having brought institutions into being, granted privileges to certain interests, and conferred office and power on particular individuals, government may find them recalcitrant and capable of arousing political hostility against itself that government would prefer not to have to confront. This, however, is government's normal lot - to have to choose between unpleasant alternatives - so if a public enterprise has excessive costs, loses money, gives bad service, and the government tolerates the continuance of such shortcomings, it must be assumed that government prefers their continuance to the consequences of enforcing change. Government is ultimately responsible and can alter public enterprise's performance for good or ill whenever it will accept the political consequences of so doing. It is important that this should be understood.

Some fair-minded readers, whilst accepting the validity of the hypothesis for the United Kingdom, may be asking themselves about its applicability to other countries. It is not only British public enterprise that has been tarred with allegations of failure; other countries' public enterprises have also come in for criticism. It cannot be the case that all governments have wished upon their public enterprises the Morrisonian public corporation or some equally unsatisfactory corporate structure, or that all countries' sponsoring departments have been as maladroit as here. To such doubts about the general validity of the hypothesis, I would reply that, so long as an allegation of unsatisfactory performance relates in general to a country's public enterprise, the hypothesis is inherently probable (because government is ultimately responsible for its public sector). The precise mechanisms by which any particular government exerts its malign influence on its public enterprise has to be established by study of the country's particular circumstances. This chapter shows how the influence operated in Britain.

The illusion that public and private enterprises are undertakings fundamentally identical in character is certainly not confined to Britain: it is held with varying intensity from country to country. It draws its strength from different sources, not least from academic teaching and professional instruction designed for private enterprise which managements of public enterprise apply to themselves. Nevertheless, it is held with particular intensity in Britain and that this is so is, I think, due to the adoption here of the Morrisonian public corporation as the vehicle for British public enterprise.

SOME BROADER IMPLICATIONS

Whilst the foregoing analysis exculpates public enterprise in

Has Public Enterprise Failed?

Britain from the charge of general failure, reflection on the arguments used is likely to suggest doubts about the fitness of governments, notably those in developing countries but perhaps, also, elsewhere, to use public enterprise as an instrument of public policy. These doubts include the following:

(1) Executing the role of 'residuary risk bearer' imposes a heavy load on government departments, particularly in the area of definition of objectives and development of corporate plans. Can and will governments equip themselves with the required expertise and will ministers make the hard choices needed?

(2) Developing a theory of management of public enterprise to parallel the theory of management of private enterprise will be difficult and its application in practice to individual cases will require qualified personnel and generally increased resources. (This relates to decision-taking criteria, measures of performance, and disciplines and incentives to replace those of the market.) Can these needs to met?; will governments really try to meet them?

(3) Because public enterprises have resources that Parliament does not vote and can confer advantages in directions Parliament does not control, public enterprises are vulnerable to exploitation by government. To check such exploitation, it is necessary that accounts should be provided promptly and in considerable detail and published. Will any authority ensure that this is done?

(4) For the same reason and because it is one substitute for the disciplines of the market, there is need for all public enterprises to be submitted to regular management audit by a competent authority whose reports will be published. Will such an authority be established, given adequate resources, and allowed to publish?

It is plain that the problem of the numbers and competence of administrative personnel is particularly acute in developing countries. When, in such countries, Parliament is weak and freedom of speech and of the Press are at a discount, public enterprise is likely to find itself particularly vulnerable to managerial corruption and incompetence, and to ministerial abuse of authority. Public enterprise, therefore, should not be regarded as an instrument of public policy suited to general use, but should be reserved for application where the necessary personnel and safeguards are available and will be put to use.

NOTES

1. J. Moore, 'Why Privatise?' in J. Kay, C. Mayer, and D. Thompson (eds), Privatisation and regulation - the U.K. experience (Clarendon Press, Oxford, 1986), p. 82.

2. S.C. Littlechild, The fallacy of the mixed economy (Hobart Press no. 80, Institute of Economic Affairs, London, 1978).

3. D.N. Chester, 'The nationalised industries - external organisation' in Report of the Select Committee on Nationalised Industries, H.C.371 - II of 1967-8 (HMSO, London), p. 522.

4. Ibid., p. 523.

5. For an explanation of this term, see the two articles and by E.F. Fama and M.C. Jensen in The Journal of Law and Economics, vol. XXVI, no. 2 (June 1983), pp. 301-49.

6. The financial and economic obligations of the nationalised industries (Cmnd 1337, HMSO, London, 1961).

7. Ministerial control of the nationalised industries, H.C.371 of 1967-8 (HMSO, London).

8. Ibid., Vol. 1, para. 873.

9. Ministerial control of the nationalised industries (Cmnd 4027, HMSO, London, 1969).

10. A study of UK nationalised industries (NEDO, London, 1976), p. 8.

11. Ibid., pp. 46-50.

12. The financial and economic obligations of the nationalised industries; Nationalised industries: a review of economic and financial objectives; and The nationalised industries (respectively, Cmnd. 1337, 3437, and 7131, HMSO, London, 1961, 1967, and 1978).

13. For example, in 1980, vide Section V of the Financing of the nationalised industries, a report by the Treasury and Civil Service Committee, H.C.348 - I of 1980-81 (HMSO, London, 1981).

14. Report by the Comptroller and Auditor General, Departments of Energy, Trade and Industry and Transport: monitoring and control of nationalised industries, H.C.553 of 1983-4 (HMSO, London, 1984), p. 3.

15. Railway finances (HMSO, London, 1983), especially part 4 of the Minority Report.

16. Report by the Comptroller and Auditor General, Department of Energy, Transport and Trade Industry: effectiveness of Government financial controls over the nationalised industries, H.C.253 of 1985-6 (HMSO, London), pp. 5 and 6.

17. Ministerial control of the nationalised industries, H.C.371-I of 1967-8 (HMSO, London, 1967), para. 842.

18. A study of UK nationalised industries (NEDO, London, 1976), p. 40.

19. Effectiveness of Government controls over the nationalised industries, H.C.343 of 1985-6 (HMSO, London, 1986), para. 22.

20. 'A thousand ages in Thy sight
   Are like an evening gone.'

3

Privatisation: Introducing Competition, Opportunities and Constraints

David Thompson*

INTRODUCTION

The implementation of privatisation policy in the UK suggests a paradox. On the one hand, much emphasis has been placed on the importance of competition. The introduction of competition has been seen as central in raising the efficiency of public sector enterprises. Thus, in a keynote speech in 1983 the thenFinancial Secretary to the treasury, John Moore MP, concluded that 'The long-term success of the privatisation programme will stand or fall by the extent to which it maximises competition'.

Yet in practice, privatisation policy has come to be increasingly focused upon the transfer of the assets of state enterprises into the private sector. The promotion of competition, the 'main objective' of policy in the afore-mentioned speech has increasingly taken a back seat. Thus, the privatisation of British Telecom in 1983 was associated with only limited initiatives to introduce competition with the former nationalised industry - in particular through the licensing of a competing trunk supplier, Mercury, and through liberalisation of the supply of ancilliary apparatus (for example, phone sets). By the time of the privatisation

* David Thompson is a former Programme Director at the Institute for Fiscal Studies. The financial support of the Economic and Social Research Council in carrying out the research upon which this chapter is based is gratefully acknowledged. Helpful comments on an earlier draft of this paper came from John Kay and from participants at a Privatisation Seminar at Templeton College in December 1987. The usual disclaimer applies.

of British Gas in 1986 it is difficult to regard the associated provisions for liberalisation as anything more than window dressing.

On further examination, however, it seems that this paradox is more apparent than real. The sectors in which public enterprises have operated are generally those in which competitive private markets were considered to have failed. Indeed it was frequently a perception that private markets were failing to operate efficiently in these sectors that prompted government intervention in the first place. Thus, it might be argued that the ambition to introduce competition into the state enterprise sector, whilst desirable in principle, was misplaced. It was effectively in these terms that the Financial Secretary presented the re-direction of privatisation policy in a second keynote speech in 1985: he concluded that 'we will encourage competition where appropriate but where it does not make business or economic sense we will not hesitate to extend the benefits of privatisation to natural monopolies'.

However, technical limitations on the introduction of competition are not the only possible reasons for the reduced prominence of liberalisation policies. The existence of monopoly creates the potential for the creation and appropriation of monopoly rents. It has been suggested that both the management and work-force of public enterprises have had an interest in opposing policies of liberalisation (see Kay and Thompson, 1986), whilst the Treasury also has an interest in the proceeds from the sale of assets.

The objective of this chapter is to discuss how, and in what ways, the incidence of market failure in the state enterprise sector has limited the introduction of compet-ition and to consider what impact liberalisation policies have had in those cases where they have been introduced. The second part considers the characteristics of market failure in the state enterprise sector, and the implications of this for the introduction of competition are then assessed. The fourth section focuses upon sectors in which liberalisation policies appear most promising - potentially contestable markets - and considers the obstacles to the introduction of effective competition. In the penultimate section we consider liberalisation policy in practice and the discussion is illustrated with analysis of one of the first sectors to be liberalised after the present government came to power - the case of express coaching. The final part draws out implications for the formulation of liberalisation policy.

MARKET FAILURE IN THE STATE ENTERPRISE SECTOR

Under familiar conditions, competitive private markets ensure the achievement of economically efficient outcomes. Allocative efficiency is achieved because firms in competitive product markets have incentives to provide the range of goods and services desired by consumers at prices which reflect the relative costs of supply. Productive efficiency is achieved because firms in a competitive capital market can only survive and prosper if they adopt the most efficient technologies and the cost-minimising combination of factor inputs.

Once the fundamental theorems of welfare economies are relaxed, however, then this highly favourable outcome can no longer be guaranteed. This possibility is referred to as market failure. The types of market failure which are relevant to the state enterprise sectors of the economy can usefully be divided into three categories, and we will consider each of these in turn. Market failure arises where:

- competitive solutions do not exist;

- they exist but are not being achieved; or

- they exist and are achieved but are not efficient.

Natural monopoly is characteristic of many parts of the state enterprise sector. Where natural monopoly exists, production by a single firm is the most efficient outcome (Sharkey, 1982). Economies of scale or scope mean that a single firm is able to serve the market at lower unit costs than if the market is divided between several firms. Natural monopoly is most likely to occur in industries with extensive distribution networks: for example, the costs of two separate gas pipelines serving the same street are likely to be very much greater than a single, larger volume, pipeline. The existence of natural monopoly is not, however, sufficient by itself to prevent the achievement of competitive outcomes. The development of contestability theory (Baulmol et al., 1982) has shown that where a natural monopoly is perfectly contestable, the incumbent firm is constrained to act efficiently by the threat of potential competitive entry.

However, a requirement for perfect contestability is that there are no irrecoverable ('sunk') costs associated with entry and exit from the market by potential competitors. It is clear that in those parts of the public sector which have traditionally been regarded as natural monopolies, the sunk costs of market entry are substantial -for example in the case of the distribution networks for electricity, gas, water, railways and local telecom services. These sectors are therefore not only natural monopolies; they are uncontestable natural monopolies and the possibility of competitive entry will not be sufficient to ensure that incumbent firms act efficiently. In these sectors, liberalisation is likely to be an ineffective policy instrument.

Not all natural monopolies in the public enterprise sector are necessarily uncontestable, however. In particular it has been suggested that aviation and bus services may be natural monopolies at the level of the individual route but that the threat of entry may make each route contestable (see, for example, Bailey et al. 1985) and the White Paper 'Buses' (1984). We will consider this further when we look at the case of express coaching in the penultimate section.

In the parts of the public enterprise sector in which competitive solutions exist it might appear, at least at first sight, that a strategy of liberalisation is all that is required to achieve competitive outcomes. Even where competitive solutions exist, however, they may not be achieved. In general enterprises' interests (whether they be profit-maximisation, output maximisation or more diffuse objectives) will be best served by reducing the extent of product market competition which they face. The more direct routes to achieving this - merger with competitors or the formation of a cartel - are generally precluded by competition policy. However, whilst the most visible horizontal restrictions on competition are thus prevented, others are more difficult to detect and adjudicate against. Firms in oligopolistic markets may engage in a range of actions to deter market entry by potential competitors or to encourage the exit from the market of existing rivals. These include price predation, tie-in-sales, geographical or other restrictions on supply, investment in capacity and brand proliferation. The essential problem is that whilst in some circumstances each of these actions may be anti-competitive in intent and effect, it is equally plausible that in other circumstances they may reflect more benign motives. Thus, for example, tie-in-sales may reflect a genuine concern on the part of manufacturers for the association of their reputation with the way in which a product is marketed. Competitive pricing by incumbents in response to market entry may be very difficult to distinguish in practice from price predation. The achievement of competitive outcomes is, therefore, a complex policy task.

In circumstances in which competitive solutions are achieved, the outcome may nevertheless be perceived as unsatisfactory. Benefits and costs which are external to the decisions made by individual firms and consumers may result in a divergence between the outcome of the competitive process and the achievement of economic efficiency. Environmental pollution, road traffic congestion and research and development (R & D) activities are examples of externalities which have often been regarded as important to the formulation of, respectively, energy policy, public transport policy and industrial policy. Asymmetries in information between producers and consumers or between manufacturers and their supplies may also result in imperfections in market outcomes. In sectors which can be characterised in terms of unsustainable natural monopoly (that is, where production by a single firm provides the lowest cost of supply but where the incumbent cannot price at levels which prevent inefficient market entry), then a competitive outcome may be inferior to a situation in which market entry is restricted. It has been suggested that this 'wasteful competition' argument can be applied to, amongst other industries, container shipping and telecoms.

MARKET FAILURE AND THE INTRODUCTION OF COMPETITION

It will be clear that market failure of various types is endemic to the sectors in which state enterprises have traditionally operated. This is not, of course, to conclude that market solutions should be abandoned, or even modified, in these sectors. Government intervention to tackle market failure introduces the danger of 'regulatory failure' - that is, the possibility that intervention may have detrimental, although unintended, consequences for efficiency. Policy choice in these sectors therefore involves a balancing of the risks and consequences of both market failure and regulatory failure (for a wider discussion, see Kay and Thompson, 1988). What the incidence of market failure in the public enterprise sector does mean, however, is that there are limits to the introduction of competition. Nevertheless, I will argue that these limits are not as restrictive as is often assumed.

Where competitive solutions do not exist - that is, where there is uncontestable natural monopoly - then introducing the possibility of product market competition will be irrelevant. However, whilst many activities carried out by state (and former state) enterprises can be characterised as natural monopolies, there are many other activities which are not. Most UK nationalised industries carry out a mix of activities, some of which are potentially competitive even if others are not. The electricity supply industry (ESI) provides a good example: electricity distribution can be regarded as a natural monopoly, but clearly retailing electrical appliances is not. In the case of electricity generation, powerful arguments have been advanced either way. All three activities are carried out by the public sector electricity supply industry in the UK. The first is a statutory public sector monopoly and so, until recently, was the third. The retailing of appliances has always been liberalised, however.

This single example shows that any simple categorisation of the UK's nationalised industries into 'natural monopolies' - where competition can be assumed not to be appropriate - and 'contestable' industries - where competition is appropriate - is a misleading simplification.

Furthermore, even where natural monopoly precludes the introduction of competition within the product market, it may nevertheless be feasible to introduce competition for the market through franchising or competitive tendering (see Domberger (1986) for a discussion). It may also be feasible to introduce capital market incentives in these sectors through private ownership, although the absence of product market competition means that regulation of the possible exploitation of the monopoly is required.

The scope for the introduction of competitive incentives in industries traditionally regarded as 'natural monopolies' is clearly wide. However, this raises complex issues relating to the appropriate industrial structure, pattern of ownership and framework of regulation in these sectors. Many of the other chapters in this volume consider these questions in relation to individual industries and for this reason I do not propose to provide more detailed discussion here. For a more general discussion the reader is referred also to Vickers and Yarrow (1985) and Kay et al. (1986).

Where competitive solutions exist but are not efficient, then the appropriate policy response generally lies not in suspending the operation of market forces but rather in modifying their outcome. Thus, in the case of externalities (such as environmental pollution, for example) the appropriate solution may be to tax the output of the pollutant, subsidise pollution control, establish property rights in a pollution-free environment or, where the pollutant has significant public good characteristics to determine regulatory standards. The detrimental consequences of information asymmetries may in some cases be eliminated by the establishment of regulatory standards and requirements to provide information on their achievement (e.g. food additives). Distributional concerns in relation to the outputs of the state enterprises sector may best be dealt with within the framework of tax and benefit policy (see Dilnot and Helm (1987) for a discussion in relation to energy prices). The list of possible market failures, and their potential solutions, is long. Many of the other chapters in this volume consider particular market failures which are relevant to individual industries, and again, for this reason we will not pursue a more detailed analysis here (see also Mayer (1985) and Kay and Thompson (1988) for further discussion). Rather, we will now focus upon the third category of market failures - situations in which competitive solutions exist and are efficient but where they are not achieved. In the next section we will consider the possible barriers to effective competition before moving on to look at liberalisation policy in practice.

LIBERALISATION POLICIES AND CONTESTABILITY

The theory of contestable markets provides a useful reference point for the consideration of liberalisation policy. A perfectly contestable market ensures, like the more familiar model of perfect competition, the achievement of allocative and productive efficiency, subject to the familiar assumptions of welfare economics. Unlike the model of perfect competition, contestability can be generalised to consider outcomes where economies of scale or scope are significant. Perfect contestability ensures the

achievement of productive efficiency in these circumstances, and provides incentives to the achievement of an
efficient second-best allocative outcome. The requirements
for a market to be perfectly contestable are the following:

- all firms, incumbents and potential competitors
  have access to the same technology;
- there are no irrecoverable (or sunk) costs
  associated with entry and exit from the market;
  and
- incumbent firms' prices are 'sticky' in adjusting in
  response to market entry.

The consequence of these assumptions is that incumbent
firms which set prices above efficient levels will be
vulnerable to 'hit and run' entry by firms who are able to
enter the market, make a profit (by undercutting the
incumbent), and exit (without incurring any sunk costs)
before the incumbent is able to reduce his 'sticky' prices.
The implication is that incumbents are constrained to
achieve both allocative and productive efficiency by the
threat of hit-and-run entry. Where economies of scale or
scope are present, incumbents are constrained to set prices
no higher than is sufficient to yield normal profits. In these
circumstances, there are also incentives to structure the
mark-up of prices above marginal costs in each market in a
manner which is efficient, subject to the constraint of just
covering total costs; that is, to mark up prices in proportion
to the price elasticity of demand in each market (the
familiar Ramsey pricing rule).

Contestability theory thus provides a benchmark for
identifying the conditions required for a liberalised market
to achieve economic efficiency. Where these conditions do
not hold then the market will be only imperfectly
contestable. This might arise because incumbents follow
more flexible (and perhaps predatory) pricing policies or it
might arise because potential competitors face sunk costs
associated with entry and exit. Oligopoly theory identifies a
whole range of potential barriers to market entry (see
Waterson (1984) and Vickers (1985) for surveys), and it is
useful to divide these into 'innocent' and 'strategic' barriers
as suggested by Salop (1979). 'Innocent' barriers to entry
arise from the characteristics of the incumbent and the
market concerned; they are often a consequence simply of

the incumbent 'being there'. British Telecom, for example, is by far the best-known supplier of branch-exchanges because for many years it was the only supplier. 'Strategic' barriers to entry refer to actions taken by incumbents to deter the market entry of new competitors or to encourage the exit of existing rivals. The nature of such strategic actions is that usually they will leave the incumbent worse off in the short run. The pay-off arises from the anticipated reduction in potential competition, and hence greater profit opportunities, for incumbents in the longer term. The key to the effectiveness of strategic actions is thus the effect which they have upon the expectations of potential competitors. Price predation, for example, would be worthwhile only if it was successful not only in driving an existing competitor from the market but also in persuading future competitors that market entry is not worthwhile because there is a possibility that it would be met with retaliation (see Vickers (1985) for a discussion of the 'chain store paradox').

The literature suggests a whole range of strategic actions which might be followed (again see ibid., and Waterson, 1984). Some of these are directed towards reducing the profitability of entrants whilst they are operating in the market (for example, by reducing prices, proliferating brands, or raising industry operating costs); others are directed toward raising the costs associated with entry and exit (for example, by requiring simultaneous entry into related markets, or by raising product quality); and some are directed towards raising entrants' expectations that entry will be met with retaliation (e.g. investment in capacity).

It will be clear that there is an interaction between 'innocent' and 'strategic' barriers to entry. The 'higher' are the innocent barriers then the lower is the investment required in strategic action to drive a competitor from the market. Because potential entrants are aware of this, however, the existence of innocent entry barriers not only increases the likelihood that strategic action will be successful but also increases the probability that it will be carried out. Innocent barriers to entry therefore provide both a basis and an incentive for strategic action.

This discussion suggests that the objectives of liberalisation policy should be to reduce where feasible the significance of innocent barriers to entry prior to a market being liberalised and to police and forestall the implementation of strategic barriers by incumbent firms once liberalisation has been implemented. To illustrate the potential significance of this in practice we now turn to consideration of the implementation of liberalisation policy in the UK.

LIBERALISATION IN PRACTICE

One of the first sectors to be deregulated by the present government was express (that is, inter-city) coach services. Legislation was introduced soon after the government took power in 1979 and deregulation came into effect in October of 1980. Although not a major part of the public sector, express coaching provides a striking illustration of the development of competition in a market in which state monopoly has been liberalised. Many of the themes which emerge are, as we shall note, being repeated in the more significant parts of the public sector which have been liberalised more recently.

Prior to liberalisation, the regulatory system for express coaching conferred effective monopoly rights for the operation of individual routes. Rights to the more important routes were generally held by public sector enterprises. In England, and on routes between the provincial English cities and Scotland, rights were held by National Express (a part of the National Bus Company). In Scotland, and on routes between London and Scotland, rights were held by companies in the Scottish Bus Group. In addition, private sector companies held rights to a small number of less important routes.

Deregulation removed restrictions on market entry. From October 1980, anyone could start up a coach service and compete with existing services provided only that they met various quality criteria: these relate to the entrants' financial probity, the safety of their vehicles and the competence of their drivers. Although most existing route rights were held by the two public sector groups, there also existed a large and highly competitive market in the provision of contract coach services. These were services in which a whole coach was contracted by the customer, for example to carry employees to their work-place or to carry children to school. The private sector companies operating in this market were thus an important source of potential cross-entry into the newly deregulated market for express coach services.

On a priori grounds, express coach services appeared to be a sector which was likely to fulfil the requirements of contestability theory. In particular, a wide range of companies had immediate access to the basic technology of the industry, either because they were already supplying express coach services or, more usually, through operation in the contract coach market. The sunk costs associated with entry (and potential exit) on to a particular route appeared low; the most important factor inputs, coaches and drivers, could be readily deployed between different routes or between different kinds of coaching services. The 'stickiness' of incumbents' prices was the requirement which appeared least likely to hold; however, the need to publicise price changes to a market containing a significant number of infrequent purchasers suggested the possibility of some 'stickiness'.

The immediate impact of deregulation suggested, however, that any doubts concerning the contestability of express coach markets were unfounded. In anticipation of deregulation a consortium of ten of the contract coach companies established plans for a national network of services in competition with the public sector incumbents. In addition, several other private coach companies entered on a smaller scale - serving a handful of routes radiating from their home base.

This significant scale of market entry was reflected in market performance. Deregulation was followed by substantial reductions in prices on most of the major inter-city routes and by significant innovation both in the types of service offered (new 'luxury' coaches were introduced offering in-journey videos and food and drink) and in the types of ticket product (with new types of discount fares). A progressive re-shaping of the network took place, with service levels being cut back on less densely trafficked routes and expanded on the more popular routes. This outcome is consistent with the view that in a regulated environment, networks had become ossified and, as in the case of local bus services (see MMC, 1982), had failed to respond to changes in the pattern of demand. Deregulation was followed - not surprisingly in view of these developments - by a reversal in the declining trend in passenger traffic (see Barton and Everest (1984) and Robbins and White (1986) for an account of the development of the liberalised express coach market).

Deregulation thus appeared, and indeed was, an

49

immediate success. However, a market with many competing companies proved to be only a transitory phase. Companies soon started to leave the private sector consortium and by early 1983 (little more than two years after deregulation) it was formally dissolved. Many of the private coach companies either exited the market or entered into joint ventures with National Express. By 1984 National Express faced competition on only a handful of its routes, although competitors with companies in the Scottish Bus Group were more successful in retaining market share.

The achievement of a high market share by National Express in the deregulated market is, of course, not necessarily inconsistent with an efficient outcome. Provided that the markets are contestable, the incumbent will be constrained to act efficiently by the threat of market entry. In these circumstances a high market share can be regarded as a sign of virtue, reflecting favourably on the incumbent's efficiency, rather than of vice. The key question to determining the success of express coach deregulation is thus whether markets have remained contestable or whether, alternatively, incumbents' high market shares are a consequence of innocent or strategic barriers to entry.

Analysis of price levels on different express coach routes shows that the pattern of relative prices is not consistent with the contestability hypothesis (see Jaffer and Thompson, 1986, 1987). Prices are higher, in relation to underlying cost and demand characteristics, on routes where market concentration is high and are lower on routes where market entrants have been successful in retaining a significant share of the deregulated market. The most important distinction (although not the only relevant one) is between routes where National Express was incumbent at the time of deregulation and routes where companies in the Scottish Bus Group were incumbent. In the case of the former, as noted earlier, entrants have usually exited the market and prices are comparatively high in relation to the cost and demand characteristics relevant to each route. In the case of the latter, entrants have been successful in retaining a significant market share on many routes and prices are comparatively lower.

Further examination indicates a number of barriers to entry which have enabled National Express to deter market entry successfully whilst sustaining a level of prices which is significantly above that prevailing in markets in which entrants have remained in the market. National Express benefited from two innocent barriers to entry. Firstly, it had a well-established (although not necessarily well-regarded) product name stemming from its predominant position in the regulatory era. Entrants faced considerable costs if they wished to match this product goodwill. Furthermore, the expenditure involved in advertising and establishing sales networks is in substantial part a sunk cost. In contrast, prior to deregulation the companies in the Scottish Bus Group had not marketed their services under a single brand name and indeed, did not start to do so until three years after deregulation was implemented. In these markets, therefore, the sunk costs faced by potential entrants in establishing product goodwill were not significantly higher than those faced by the incumbent.

The second 'innocent' entry barrier from which National Express benefited relates to its scope for responding to market entry. Oligopoly theory identifies the importance of the bankruptcy constraint and incumbent firms' objectives. A firm with a weak bankruptcy constraint is more likely to win a post-entry price (or non-price) war, whilst an output-maximising firm is more likely to respond to entry with retaliation rather than accommodation, than is a profit-maximiser. At the time of deregulation National Express was a small subsidiary company of a large public sector enterprise which operated in markets where, typically, competition was precluded by regulatory controls. As such its bankruptcy constraint was probably perceived to be weak, despite government financial controls which required its activities to be accounted for separately from the rest of the National Bus Company. Furthermore, the new positive theory of public enterprise (see Rees, 1984) suggests that public enterprises can be characterised as output-maximisers subject to a financial constraint. Both of these characteristics of National Express can have been expected to signal to potential entrants that market entry might be met with retaliation. In principle, both factors apply equally to the companies in the Scottish Bus Group. However, the far larger size of the National Bus Company suggests that they are likely to have proved more significant in its case.

We noted earlier that the presence of 'innocent' barriers to entry increases the potential returns, and hence the probability, of strategic action. The development of competition in the newly deregulated express coach market shows a number of actions by National Express which have the characteristics of entry deterrence. The company used its rights of ownership or control over many city centre coaching terminals to bar access by competitors (see Davis, 1984). The sunk costs associated with the development of competing facilities would have been substantial, although joint ventures developed with central London hotels by some successful entrants demonstrated an ingenious method of minimising these sunk costs. However, refusal of access also had the effect of raising consumer search costs for passengers. Many consumers wishing to consider the option of travelling on a competitor's service would start by simply contacting the best-known coach terminal.

This action by National Express also acted to the benefit of the Scottish Bus Group companies in relation to Victoria Coach Station - the predominant London terminal. In the Scottish cities, however, there was often less scope for incumbents to secure favourable terminal access than in the English provincial cities served by National Express.

It will be clear that National Express was only able to take this particular type of strategic action because it carried out two separate - although vertically linked - activities in the deregulated coaching market. Firstly, it provided express coaching services - a potentially competitive activity. Secondly, it provided coaching terminal services - an activity in which competition can be expected to be highly imperfect because of the potentially high sunk costs associated with entry. It was because of its common ownership of both these activities that National Express was able to use its dominant position in the latter activity - terminal services - as a basis for deterring entry in the potentially competitive activity - coaching services. The common ownership of these two vertically linked activities can be viewed as a third type of 'innocent' barrier to entry.

As the deregulated market developed, National Express was able to use this control of access to Victoria Coach Station as an inducement to selected competitors to participate in joint ventures with it. This had the effect of removing one source of competition on particular routes - in some cases at the expense of other entrants.

National Express's most significant response to entry was, however, an announced policy that it would match the prices offered by entrants, a policy which was put into practice. This policy had the effect of reducing the potential 'stickiness' of its pricing response to entry. Consumers were effectively told that the company's prices would always equal the opposition and specific marketing initiatives which responded to entrant's actions were supplementary, rather than central, to informing consumers of this. Taken together with its access to city centre coaching terminals and its high service frequencies, this pricing policy had the effect that National Express was generally offering a more attractive package of price and service quality than its rivals. In contrast, the companies in the Scottish Bus Group did not follow a policy of matching entrants prices and in practice usually allowed themselves to be undercut by between 10 and 20 per cent.

The outcome has been a situation in which, as already described, competitors to National Express have generally exited from the market and where a higher level of prices has been sustained than on the Scottish Bus Group routes. This outcome has been reflected in the trend in prices since deregulation. On routes on which National Express was incumbent at the time of deregulation, the initial steep cut in prices has been followed by a steady real increase. Fare levels are still lower, in real terms, than prior to deregulation, but only by a modest amount. In contrast, fare levels on the routes on which the Scottish Bus Group companies were incumbent remain over 20 per cent lower, in real terms, than the level prior to deregulation.

This clearly does not suggest that the deregulation of express coach services has failed. The innovation which has taken in products and services, the progressive re-balancing of the network towards areas of high demand, and the lower overall level of real prices, all point to significant benefits. It does suggest, however, that deregulation has fallen well short of achieving the full benefits of effective competition on many of the deregulated routes.

This pattern of continued incumbent dominance is one which is mirrored in many other sectors in which deregulation policies have introduced competition into what were formerly state monopoly activities. In the case of telecoms' private branch exchanges (PBXs), British Telecom has continued to hold a large share of the deregulated market (see Gist and Meadowcroft, 1986), although, as in the case of express coaches, deregulation has been followed by a significant product differentiation and a decline in real price levels.

In the energy sector, the deregulation of gas supply (in 1982) and electricity supply (in 1983) has been followed by negligible market entry and it is difficult to detect any significant change in consumer prices or the range of products offered (see Hammond et al., 1985, 1986). In contrast, the liberalisation of domestic air services in the UK and international services to some European countries has been followed by more significant market entry and by a favourable impact upon prices and the range of products offered (see McGowan and Trengove, 1986 and CAA, 1987). Nevertheless, incumbents remain the largest players in these markets and deregulation has not resulted in the significant increase in efficiency which followed US deregulation, despite the frequently made claim that significant scope for improvement exists in European air services (see, for example, Sawers (1987), National Consumer Council (1986), McGowan and Trengove, 1986).

In each of these markets, incumbents have benefited from the innocent barriers to entry identified in the case of National Express - product goodwill established from the regulated era, financial strength provided by continued access to many markets in which competition remains prohibited, and common ownership of potentially competitive activities, where deregulation has been implemented, and vertically related activities where competition is imperfect or absent. There are also suggestions of strategic actions which have built upon these innocent barriers - exclusive supply arrangements and the takeover of a principal competitor in the case of PBXs (see Gist and Meadowcroft (1986) for a discussion), and attempted takeover of a principal competitor in the case of aviation.

The common ownership of potentially competitive and of imperfectly competitive activities is of particular significance in the case of PBXs and the energy industries. We saw that in the coaching case, common ownership of coaching and terminals provided the basis for strategic action by effectively requiring simultaneous entry into both activities, the latter activity involving significant sunk costs. In the case of PBXs, gas production and electricity generation the deregulated activity is vertically linked to an uncontestable natural monopoly activity (the relevant distribution network) which is owned, in each case by the incumbent. To enter the deregulated market, therefore, a potential competitor, or his customer, must enter into a contractual relationship with the incumbent to obtain the required vertical linkage with the natural monopoly activity. This provides obvious opportunities for abuse and, equally importantly, signals to entrants the possibility that abuse will occur. Furthermore, the dominance of information and expertise enjoyed by incumbents is such that any abuse is difficult both to detect and to police (see Hammond et al. (1986) for a discussion of the difficulties in determining whether or not the public sector electricity supply industry has acted anti-competitively in setting the terms of entry into the deregulated market for electricity generation).

We now turn finally to consideration of how liberalisation policy can be framed so as to minimise more effectively the effect of these entry barriers, which appear to be almost universal in recently deregulated state monopoly activities.

PROMOTING COMPETITION IN POTENTIALLY CONTESTABLE MARKETS

The discussion in the previous section distinguished the separate, although interrelated, importance of innocent and strategic barriers to entry. This distinction suggests that a successful liberalisation strategy requires two distinct parts. The objective of the first part, prior to deregulation, is to reduce the effect of innocent entry barriers upon the development of competition in the deregulated market. The objective of the second part, post deregulation, is to inhibit strategic action by incumbents to deter entry or to encourage the exit of existing competitors.

The dismantling of innocent entry barriers points to two implications in particular. The first is minimisation of the financial strength which incumbents in many deregulated markets have drawn from their access to markets where competition is limited. This suggests separation of the ownership of deregulated activities from activities where competition remains imperfect (whether because of natural monopoly or because of remaining statutory restrictions). The second is minimisation of the scope for strategic action in deregulated markets which is provided by common ownership of potentially contestable activities and vertically linked activities which have high sunk costs of entry. This again suggests separation of the ownership of the relevant activities. In the case of express coaches the first consideration would suggest separation of the ownership of National Express and the rest of the National Bus Group, whilst the second consideration suggests separation of the ownership of National Express's coaching activities from their ownership of coaching terminal services. This is a policy which is, somewhat belatedly, being implemented as part of the privatisation of the National Bus Group. The prohibition of strategic action by incumbents is a more general problem, but one which has particular significance in newly deregulated markets in which the comparative advantage of incumbents is unusually large. The success of incumbents in protecting their position in newly deregulated markets raises the question of whether UK competition policy is sufficiently strong to guarantee effective competition in markets in which there is a substantial imbalance in the strength of incumbents and potential entrants. One solution to this is the restructuring of industries prior to deregulation, even in circumstances in which this is not suggested by the preceding discussion, to provide for more evenly balanced competition. The breakup of the National Bus Company which has accompanied the liberalisation of local bus services has provided significant scope for cross-entry from one local geographic area to another.

However, this also suggests that the development of competition in newly liberalised markets requires more than the removal of statutory restrictions on competition, even if this is accompanied by appropriate restructuring. It is clear that effective competition also requires an effective competition policy to detect and inhibit anti-competitive activity in the newly deregulated markets.

REFERENCES

Bailey, E.E., D.R. Graham and D.P. Kaplan (1985) Deregulating the airlines, MIT Press, Cambridge, MA

Barton, A.J. and J.T. Everest (1984) Express coaches in the three years following the 1980 Transport Act. TRRL Report, 1127

Baulmol, W.J., J.C. Panzar and R.D. Willig (1982) Contestable markets and the theory of industry structure. Harcourt Brace Jovanovich, New York

Civil Aviation Authority (CAA) (1987) Competition on the main domestic trunk routes. CAA Paper, 87005

Davis, E.H. (1984) Express coaching since 1980: liberalisation in practice. Fiscal Studies, 5, (1), 76-86

Department of Transport (1984) Buses. Cmnd 9300, HMSO, London

Dilnot, A.W. and D.R. Helm (1987) Energy policy, merit

goods and social security. Fiscal Studies, 8, (3)

Domberger, S. (1986) Economic regulation through franchise contracts. In J.A. Kay, C.P. Mayer and D.J. Thompson (eds), Privatisation and regulation - the UK experience, Oxford University Press

Gist, P. and S.M. Meadowcroft (1986) Regulating for competition: the newly liberalised market for private branch exchanges. Fiscal Studies, 7 (3), 41-66

Hammond, E.M., D.R. Helm and D. J. Thompson (1985) British Gas: options for privatisation. Fiscal Studies, 6 (4), 1-20

_____ (1986) Has the Energy Act failed? Fiscal Studies, 7 (1)

Jaffer, S.M. and D.J. Thompson (1986) Deregulating express coaches: a reassessment. Fiscal Studies, November

_____ (1987) Express coaching: an analysis of contestability in practice. Institute of Fiscal Studies Working Paper, 79

Kay, J.A., C.P. Mayer and D.J. Thompson (eds) (1986) Privatisation and regulation - the UK experience. Oxford University Press

Kay, J.A. and D.J. Thompson (1986) Privatisation: a policy in search of a rationale. Economic Journal, March

_____ (1988) Policy for industry. In R.G. Layard and R. Dornbusch (eds), Britain's economic performance, Oxford University Press

Mayer, C.P. (1985) Recent developments in industrial economics and their implications for policy. Oxford Review of Economic Policy, 1, (3)

McGowan, F. and C. Trengove (1986) European aviation - a common market? Institute of Fiscal Studies Report Series, 23

Monopolies and Mergers Commission (MMC) (1982) HC 442. HMSO, London

Rees, R. (1984) A positive theory of public enterprise. In M. Marchand, P. Pestieau and H. Tulkens (eds), The performance of public enterprises, North Holland, Amsterdam

Robbins, D.K. and D.W. White (1986) The experience of express coaching deregulation in Great Britain. Transportation

Salop, S. (1979) Strategic entry deterrence. American Economic Review, Papers and Proceedings, 69, 335-8

Sawers, D. (1987) Competition in the air. Institute of Economic Affairs, London

Sharkey, W.M. (1982) The theory of natural monopoly.

Cambridge University Press, Cambridge

Vickers, J. (1985) Strategic competition among the few - some recent developments in the economics of industry. Oxford Review of Economic Policy, 1 (3)

_____ and G. Yarrow (1985) Privatization and the natural monopolies. Public Policy Centre, London

Waterson, M. (1984) Economic theory of the industry. Cambridge University Press, Cambridge

4

Privatisation and the Consumer

John Hatch*

This chapter considers the ways in which privatisation of the nationalised industries affects the consumer; but it is impossible to consider the effects on consumers without first looking at the more general rationale for privatisation. I will therefore start by examining the theory behind privatisation, before focusing on the consumers' experience of privatisation to date. I will then move on to electricity, establish some key principles for safeguarding consumers in a privatised electricity supply industry (ESI), and suggest a possible institutional framework to ensure that this happens.

THE RATIONALE FOR PRIVATISATION

As is well known, the privatisation programme under the Conservative administrations since 1979 has grown to the point where, to quote John Moore's famous contention, 'nothing is sacred... except for the Treasury'. From the sale of 25 per cent of ICL in December 1979, through the landmark £4 billion flotation of British Telecom, and the £5.6 billion of British Gas, we now contemplate something in the order of £18 billion for the electricity industry in England and Wales.

Before we become transfixed by the figures, however, we should remind ourselves why it is that the boundaries between the public and private sectors have been re-drawn. Essentially, the objectives of the programme fall into four

* Chairman, Electricity Consumers' Council. The author acknowledges the great assistance received from Mr Stephen Young in the preparation of this paper

59

categories:

(1) to increase competition and spread consumer choice;

(2) to reduce the Public Sector Borrowing Requirement (PSBR)/increase government revenues;

(3) to give the public and the work-force a stake in industry; and

(4) to allow nationalised industry management to escape from 'the dead hand of Whitehall'.

These objectives will be considered briefly below, starting with competition.

Competition and consumer choice

The switch to supply side economics, and the rebirth of neo-classical economic theory, have revived the notion that the unimpeded operation of firms in freely competitive markets maximises consumer satisfaction - producing optimum outcomes for society. What Keynes described as the unquestioned elegance and logical appeal of the classical model has been re-inserted into economic policy-making.

As the 1987 Conservative Party Manifesto put it, 'Competition forces the economy to respond to the needs of the consumer, it promotes efficiency, holds down costs, drives companies to innovate, and ensures that customers get the best possible value for money.' Cecil Parkinson, when Secretary of State for Industry, remarked,

> The truth is that public service and private profit go hand in hand. Public service means serving the public and giving them what they want. Marks and Spencer, Sainsbury, the local newsagent - they all give an excellent public service but they are all trying to make a profit.

Cutting state expenditures/raising state revenues

The second objective of privatisation, to reduce the drain caused by the public sector and increase the flow of revenues to the Treasury, has a number of components. These include the effects on the money supply and interest rates, the impact on the equity market and the problem of crowding out. The 'crowding out' thesis contends that the growth of the state imposes undesirable constraints on the development of the private sector - either through producing higher tax burdens, thus reducing profits and incentives to invest, or through high PSBR levels, which raise interest rates and the costs of investment.

When an industry is transferred to the private sector, the Treasury treats the business's net spending, previously its cash limit within the PSBR, as outside the PSBR. Furthermore, proceeds from flotation are counted as negative PSBR, reducing the government's requirements for finance. While this may not be the place to join the debate, it is worth noting that the nature of the causal relationships between the PSBR and the money supply, and their relationship to the mechanics of privatisation, remain controversial.

The capital-owning democracy

The third objective of privatisation has been, to quote the 1987 Conservative Party Manifesto, 'to make share ownership available to the whole nation. Just as with cars, television sets, washing machines and foreign holidays...'; or as Nicholas Ridley put it, when Financial Secretary to the Treasury (1982), 'Real public ownership - that is, ownership by the people - must be and is our ultimate goal.' Purchasers of equity in privatised companies have both a financial stake and a direct source of influence over the company - both of which had been lacking from the Morrisonian model of the public corporation.

Thus, privatisation has curtailed the decline in individual share ownership in the UK, with almost a quarter of Britain's adult population now owning shares. The BT flotation raised the number of shareholders from 2 million to 3.2 million. After the Trustee Savings Bank privatisation, the figure grew to 7 million. British Gas took the total to over 8 million, and a recent poll by Dewe Rogerson indicates that, since Rolls Royce and the British Airports Authority flotations, the figure has now reached 9.4 million. Clearly, there are many more Sids now than we would have thought possible a few years ago.

Privatisation and the Consumer

The dead hand of Whitehall

The fourth objective is that of allowing nationalised industry managements to escape 'the dead hand of Whitehall'. Privatisation will, it is said, free an industry from the contradictory nexus of political interference and non-market criteria, permitting that industry to make more rational economic decisions. Removing nationalised industries from the entanglement of red tape and the interfering expediency of politicians, replacing bureaucracy with the market, will clarify the objectives of the industry and lead to enhanced economic performance.

One example of state control hampering a utility's plans would be British Telecom, which, barred from raising loans on the domestic capital market, was unable to finance its much-needed modernisation programme - with results that have now become apparent.

A CONTRADICTORY RATIONALE?

Whilst these objectives are laudable individually, in toto they can be shown to be incompatible. The resulting diffusion, and even conflict of objectives, has produced sub-optimal outcomes for the programme as a whole - and the consumer has often been left to carry the can.

How can this come about? There are two main areas of conflict between the objectives described above, but each impacts directly on the notion of competition. Firstly, there is the Treasury's requirement for maximum proceeds from a flotation - and a strong case could be made that the revenue-generating potential of a company being floated is inversely related to the degree of competition in its markets. A similar conflict is generated by the government's intention to create a share-owning democracy, with the maximum take-up of an industry's shares. Again, the injection of more competition would be likely to reduce investors' willingness to participate in a flotation.

The airline industry provided a clear example of this when, in 1984, the Civil Aviation Authority recommended that a number of prime routes be transferred from British Airways (BA) to British Caledonian. BA Chairman Lord King threatened to resign if the re-allocation went ahead, claiming, 'There is no way you could ever get a prospectus written for privatisation if these proposals were allowed to stand.' The OECD later commented:

> British Airways route monopolies were hardly affected in the review which preceded privatisation plans. While this will ensure that the sale price is not affected in an unfavourable way, it does not auger well. The government has been inhibited from breaking up public sector monopolies before sale because of the effect on the sale price. The mixture of motives - desire for increased competition and the need to secure maximum proceeds for the taxpayer - may have reduced policy effectiveness. (OECD, Economic Surveys 'United Kingdom 1984-85', 1985)

Why should any of this concern the consumer? The theoretical theme, strongly supported by empirical evidence (of which more later), is that the key to consumer sovereignty is market structure. The act of privatisation does not, in itself, produce changes in market structure. Markets are a form of organisation, not a form of ownership - public ownership is not synonymous with non-market mechanisms, while private ownership does not, in itself, imply that the market holds sway.

The returns available to a firm depend much less on ownership than on the nature of the market in which it operates. Privatisation, if it is to produce the claimed benefits, must operate in tandem with more competition, and an abrogation of monopoly powers: or as the Financial Times (5 October 1983) has noted, '...the introduction of competitive pressure to public sector enterprise is a far greater spur to efficiency than the act of privatisation'.

Hence, if the public is to benefit from privatisation as a consumer, rather than as a taxpayer, a worker, or a shareowner, privatisation must proceed hand in hand with the introduction of competition.

COMPETITION AND THE CONSUMER - A LOOK AT THE EVIDENCE

The evidence on performance of privatised utilities to date is mixed.

Privatisation and the Consumer

British Telecom (BT)

For the mainstream areas of BT's business, the company is still effectively a monopoly, or at best a duopoly. Mercury, primarily aimed at business users, is aiming at about 5 per cent of the market - arguably not effective competition. Over the past few months, BT's apparent indifference to the consumer has generated much comment.

As soon as it was privatised, BT stopped publishing the quality of service measurements it had previously produced on the grounds that the information was 'commercially sensitive'. This prompted Bryan Carsberg, Director-General of the Office of Telecommunications (OFTEL), to set up his own monitoring system. Since privatisation, consumer complaints received by OFTEL are running at higher levels than before privatisation, with call boxes causing particular problems for 48 per cent of complainants. BT expects that, at any one time, between 16 and 18 per cent of its 78,000 call boxes will be out of order - in November 1986 OFTEL reported that 21 per cent of call boxes were unusable. By way of comparison, New York Telephone expects between 2 and 3 per cent of its 55,000 boxes will be out of order at any time.

In the recent utilities survey conducted by the National Consumer Council, 18 per cent of respondents considered that BT was 'not very' or 'not at all' effective in sorting out consumer problems, compared with a figure of 12 or 13 per cent in other utilities. Three times as many respondents wanted to complain about telephones as about water and electricity. In similar vein, the Telecom Users' Association received as many complaints in the first half of 1987 as in the whole of 1986.

However, if we turn to areas of the telecom market in which genuine competition exists, the experience has been different. While Mercury has yet to make an impact in the domestic market, with barely 2,000 customers, its cables now pass over 1,000 buildings in the City of London, and have penetrated over half of these. While domestic tariffs are among the highest in Europe, evidence is beginning to emerge that long distance and international customers are better served.

Looking at the market for equipment, the ending of the Prime Instrument Monopoly has given consumers the option of attaching any telecom equipment with a green 'approved' label to the end of their telephone line. The result has been a proliferation of phone shops in the High Street, and a severe shock for BT, which is losing market share in both the private exchange sector and the telephone sector. BT's share of the telephone market fell from 79 per cent in 1985 to 66 per cent in 1986, and is expected to decline to 44 per cent by 1989. Meanwhile, the High Street telephone market, which almost doubled in size in 1986, to reach £46 million, is predicted to double again by 1989. The biggest share of the retail phone market was supplied by Dixons (19 per cent), followed by Comet (15 per cent), Argos (11 per cent) and Boots (10 per cent). BT shops took only 4 per cent. In much the same way, the market for answerphones, previously another expensive BT monopoly, is expected to reach 590,000 machines by 1989, up from 300,000 in 1986 (Financial Times, 17 August 1987).

The result of the liberalisation of markets for phone equipment has been a rapid advance in consumer access to advanced telephone technology, and an equally dramatic fall in the price of equipment - buying a phone outright now costs less than a year's rental.

British Gas

Ostensibly, the experience of gas consumers since privatisation has been favourable. Domestic tariffs were cut by an average of 4.5 per cent in June 1987, slightly more generous than the price changes allowed under the Retail Price Index minus x plus y formula, according to Sir Denis Rooke. However, the OFGAS Director-General, James McKinnon, was concerned that British Gas was not passing on the full benefits of falling gas prices to consumers. In the ensuing struggle for information, OFGAS eventually resorted to threats of legal action against British Gas to obtain the information it needed to perform its statutory duty. British Gas eventually complied with the OFGAS request by delivering a brown envelope to OFGAS on the morning of the British Gas's Annual General Meeting. As far as we know, McKinnon is still digesting the contents.

For unregulated customers, heavy industrial users, the experience has been different. A survey by National Utility Services shows that the average price of 34.2p a therm paid by British business this year is the highest in Europe, a marked change from 1986, when UK gas was cheaper than West German, French or Belgian gas. Average prices for industrial gas in the UK have fallen by 1 per cent since last year, whereas in other European countries the reduction has been in the order of one-third (Financial Times, 1 October 1987). Little wonder that the Office of Fair Trading has received complaints from the British Iron and Steel Producers Association, the Chemical Industries Association, and the British Data Management Foundation, while Sheffield Foregemasters has taken its complaint to the Office of Fair Trading (OFT) and the European Community.

Coach and bus travel

The provision of long and short distance bus services was deregulated in 1980 and 1986 respectively, with widespread relaxation of the licensing requirements on coach and bus operators. At this stage, evidence of the results is mixed.

Long distance road passengers have benefited from a wider range of cheaper services, but the experience of the more recent local bus deregulation is less clear, and seems to depend on location - some areas having benefited from more buses and lower fares, while others have had the reverse experience. Research by the Transport and Road Research Laboratory shows that the number of bus operators has gone up by 4 per cent since deregulation, while 83 per cent are now run without subsidy. Minibuses, more appropriate for many routes, have been widely introduced. The proportion of services run by the private sector has increased by half, from 8 to 12 per cent. Drawbacks have included withdrawal of fares concessions, and reduction in off-peak services, loss of cross-ticketing facilities, and lack of timetabling co-ordination.

The three industries considered above demonstrate that, on the whole, the key to delivering better performance to the consumer is liberalisation - the process by which an industry which has previously been able to protect itself from competition, either because of its statutory monopoly, or because it has erected barriers to entry, is exposed to competitive forces when government changes the rules of the game. Privatisation itself is relatively unimportant.

ELECTRICITY - COMPETITION OR CONSOLIDATION?

We now turn to potentially the biggest privatisation of all -

electricity. As shown above, for BT, some competition has been introduced; but the very nature of telecommunications, with rapid advances in new technology, means that BT will be subject to a continuing increase in competitive pressure - the 'naturalness' of the monopoly will be eroded by devlopments in satellites, cellular communication, fibre optics, and so on. Such pressures will not be evident in the case of electricity, where the insertion of competitive pressures will depend on governmental will rather than leading-edge technological change.

For the consumer, contact with the electricity industry is with the Area Board. Distribution is a locational monopoly, however, and likely to remain so; and effective competition in transmission would require confutation of the textbook logic of economic efficiency. Hence, it is widely recognised that the only real scope for competition is in the generation of electricity. An example of why this might be desirable was provided when the ESI released its Annual Report and Accounts in July 1987. The industry's financial performance in 1986-7 was impressive, with an operating profit of £1,150 million; but while the costs of fuel inputs fell by 8.3 per cent, the Central Electricity Generating Board's other costs rose by 8.2 per cent. Nuclear power stations continued to show poor economic performance, to the extent that a price rise was threatened in order to recover increased costs - partly caused by inefficient advanced gas-cooled reactor plant. While this threat has now receded - partly due to intervention by the Electricity Consumers' Council (ECC) - it provides a perfect illustration of the way in which a monopoly supplier can exploit its position, and ride roughshod over consumers.

However, the introduction of competition into electricity generation will be neither quick nor easy. Electricity is unlike other products - it cannot be stored, its costs of production vary from minute to minute, and it must be available on demand. While there are various models available for the industry post-privatisation, the benefits for consumers are uncertain. It looks increasingly certain that the key to the industry's effective operation will be regulation - to control prices, protect service standards, and stimulate competition. I will now look briefly at the question of regulation - briefly because this is a theme which George Yarrow will explore in more depth in Chapter 14.

REGULATION AND CONSUMER PROTECTION

Signposting the criteria

The kind of regulation required for the ESI will depend on the structure chosen by the Energy Secretary, which, at the time of writing (October 1987), is still to be decided. In essence, the need for regulation is inversely related to the degree of competition - if the industry is privatised with its monopoly status intact, there will be a need for strong and effective regulation.

The task for regulators can cover a wide range of functions - from industry pricing policy to environmental policing or technical standards. The responsibilities of the regulators of electricity have yet to be clarified, but consumers, of whom there are 21 million, will be looking for their interests to be effectively protected. Consumers will want to know that their electricity supply is safe, reliable, available and affordable. Specifically, consumers will look to the reshaped ESI to:

(1) introduce desirable competition;

(2) provide a safe and secure supply of good quality electricity into the next century and beyond;

(3) provide electricity as cheaply as possible;

(4) offer a stable and fair pricing framework for all consumers;

(5) lead to better service.

Given that the distribution side of the industry is always likely to remain a monopoly, the industry's interface with the consumer is unlikely to become fragmented. In these circumstances, consumers will look for their interests to be protected by an agency which:

(1) fully protects the consumer against the abuse of all residual monopoly power;

(2) fully protects the consumer against unfair pricing regimes;

(3) ensures that electricity is produced as cheaply as possible, consistent with ensuring consistency of supply in the long term;

68

(4) provides the consumer with easy access to advice, intercession, representation and arbitration;

(5) preserves and improves upon the existing provisions under the Code of Practice.

An institutional framework

If we look at the specific regulatory and consumer protection agencies established to police the activities of privatised monopoly utilities in the UK, two models exist.

The Gas model

When British Gas was privatised in 1986, the Gas Act established two bodies to police the industry: the Gas Consumers' Council, mainly a complaint-handling body, and OFGAS, the Office of Gas Supply, which is responsible for regulation.

OFGAS is responsible for monitoring and enforcing the authorisation granted to British Gas PLC by the Secretary of State for Energy, and for issuing authorisations to other suppliers of gas through pipes in Great Britain. OFGAS's primary responsibility is to enforce the price formula which governs the maximum average price British Gas can charge to its tariff customers, as well as ensuring that standing charges rise no faster then the rate of inflation.

Other functions of the Director-General of OFGAS include:

(a) granting authorisations to other suppliers of gas through pipes;

(b) investigating complaints on matters where his enforcement powers may be exercisable;

(c) fixing and publishing maximum charges for reselling gas;

(d) reviewing developments affecting the gas industry;

(e) obtaining all the information necessary to carry out his functions

Complementary with OFGAS is the Gas Consumers' Council (GCC), superseding the former National Gas Consumers' Council. Its functions are to investigate other complaints from gas consumers - principally British Gas domestic and commercial tariff customers. The GCC has offices in each of the twelve British Gas regions where consumers can seek help, and has a statutory reporting role to the OFT and OFGAS.

I have already looked at the difficulty OFGAS has experienced in obtaining information from British Gas. What of consumers' general experience of the privatised British Gas? One indicator of the effectiveness of consumer protection arrangements for gas could be the operation of the Code of Practice which polices the fuel industries' disconnection procedures. According to figures from the GCC, the number went up from 35,626 in 1985-6 to 45,255 in 1986-7, a national increase of 27 per cent. Taking the first six months of 1987 against the same period in 1986, the number of disconnections was up by 40 per cent.

The British Telecom model

The Telecommunications Act 1984 established the Office of Telecommunications, or OFTEL, as an independent body to monitor and regulate telecommunications in the UK. The principal functions of OFTEL are:

(1) to ensure that holders of telecommunications licences comply with their licence conditions:

(2) to maintain and promote effective competition in telecommunications;

(3) to promote, in respect of prices, quality and variety the interests of consumers, purchasers and other users of telecommunications services and apparatus

In August 1984 OFTEL took over the responsibilities previously held by the Post Office Users' National Council, with assistance for its consumer protection functions provided by the Advisory Committees on Telecommunications in Wales, Scotland, Northern Ireland and England. (In some areas there is also a Post and Telecoms Advisory Committee from which advice and assistance can also be sought.)

From the evidence provided above, it can be seen that public perceptions have not been favourable to BT since privatisation, which puts the spotlight firmly on the regulatory/consumer protection agency. However, according to the National Consumers' Council, OFTEL is not seen as an effective source of redress: only 6 per cent of respondents to their survey knew about OFTEL, compared with 65 per cent for the GCC and 53 per cent for the ECC.

BT's unpopularity therefore fuels public pressure, which remains unrelieved by the safety valve of effective consumer protection: and BT's practices are untempered by the regulator's ability to reduce revenues as the corollary of poor service.

Policing a privatised ESI

When electricity is privatised, there will be a need for a more effective regulatory/consumer protection mechanism than OFTEL or OFGAS. Indeed, shortly after his appointment, the Energy Secretary, Cecil Parkinson, affirmed that the public 'will not be left at the mercy of a privatised industry which can charge what it likes'. (BBC Radio 4, 14 June 1987).

When addressing the recent Conservative Party Conference (October 1987), Mr Parkinson tacitly accepted the criticisms of telecoms and gas, some of which had been voiced by previous speakers, and pledged that the consumer will receive top priority when electricity is privatised. The Energy Secretary said he was examining 'radical new ideas for guaranteeing better standards of service', including, 'proposals for rebates and vouchers for customers who receive service that falls short of agreed standards'. (Financial Times, 8 October 1987).

This recognition that, for customers of a monopoly, a reduced standard of service is equal to an increase in price, calls for a new kind of regulatory and consumer protection agency, with the ability to measure the trade-off and incorporate the results in the price control formula. A possible institutional framework would be one organisation to cover all aspects of the industry's operations after privatisation. Such a body, perhaps an Electricity Commission, would have two major functions: regulation and consumer protection. Each function would need, and could share, the most complete access to information, and each would be informed by the knowledge, experience and perspectives of the other. Both elements would share the same statutory status, and the occasional conflicts of interest could find both expression and solution - with arbitration by an Electricity supremo. In order that the inevitably monopolistic activities of the distribution side are effectively monitored and regulated, there would need to be a considerable local presence for the Electricity Commission: this would be the main interface with actual consumers of electricity.

Electricity is a difficult industry to privatise. Its size and complexity, combined with the indispensable nature of its product, will require an imaginative and carefully chosen strategy. We await the announcement from the Secretary of State with interest.

5

Privatisation and the Employee

Lord McCarthy of Headington*

I take it that by privatisation we mean four rather different developments: firstly, the denationalisation of public corporations such as British Gas, British Airways and British Telecom; secondly, returning to the private sector limited liability companies which were previously bought by the government - for the most part to prevent them going bankrupt (e.g. Jaguar and Rolls Royce); thirdly, the deregulation of road transport services and the breakup of the public sector; and fourthly, 'contracting out' work previously done by direct labour in the National Health Service, local government and the Civil Service.

I undertook to talk about the impact of measures of this kind on the employees concerned. My main problem has been data. I am not aware of an in-depth analysis of worker opinion both before and after privatisation - although it would make an excellent thesis topic for a Templeton student, or an OXIFER research project. However, I have come across an NOP survey on attitudes to public ownership and privatisation in the population as a whole. I refer to it in the final section of this chapter and summarise the main contents.

In the absence of adequate direct data I have had to focus on the expressed views of those institutions whose job it is to reflect worker opinion and safeguard workers' interests - i.e. trade unions with members in the public sector. This may well be what was expected of me anyway.

Unions organising in the public sector have opposed privatisation from its inception. Their arguments may be summarised under four broad heads:

* Nuffield College, Oxford

(1) privatisation has been denounced as a form of 'asset stripping' - the sale of the family silver at knock-down prices;

(2) doubts have been expressed about the extent to which privatisation will result in increased competition;

(3) unions have argued that it was unlikely to improve services to the consumer; and

(4) privatisation has been attacked because of its effect on the terms and conditions of union members.

I devote a section of the chapter to what unions and the TUC have said under each of these heads. My aim thoughout is to hold a dock brief for the union point of view, presenting it in a fair and objective way. In the course of the argument I shall allow myself a few personal opinions and judgements.

PRIVATISATION AS ASSET STRIPPING

The government has estimated that so far, privatisation has earned the Exchequer about £11 billion.[1] The extimate for 1987-8 is £5 billion. This is the result of 29 major privatisation sales. Thirteen of them involved the disposal of assets through the Stock Exchange. Sixteen involved sales to other companies or buy-outs. As a result about 600,000 employees have left public sector employment and 30 per cent of total assets have been disposed of.

However, we have it on the authority of the government that this is just the beginning. The minister responsible has said that 'no state monopoly is sacrosanct'.[2] Thus, another 850,000 workers - who are almost all trade union members - await privatisation in what remains of the public trading sector - e.g. in British Rail, British Coal and Electricity Generation and Supply. In addition, an unknown number of public sector employees may yet find themselves out of a job in the National Health Service, the Civil Service and local government.

It is a central plank of the trade union argument against privatisation that so far almost all assets sold have been undervalued. (The only admitted exceptions are Britoil and Enterprise Oil, where price fluctuations inadvertently produced over-priced and under-subscribed flotations.)[3] The

Trades Union Congress's (TUC's) measure of undervaluation is the difference between the value of the offer price and the value of shares when trading begins on the Stock Exchange. By this yardstick they claim that so far total undervaluation amounts to some £3.5 billion; the equivalent of over £180 for every household in the country, or the product of threepence on the standard rate of tax.

The charge of undervaluation is supported by the work of Mayer and Meadowcroft for the Institute of Fiscal Studies. They calculate that discounts on privatisation sales have been running at roughly twice the normal rate - i.e. more than 26 per cent as against the more usual 12 per cent. They conclude 'Discounts on offers for the sale of public assets thus seem well in excess of the average for private issues.'[4]

But it is part of the trade union argument that undervaluation is only one form of asset stripping. There is also what needs to be done, in some cases, to attract buyers at any price. The most common tactic used has been the wiping out of past liabilities in the form of government loans. In this way British Airways was made an attractive market proposition. Conversely, parts of British Shipbuilding were sold off upon the basis of guaranteed orders from the Defence Department - e.g. at Scott Lithgow and Yarrow Shipbuilders.

Finally, a further cost of privatisation is said to be the high fees paid to all the accountants, bankers, solicitors and underwriters who handled asset sales. The House of Commons Public Accounts Committee estimates that so far this bill for privatisation is in the region of £600 million.[5]

Of course the government's reply to criticism of this kind is that it leaves out of account the opportunities provided by privatisation to extend share ownership. Before the stock market slump we were always being told that the government had created a new form of 'risk free' equity holding which had attacted a new race of shareholders - especially the past employees of state monoplies. Enthusiasts of this development often spoke as if it had already changed the British class structure in some vague but fundamental way - ushering in a new and novel form of worker capitalism.

Trade unions had several replies to make to arguments of this kind. Firstly, they pointed out that the public, through Parliament, already owned the enterprises concerned. If profits were made they benefited as taxpayers.

Privatisation and the Employee

All privatisation has done is take away 'the people's stake in an enterprise like British Telecom' and hand it over to the minority able to 'buy shares in something they already owned'.[6] Secondly, the facts suggest that the financial institutions quickly acquired control of most privatised companies. The majority of small shareholders sold out for easy profits. Thus British Aerospace had an 83 per cent reduction in the number of shareholders within a year of privatisation. In Cable and Wireless the initial 150,000 slumped to less than 26,000 within a year.[7] It is also claimed that before the slump, selling was particularly brisk amongst trade union members - especially those threatened with redundancy. Finally, and most importantly, it is argued that any extension of share ownership cannot function as a justification for this kind of public sector asset stripping. The fact remains that what ought to have been retained as a national asset has been disposed of on bargain-basement terms.

PRIVATISATION AND COMPETITION

One of the main claims made for privatisation was that it would make state monopolies profitable by subjecting them to the winds of competition. Trade unions also have several answers to this contention.[8] Firstly, almost all privatised public utilities were already making profits. Secondly, most of them managed to remain profitable while being subjected to competition in some form - for example, gas and electricity competed against each other, while British Airways was expected to hold its own against world-wide competition. More importantly, privatisation has usually taken a form which did not subject the new enterprises to significant additional competition. All that has happened is that market dominance is no longer qualified by effective public control.[9]

Of course it is true that after severe public criticism of several privatised companies - notably British Telecom - government spokesmen promised that in future they would try to privatise in a way which did increase competition - presumably by breaking up bits of electricity supply, or the railways, and setting them up as rivals to each other. We have no proof, however, that effective action will be possible along these lines. It may be that the need to find willing investors will prevent fragmentation. In any case the idea of the South Thames Electricity Board fighting it out with the South Thames Electricity Board is not especially attractive. While Western Region versus Southern Region looks like a silly game.

After all, much of public ownership arose out of the need to prevent wasteful competition in services which were regarded as natural monopolies - for example, electricity and gas. Others were formed because the existing owners were unable to guarantee expansion and development, although they were already heavily subsidised by the state - for example British Airways and British Aerospace. The British Transport Commission was needed because the old railway owners had run their industry into the ground.

Moreover, in almost all cases, with the exception of British Steel, there was substantial cross-party support for what the post-war Labour Government proposed - and it had little to do with socialism, or with hostility to private enterprise. The point was that a detailed knowledge of the state of these industries and services appeared to suggest, to most informed observers at the time, that the existing pattern of organisation and management was in need of a drastic overhaul. Public ownership appeared to be the best way of ensuring that what needed to be done was done.[10]

For reasons of this kind the Conservative Party, when returned to power in 1951, saw no need to tamper with the greater part of the post-war Labour Government's programme of public ownership. As late as the early seventies, it is said the Tories, under Ted Heath, took the view that important national companies which had been bought to the brink of bankruptcy ought to be taken into public ownership - for example, Rolls Royce. It was only with the entry of Mrs Thatcher into Downing Street that a government arose which took the novel view that a case against public ownership could be sustained on a priori grounds. Only Thatcherism asserts that nationalised industries must be 'failing the nation' simply because they belong to the people. Only Thatcherism assumes that selling them off is an infallible way of providing the public with improved services at lower costs. Naturally enough, trade unions with members in the public sector see no reason why they should subscribe to novel doctrines of this kind.

PRIVATISATION AND IMPROVED SERVICES

Trade unions also claim to have direct evidence that in many areas the coming of privatisation has already resulted in a deterioration of services. Thus, the privatisation of bus routes is said, by the major union involved, the Transport and General Workers Union (T&GWU), to have been followed by inner-city congestion and a lack of rural services - especially in off-peak periods. In London, they allege, the newly created London Regional Transport has relied on much higher fares and the cancellation of unprofitable routes. Similarly the break up of the National Bus Company, and the restrictions placed on local authority subsidies by the 1985 Transport Act, has caused the cancellation of essential routes, leaving rural areas without transportation of any kind. Of course the T&GWU does not deny that in many instances commuters are offered additional services at bargain prices; but claim that this has only been possible at the cost of running down, or refusing to cover, unprofitable routes.

In the case of the National Health Service, the TUC has made a concerted attempt to collect evidence from all major unions with members in the service. They have sought to monitor the progress of 'contracting out' ever since 1983, when the Department of Health and Social Security (DHSS) informed health authorities that they must 'put out to private tender' all cleaning, catering and laundry work. As a result, since 1983, Area Health Authorities have only been able to use 'in house' labour if they could demonstrate that the costs would be lower than the lowest private tender.

Yet the latest figures from the DHSS suggest that even on these terms the bulk of the work has been retained 'in house'. Thus, out of 1,287 contracts put out to tender in 1986, NHS teams were able to underbid all but 274 private firms - i.e. about 80 per cent of the total.[11] Moreover, there is TUC evidence to suggest that many private contractors chosen failed to give satisfaction. In its two publications Contracting failures and More contracting failures, the TUC records, with ill-concealed glee the complaints of dozens of doctors, nurses and hospital managers since 1983 - complaints of non completion, defective work, bad food, dirty laundry and so on.[12]

With special relish Congress House also records how many health authorities came to discover that their first private contract price was really a loss leader. After dismantling their own internal departments, they found that a new contract was not obtainable at anything like the original price. Yet it proved to be almost impossible to persuade the DHSS to allow them to swich back to direct labour: management found themselves locked into the private sector!

Similar stories abound in the same TUC publications concerning local government. Here, the pace has been set by Conservative local authorities, who have pioneered the 'contracting out' of cleaning and catering services. According to the TUC, the result has been a further stream of complaints from head masters, office workers and members of the public - most notably, those who have suffered from the non-collection of business and household refuse.

PRIVATISATION AND TERMS AND CONDITIONS OF WORK

So we come finally to the views of trade unions concerning the impact of privatisation on terms and conditions of work. Here the evidence is considerable and is best considered under four sub-headings: jobs, pay, fringe benefits and rights of representations. Most of the relevant data is summarised in yet another TUC publication, Bargaining in privatised companies.[13] This suggests that virtually all companies have instituted major redundancies since privatisation. The chances are that British Steel heads the list with a manpower reduction of about 60 per cent. Other organisations with larger than the average reductions include British Airways and British Telecom. At Rolls Royce, we are told, there was a 'pre-privatisation slimming down process' which cut the labour force by some 30 per cent. Further redundancies may be expected since 'an increasing amount of RR work is being subcontracted out to private firms'.[14]

On pay the evidence suggests that a sharp distinction must be drawn between management, especially top management, and the rest of the labour force. In most privatised firms the rate of increase for manual workers and clerical grades has been just above the rate of inflation -i.e. something near the median rate of increase for these grades in the private sector as a whole since 1982. This has permitted an improvement in real wages of something like 3 per cent a year. In many privatised firms the unions involved have had to make significant concessions to obtain increases of this size - for example, a change in shift patterns in Associated British Ports, large scale redundancies in British Telecom and the erosion of overseas allowances in Cable and Wireless.

In contrast to this picture, virtually all the privatised concerns began their operations by awarding very significant pay increases to management, and the higher up the manager the greater has been the increase. Once again the TUC provides the best overall assessment of the size of this movement. They calculate that 'top executives' (i.e. full-time board members) received an average increase of £18,993 in the first year of privatisation - i.e. an improvement of some 34.3 per cent. In the second year increases since privatisation were raised to an average of £45,413 - i.e. an improvement of 85.1 per cent.[15] Naturally enough trade union negotiators have sought explanations for this unprecedented widening of differentials. Two types of defence have been advanced. In a minority of cases the answer has been that the board needed to attract a higher calibre of manager from outside the industry. In other cases the argument has been that existing management morale was dangerously low, more money was essential to induce a higher level of commitment and performance.

The position on fringe benefits is more varied. There are widespread complaints about the introduction of new pension schemes which are much less attractive than those obtainable under public enterprise - for example, in British Airways, British Shipbuilder, British Telecom, and so on. Ex-British Transport Hotels have also reneged on established travel facilities. On the other hand, the new pension schemes at Jaguar and Redpath Dorman Long are said to be an improvement on what the workers enjoyed before. The position on representation rights and trade union facilities is that the unions claim that they have invariably worsened with the coming of privatisation. The section on 'the bargaining climate' in Bargaining in privatised companies contains detailed complaints against the management of virtually all privatised companies. At Amersham International the new race of managers do not always see the need for consultation and try to cut corners in accepted consultation procedures. The new owners of British Transport Hotels have cancelled negotiating rights with the TSSA and NUR - despite solemn promises made to both unions at the time of take-over. At Bristol, it is claimed, certain jobs have been excluded from trade union membership. The union ASTMS says that during a recent dispute at Cable and Wireless there were veiled threats about promotion and disciplinary action made to their members - after management had 'abrogated' a long-standing arbitration agreement.

At Hoverspeed 'all union recognition has been refused' - despite promises made to British Rail and a call for recognition from the arbitration service ACAS. At Redpath Dorman Long it is admitted that the parent company - Trafalgar House - 'prefers not to have collective bargaining relationships with its staff employees'. At Scott Lithgow - another Trafalgar subsidiary - the EMA complains that most questions affecting their members are regarded as the 'sole prerogative of the Board'. At Sea Containers, the new owners of Sea Link, the TSSA has been denied recognition - another alleged breach of assurances. At Wynch Farm Oilfield, previously owned by British Gas and BP, the union membership agreement has been withdrawn. At British Airways the T&GWU complains of reductions in time off for union work.

Summing up the position in the privatised parts of British Shipbuilders the General Secretary of the CSEU has said that management's record over the introduction of privatisation is best described as 'incompetence mixed with arrogance leading to chaos.'[16] In British Telecom the UCW has described the industrial relations climate as 'increasingly hostile'. According to the STE some agreements are being systematically ignored or broken - for example accommodation standards. Meanwhile, 'unions are being denied access to information, sometimes with no explanation'. Moreover, BT is attempting to de-unionise the management structure by offering personal contracts to senior management, to remove them from the collective bargaining process. It is also alleged that there have been implications that continued union membership, though not specifically forbidden, may retard a person's career; and inducements, such as company cars, have been offered to those accepting a personal contract.[17]

It should perhaps be mentioned in passing that the statute book still contains an employment protection law which makes it unlawful to place any pressure on an employee to leave a union or remain a non-unionist. For what it is worth the anti-union pressures which the TUC alleges exist in the privatised sector are all quite illegal.

In their introduction to <u>Bargaining in privatised</u>

companies, the TUC asserts that attempts to roll back the frontier of union influence and depress the standards of their members should not be seen in isolation. They should be viewed as the final proof that the Thatcherite commitment to privatisation has little to do with either the improvement of services or the extension of competition. The central aim has been to provide greater rewards for private shareholders at the expense of the employees in each concern. Moreover, concludes the TUC:[18] 'there is every indication that it is one of the Government's deliberate objectives; privatisation is supposed to undermine workers' conditions. That is one of the ways to make companies more profitable for their new owners.'

THE NOP SURVEY ON PUBLIC OWNERSHIP

As part of their campaign against privatisation the TUC commissioned an opinion poll from NOP Market Research.[19] It was undertaken in October 1986, and consisted of a quota sample of 1,969 adults taken from throughout Great Britain. The full survey report breaks the results down under various headings, including trade unionists and non-unionists. This allows us to make a few broad generalisations about what workers feel about privatisation and how representative the TUC's position is in the case of union members. Unfortunately there is no further breakdown of union members which allows us to extract the views of those who have been directly affected by privatisation. However, it seems worthwhile presenting a short summary of the main results of the survey.

The first point to make is that there is a solid, and in several cases overwhelming, majority of the public which continues to favour the public ownership of services already privatised - for example, defence factories and naval dockyards, local bus services, British Telecom, and so on. There is also wide concern about the impact of private contractors in local and NHS services. Government plans to force tendering for local authority services, for example, are opposed by a majority of five to one.

As one would expect trade unionists are more likely to support public ownership, and fear the results of privatisation, than non-unionists - although sometimes the differences are relatively small. Thus, for example, 80 per cent of trade union respondents considered that defence factories and naval dockyards should remain within the public sector; the comparable figure for non-unionists was 69 per cent. Asked if they thought that standards of service would deteriorate if privatisation was introduced into the NHS or local government, 57 per cent of trade unionists expressing an opinion thought that matters would get worse; the comparable figure for non-unionists was only 43 per cent.

Naturally enough the TUC expressed pleasure at the results of their NOP survey. They claimed that it indicated that the government is losing the debate about public ownership. Unfortunately for them some eight months later Mrs Thatcher went to the country with a manifesto which promised much more privatisation. This time the people appeared to agree with her.

NOTES

1. House of Commons Parliamentary Debates, 26 February 1987, Col. 372.
2. The Rt Hon John Moore MP, speech to a conference of stockbrokers, Fielding and Newson Smith, 1 November 1983.
3. The UK privatisation programme (Trades Union Congress, June 1987).
4. Fiscal Studies, 1985, p.6.
5. Quoted in J. Kay, C. Mayer and D. Thompson (eds), Privatisation and regulation (Institute of Fiscal Studies, London, 1986), p. 328.
6. The UK privatisation programme.
7. Ibid.
8. See Stripping our assets: the City's privatisation killing (Trades Union Congress, May 1985).
9. See The £16 billion gas bill: the real cost of privatisation (Trades Union Congress, November 1985).
10. See Norman Chester, The nationalisation of British industry, 1945-51 (HMSO, London, 1975)
11. The UK privatisation programme.
12. TUC, February 1985 and December 1986, respectively.
13. TUC, February 1986.
14. Ibid.
15. Privatisation and top pay (Trades Union Congress, December 1985).
16. Bargaining in privatised companies, pp. 4-10.

17. Ibid.
18. Ibid.
19. <u>Report on a Survey carried out by NOP for the TUC on public ownership</u> (October 1986).

6

'Managing' Cultural Change on Privatisation

Nick Woodward*

INTRODUCTION

At the 1987 Conservative Party Conference, the Prime Minister called for an 'enterprise culture'. Peters and Waterman's In search of excellence has reached the US best-seller lists, and been put on the required reading list by the Chairman of Courtaulds. Articles on cultural change, symbolic leadership and organisational transformation have invaded journals and magazines, whether academic, journalistic or evangelistic. In short, cultural analysis is high fashion, and cultural change is widely advanced as the way to achieve organisational results.

In a world of management, therefore, it must seem obvious that managers' responsibility must be to manage the culture, or, for improvement, to manage cultural change: for managers are supposedly responsible for organisations, their behaviour and their financial results, though perhaps less so when the results are adverse.

I have argued that this view of management as prime mover and decision-maker, repository of wisdom and knowledge, and the only legitimate authority can have adverse consequences when used to legitimise a system of power, status and rewards divorced from task (Woodward, 1985). Thus, the notion of management is itself part of a system of beliefs and values predicated on assumptions about the nature and function of organisation, about the distribution and legitimacy of power, rewards and status, around which cluster sets of myths, rituals and behaviours which, according to context, may be constructive or

* Templeton College, Oxford

destructive, enlightening or deadening. For this reason, I have put 'management' in inverted commas: for does it make sense to talk of 'managing' cultural change, when management, as person or function, is itself part of the culture to be changed? It is like pulling oneself up by the bootstraps: worse, if managers are not part of the solution, they are likely to be part of the problem. This point is addressed in the next two sections.

One of the widely expressed rationales for privatisation is that of improving internal efficiency and enhancing customer service, through two mechanisms: firstly, by transfer to private ownership, some sort of 'discipline' will be exercised through stock market processes; and secondly, in some cases, the threat or reality of competition in some or all of the privatised organisations' markets will enforce customer sensitivity. But how these effects will be achieved is rarely specified. The underlying model assumes some stimulus/response mechanism, some form of ecological adaptation.

The purpose of this chapter is to cast some light into the black box of organisation and to suggest some implications of taking the notion of 'cultural change' seriously. Firstly, however, we will touch on the notion of culture and organisational culture, and the background to its current popularity.

THE NOTION OF CULTURE

The root of 'culture' is concerned with the act of cultivation. By transference the term now applies to the transmission of values, beliefs and associated behaviours, both collective and individual, which give meaning to life: the integrated pattern of human behaviour which, as Webster's dictionary puts it, includes thought, speech, action and artefacts, and depends on man's capacity for learning and transmitting knowledge to succeeding generations. It is this notion of transmission - the cultivation of young minds or novitiates - which lies at the root of culture.

Thus, this notion of culture encompasses the 'gestalt' of a particular society or subsection of society - in Mary Douglas's schema (1978) its attitude to and view of nature (what is 'us' and what is 'them'); of its genesis, of processes relating to space, to agriculture, cookery, medicine, and so on; of time (old age, youth, times past and future); of human nature (sickness, health, death, abnormality and relation-ships); and of society (distributive justice and punishment). At the personal level it concerns 'meaning', in terms of valid answers to questions such as 'who am I', 'where do I come from', 'what is life about?'. The answers are often transmitted through stories relating to the whole fabric of life, from its deepest meanings to the minutiae of personal behaviour.

To those of a positivist bent, with strong belief in scientific knowledge, there may seem valid and compre-hensive, rational and scientific views on many of these questions; but many diverse cultures can incorporate and successfully practise scientific methods without sacrificing their cultural integrity, their religion, traditions and their way of life. At the other extreme, an exclusively ' rational' view can diminish rituals, myths and behaviours which give meaning to life, can drive out the human, just as the ethnocentric view of some early anthropologists evaluated 'primitive' cultures against the unconsidered yardstick of their own. Yet such views are themselves cultural artefacts which can be analysed in terms of associated myths, ideologies and rituals (often destructive of social relations and of personal growth) as validly as any other set of positions.

This does not, however, belie the truth or validity of science or rationality. Cultural analysis is concerned with meanings, beliefs and values, not with truth or falsehood, though the analysis may be valid or invalid. As Leach (1982, p. 53) puts it, 'social anthropologists should not see themselves as seekers after objective truth: their purpose is to gain insight into other people's behaviour, or for that matter, into their own'. This insight, Leach explains, is 'the quality of deep understanding which, as critics, we attribute to great artists, dramatists, novelists, composers; the difference between fully understanding the nuances of a language and simply knowing the dictionary glosses of the individual words'.

Such personal insight raises the question of the standpoint of the observer - how far an outsider uses his or her own cultural perspective in analysing and categorising another culture: or, as an insider, how far he or she is capable of self-analysis. In a similar vein, Levi-Strauss (1976) remarks that as the schizoid consequence of exploring other cultures in a deep sense one is rejecting one's own. By analogy, seriously to study management - its ideology, rituals, tools, beliefs and symbols - one must to a degree stand outside, though comprehend, the myths which serve management. Thus, the idea of 'management' as instrumental subject and 'culture' as analysable and manipulable object rests on a spurious notion of managers as outside their culture - on a category mistake.

ORGANISATIONAL CULTURE

While their are multiple perspectives on human societies, and many subdivisions and differences within the set of those who study cultures and society, for current purpose it is sufficient to accept that culture, whether of organisations or societies, embodies 'a system of shared and meaningful symbols', manifested in myths, ideology and values and in multiple cultural artefacts' (Allaire and Firsirotu, 1984, p. 213).

In the context of organisations this raises the question whether the formal set of management systems - the processes and objectives - are to be treated as separate though related to the set of myths, ideology and values. Allaire and Firsirotu suggest an analytic distinction between the 'sociostructural' system (structures, strategies, policies, processes) and the 'cultural' system (myths, values, ideology), which then enables one to ask questions about the relationship between the two in terms of the degree to which the one legitimates and supports the other, or vice versa. Schein (1984), on the other hand, suggests a schema whereby the 'visible artefacts' (dress, architecture, technology, behaviour patterns, documents) which are visible but not easily decipherable, requires analysis at a supporting level of values and behavioural standards, which in turn are supported by basic assumptions about the organisation's relationship to the environment, the nature of reality, time and space, of human nature, human activity and human relationships. These latter are at the level of 'taken for granted, invisible, preconscious' assumptions, and raise again the dilemma of the observer's standpoint.

These two views are organising schemas - not inconsistent theories or hypotheses. Thus, the first perspective points towards criteria of effectiveness (fit between organisation and environment), perhaps of organisational health (fit between expressed values and behaviour); while Schein's provides a checklist (not a manual) for gaining insight into the meanings, observed artefacts and behaviours.

These are but two of many recent essays on aspects of organisational culture, but serve to indicate that in focusing on organisational culture, analysts are coming up against problems familiar to social and cultural anthropologists. However, formal organisations present a further problem - how far and how they reflect, oppose or transform the wider cultural and social context in which they operate. If one focuses on the ambient culture, then, that will dominate analysis, but if organisations are the subject of analysis, then organisational differences and organisational imperatives are brought into focus, rendering the national, class or regional cultural content fuzzy. Pascale (1985), for instance, attempts to characterise organisational cultures on a strong-weak scale, according to their socialisation practices. However, in putting organisation in the foreground, one can miss the background, for individuals may be strongly linked to some groupings (for example, family, club, community), weakly to others, simultaneously and dynamically. Furthermore, from a psychological perspective, some individuals may have weak preferences for social interaction, just as cultures can be characterised on a scale incorporating the degree of social cohesion and the nature of norms and stratification (Douglas, 1978).

In brief, the field of cultural analysis is widely and variously defined, and the paths within this field are labyrinthine. Thus, for example, there have been many recent attempts to study Japanese firms and seek explanations for their cohesion and values in background Japanese cultural values, yet students of Japanese companies see great differences between them - though a common 'Japaneseness'; and a distinctively British firm - Marks and Spencer - in terms of its functioning, values and behaviour, bears many resemblances to some observed characteristics of some Japanese firms. The extent of similarity or difference depends partly on the observer's perspective and focus, and purpose.

A fundamental characteristic of human culture is its endless diversity (Leach, 1982), which requires particular and detailed study and interpretation. This diversity is not of a simple kind, easily reducible and quantifiable, but shifting, subtle and complex as a Shakespeare play. Attempts to map and interpret it have reflected this complexity. Why, then, has the notion of 'culture' taken such hold among

'Managing' Cultural Change on Privatisation

Anglo-Saxon managers and management students, who have tended to pursue a rationalist reductionist path? There are two reasons: firstly, in focusing on ideas, values, symbols, the notion seems to reassert the importance of human values and commitment in organisational life; and secondly, it seems to offer a way forward from the perceived failures of many management practices rooted in an ideology of rationality and control.

It was the success of Japanese corporations in penetrating US and world markets which led students of management to investigate Japanese management practices, and in turn prompted Peters and Waterman to search for 'excellence' in US companies. Their book is more symptomatic than seminal. Their argument is an attack on the excesses of rationality, structure and control - an appeal to which many senior executives have responded because the limitations of the latter have been demonstrated by their experience. In short, it represented an evangelistic belief - the more passionate because the result of conversion - that organisational objectives can be better achieved through commitment - through getting employees on one's side - rather than through mechanisms of bureaucratic control. Culture, as a solution, is used as a codeword for harnessing enthusiasm, abandoning needless controls, liberating energy and initiative. In discussing class, hierarchies and markets, Ouchi (1981 p. 84) notes that

> the monk, the marine or the Japanese auto-worker who appears to have arrived at a selfless state is in fact achieving selfish ends quite thoroughly. Both of these governance mechanisms realize human potential and maximise human freedom because they do not constrain behaviour. In contrast, only the bureaucratic mechanism explicitly says to individuals 'do not do what you want, do what we tell you to do because we pay you for it'. The bureaucratic mechanism alone produces alienation, avarice and a lowered sense of autonomy.

If this sentiment strikes a chord, then it follows that managers must concentrate on building organisations which can tap personal commitment, and consequent concern with the emotional, affective side of humans has legitimised a concentration on the symbolic and ritual aspects of organisational communication and behaviours.

CULTURE-ORIENTED MANAGEMENT

From the many books and articles which have tapped the vein of organisational culture, approaches can broadly be classified into three not inconsistent modes. Firstly, exploration of the notion of culture, drawing in particular on other desciplines - notably anthropology - with varying degrees of integration and insight. This approach, of course, depends on the competence and capacity of its authors, and the receptiveness of its intended audience. For some the discovery of organisational culture may resemble the discovery of grammar by the <u>Bourgeois Gentilhomme</u>. Secondly, to look at successful/unsuccessful organisations, to highlight differences and look for generalisable conclusions - essentially compare, contrast, extract. This approach depends critically on the definition of successful/unsuccessful, and the quality of its methodology. Peters and Waterman's eight slogans can be recipes for disaster, as well as success; and subsequent writers have pointed out that some of their 'successful' companies have subequently proved less than successful, and also cast doubts on the efficacy of some of their cultures. Thirdly, and often linked to the second, there have been many essays at providing guidelines for managers, of a normative kind. The problem here is that these managers may be seen as outside the culture they are 'managing'. This is a particular problem where their own taken-for-granted assumptions - their authority, the legitimacy of their actions, the acquisition and use of power - are themselves part of the organisational culture they are trying to influence. If they are not part of the solution, they are part of the problem.

What prescriptions emerge from this literature? Deal and Kennedy (1982, pp. 141-2) characterise 'symbolic managers' as placing a much higher level of <u>trust</u> in fellow employees, and seeing themselves as players in a daily <u>drama</u>. Peters (1980) similarly underlines the importance of setting and signals, through careful use of <u>language</u>, manipulation of <u>settings</u>, shifts of agenda and time to <u>signal</u> changes in priorities, <u>consistent</u> and frequent feedback to stress a chosen theme and 'selective seeding of ideas'. Key words here relate both to the dramatic handling of messages - in terms of language, settings, signals; and aspects of personal behaviour - trust, consistency.

Note that these look like aspects of personal style, reflecting a personal understanding and use of symbolic aspects and a personal belief in standards reflected in personal behaviour. For an observer, all organisations have their own peculiar culture: none is culture-free, however rational and purposive its mythology. The question that concerns us here is why do these cultural evangelists focus on symbol, ritual and drama? The answer seems to be that in elevating the personal and the symbolic, in speaking to the affective side of humanity, this approach reasserts the roots of social (as opposed to formal) organisation. 'Social organisations are incompatible with formality, distance and contractualism. They proceed smoothly only with intimacy, subtlety and trust.' (Ouchi, 1981, p. 93).

Over the past few years, on courses for a variety of companies, I have attempted to tease out desirable and undesirable aspects of what they term their 'culture', of their organisational behaviour. The desirable aspects (and their opposites) emerge consistently in terms like task clarity, consistency of behaviour, recognition, sharing, risk taking, integrity and authenticity, openness and trust. Perhaps 'managing cultural change' is too grand and perplexing a notion, importing methodological and conceptual problems with the notion of culture. The real issue is the quality and pattern of behaviour within organisation - up, down and across hierarchy, and in relation to customers, suppliers and other stakeholders: of wanting to reinforce desirable patterns and reduce the undesirable legitimised in the name of customer service, of personal health, and of long-term corporate survival. It also speaks to an ancient and common teleological tradition which has been sadly missing from much instrumental business school education - of 'man as he might be'. However, if this is what senior managers desire, then they must start with themselves - for their employees will judge and react to their actions, not their words, and they themselves normally exercise strong influence on the rules and structure of their organisations - on rewards, promotion, incentives, resources. If it is cultural change they seek, then it is on their own behaviour that the stories will focus which give clues as to the nature of a culture, and which reveal its values.

What external changes, then, might affect an organisation on privatisation, and what behavioural changes might they trigger or entail?

PRIVATISATION

According to Hatch (1987) the objectives of the government's privatisation programme fall into four categories:

(1) to increase competition/spread consumer choice;
(2) to reduce the PSBR/increase government revenues:
(3) to give the public/work-force a stake in the industry; and
(4) to allow nationalised industry management to escape from 'the dead hand of Whitehall'.

It is the first and fourth of these which may have strong implications for privatised organisations. They both imply a model of an organisation adapting/responding to environment - the first by introducing a threat (competition, loss of market share), the second by relaxing a constraint (Whitehall financial planning and political controls). Let us examine each category in turn.

If the effect of a privatisation programme is to reduce or eliminate barriers to entry and provide genuine competition, then consumer choice will _ipso facto_ be enhanced (disregarding social welfare issues). The case of buses seems to fit this scenario most closely (Rickard, 1987) both in terms of service provision and consumer choice - entry of new operators, management buy-outs, experimentation with routes and services, and so on. The industry has, in effect, been split up - presumably with galvanising effects on the individual companies. This is not to say that the industry will for ever foster change: most private sector markets exhibit cycles of stability and change, as a result of both internal market and technical innovation factors, and of threats from competing modes. A more interesting case of competition and 'cultural change' involves British Airways, which has always been subject to a degree of competition from competing airlines, national and international. However, it underwent a process of transformation prior to privatisation, reducing staff by some 20,000 and putting the survivors through a crash training programme aimed at underlining the customer-oriented service side of the business. This, along with the allocation of profitable routes, made the airline profitable and easier to sell off (objective 2 above). There seems no reason in principle, however, why such a transformation should not have been achieved with the airline maintained in the public sector - an argument for the possibility of 'hauling oneself up by the bootstraps', given the will and the capability.

In contrast, many industries already privatised, or on the schedule, are by nature monopolistic - the British Airports Authority, British Gas, British Telecom, the CEGB. It is not obvious a priori that these will automatically enhance consumer choice or become more customer-sensitive as a consequence of having their shares privately held. The behaviour of a discriminating monopolist should be sufficient to satisfy financial requirements, while it is not clear how far regulatory bodies can enforce appropriate behaviour, as opposed to limiting excesses. The history of government - nationalised industry relations over the past 40 years suggests that 'control' is better able to stop things happening, rather than make them happen; and regulation by an external body is likely to follow a similar, if more informed and less arbitrary, pattern. Of course there are other mechanisms and constituencies - consumer councils, publicity, complaints, and so on; but these can in turn produce a defensive public relations posture, rather than a genuine operational response.

Part of the problem with massive systems industries seems to be genuinely 'cultural' - massive capital and human investment in technology and systems, to keep the system in balance and flexible to varying demand (especially in rail, telecoms and electricity). To service this technological operating core a massive cadre of dedicated specialists, engineers and technologists has been built up, with their own norms, values and standards focusing on the maintenance and upgrading of this core, in the name of service. This 'service' is typically defined in terms of technical standards (houses cut off from electricity; trains late or cancelled; phones out of order or lines engaged), but without much understanding of the particular and personal concerns and perceptions of individual consumers. The consequence is often an insensitivity to and ignorance of consumer psychology, exacerbated by the fact that frustrated consumers cannot often take their business elsewhere; and that complaints are met with explanations in terms of system or bureaucratic inflexibility. There is surely more scope for variety, experiment and innovation in customer relations.

According to Hatch (1987) this sensitivity to consumer needs and concerns can go either way as a result of privatisation. Standards of service and/or communication seem to have fallen in the case of telecommunications and gas, whereas electricity, pre-privatisation, seems to be making genuine attempts to be more sensitive, sensible and responsive to customers. Furthermore, British Rail, for whom there are no immediate plans for privatisation, seems to be making genuine progress in improving customer service and sensitivity, partly because the current Chairman's success in negotiating with government has provided his organisation with support and trust sufficient for him to make longer-term plans.

In sum, some of Peters and Waterman's prescriptive traits (bias for action, close to the customer, productivity through people, hands on value-driven) seem applicable whether an organisation is in the private or the public sector. Ironically, one of their 'excellent' companies (IBM), while giving customers 'what they want' may do so in the manner of a discriminating monopolist - tying in sales, exploiting consumers' surplus and using predatory pricing to constrain competition (DeLamarter, 1986).

The second rationale for privatisation is release 'from the dead hand of Whitehall'. This phrase in itself nicely exemplifies one of the major problems in the history of nationalised industries - 'Governments have tended to intervene (often arbitrarily) for short term, political/ economic objectives using the rhetoric of hierarchical control, of the public interest, and of economic/financial virtue' (Woodward, 1986, p. 316) and have systematically avoided accountability for their interference. Even on privatisation, the malign effects of civil service bureaucracy are blamed, rather than the short-term and arbitrary expedience of their political masters. That said, there are no doubt benefits in being relieved from the need to submit to the PESC process, investment reviews, and so on. Ironically, in the 1970s these Whitehall-imposed disciplines were seen as a way of enforcing modern management techniques on complacent incompetent monoliths.

However, apart from release from the need to participate in these bureaucratic procedures, privatisation can have an energising and liberating effect - access to capital markets which will appraise the organisation and its projected needs on commercial criteria, rather than its effect on the PSBR (notably for Telecom), the possibility of joint ventures, diversification and export activity, where such ventures were previously statutorily or politically constrained (see Heath, 1987). Apart from releasing suppressed energy this in turn can make it easier to recruit and keep entrepreneurial talent, and offer improved opportunities for career progression, for genuine risk taking. Such opportunities were undoubtedly there before privatisation. Most industries will have their stories of heroic achievement. An ex-Area Director of what was formerly the National Coal Board, was given the chance before he was 30 of turning round a small wholly owned Coal Board subsidiary which manufactured power kits for mines. The current Chairman of British Gas is renowned for his early engineering/entrepreneurial exploits. The Wytch Farm development by British Gas offered great opportunity for the team which developed it. On its compulsory sale, the bulk of this team with demonstrated expertise and a track record were recruited into the private sector. Thus, while there is good evidence for the <u>de facto</u> liberating effect of privatisation on privatised corporations, in terms of the ownership dimension, this effect could have been achieved as successfully by relaxing these constraints and controls while maintaining public ownership.

While the benefits of entrepreneurial opportunity may sometimes accrue to managers' careers, the question remains whether this affects the core business. My guess is that if this energises existing managers and makes it easier to recruit the brightest and best, then if their career paths bring them back into the core business, their experience and capability may have an effect. Against this, however, we have an example of many of our large private sector commercial and manufacturing companies in which the rewarding career for the young or ambitious lies with overseas subsidiaries or with innovative ventures at the margin, and where it is hard to advance in, or change, the existing established core. Once again we have the case where the private sector, in a supposedly competitive environment, does not guarantee innovation, responsiveness, openness, or freedom from bureaucratic controls - indeed, quite the reverse, as evidenced by the current fashion for cultural change in large private sector companies.

It seems then that change, or a continuing commitment to change, and dynamism are needed to combat the deadening effects of size, structure and stability. The act of privatisation can provide a trigger for change, for re-evaluation of existing practices, assumptions and habits of thought. However, if the change itself is the trigger, what is there to prevent organisations undergoing a cycle of change and settling down subsequently to a new level of stability - the familiar change cycle of freeze, unfreeze, refreeze? Might not the next appropriate galvanising change be renationalisation, or some other form of exasperated government intervention?

CHANGE

Many organisations, both public and private, systematically deny or avoid the need for change - in working practices, in structure, in skills, in philosophy. Indeed, those responsible when the first signs of need become evident have often been promoted, recruited elsewhere or retired by the time that the crisis is internally evident. How is it that symptoms which are evident to outsiders (customers) and often to humble insiders, and which are critical to the organisation's survival and health, are denied by those responsible? The answer lies partly in the nature of organisation, and its excesses. Put simply, the roots of purposive organisation lie in co-operative endeavour for a common purpose (task), building on economies of scale, of specialisation, and so on. However, the advent of size brings structure, rules, divisions, hierarchy. Vertically, what began as responsibility for organisation of the common endeavour, can be subtly divorced from responsibility through pursuit of power, status, career and other rewards: while horizontally, specialisation, professionalisation and divisionalisation generate goal displacement - pursuit of territory, power, and related objects, in which the sense of common purpose as the key legitimising mechanism is lost, and in which co-operation is lost in pursuit of sub-goals. The whole is complicated and traduced by a rational but inappropriate use of modern management techniques. In apparently rational pursuit of order and control, the system produces an organised chaos. If this dynamic be accepted, then the problem in organisation is to rebuild its roots, of co-operation and purpose. It is this issue which much of the literature on corporate culture seeks to address, through emphasis on the use of slogans and stories to reinforce values, on human qualities of integrity, trust, consistency and openness, and on the signalling behaviours and rituals of senior managers.

The second problem with confronting change is psychological - fear of the unknown, fear of the unfamiliar -

which provokes defensive behaviour, rationalisation, denial and projection. It is often both more comfortable and safer to do one's prescribed job according to familiar patterns, than to confront the difficult challenge of accepting the need for change - particularly when, for senior managers, the need for change lies first with oneself. It is far easier to employ consultants to seek solutions in systems, structures and incentives - all apparently rational, valid and professionally presented - but not much use if treating symptoms of a more systemic disease. It was awareness of this dynamic that prompted Townsend (1970, p. 95) to aver that the only proper use of institutional consultants was as a threat - 'If you fellows don't get shaped up within thirty days so you're a credit to the rest of the company, I'm going to call in Booz Allen.' Of course change is most welcome when anything is preferable to the present, in crisis or under constraint, and least welcome when it disturbs existing comfortable practice - and the threat of some future crisis is easily rejected when past and present confirm the validity of current practice. The generally favourable reaction of nationalised industries to privatisation may be interpreted along the lines of the first condition (crisis). For most, however, it seems more consistent with the second (constraint) - better access to capital, freedom from Whitehall bureaucracy and arbitrary political interference. If the latter, then for those industries with elements of natural monopoly, there can be no guarantee of automatic improvements in levels and kinds of customer service, or in productivity or effectiveness.

CONCLUSION

What forces, then, might be brought to bear on these industries to render them more customer-sensitive? Firstly, the appointment of a missionary chief executive can have an effect (cf. the case of British Airways). Secondly, there may be political pressures which can be brought to bear (threat of franchising, further competition, renationalisation), though the experience of 'control' under nationalisation gives little ground for hope on this score. Thirdly, representation by organised consumer groups may induce a will, or, if there be willingness to serve the customer, may serve to educate and induce experimentation (there is some evidence of this with the Electricity Consumers' Council).

Fourthly, the regulatory body may use such statutory teeth as it has been given. With a sympathetic touch it may help to transform the industry's behaviour, at the risk of the regulators becoming the captive of the regulated; or alternatively, the use of threats and sanctions may generate defensive behaviour and an adversarial stance. The recent experiences of OFTEL and OFGAS suggest the latter.

However, accepting the will and capability, at the top, to effect a 'cultural change' in the limited sense of getting close to the customer, keeping it simple, and so on, how is this achieved and maintained? Firstly, the assertion of a set of simply stated principles, (mission statements, value statements) which clarify the organisation's basic task, and which can inform and guide behaviour at all levels of the organisation. If this seems trivial, Marks and Spencer has a simple and clear statement of mission, enunciated 50 years ago, which can still be seen today as guiding its growth. Likewise, many Japanese companies have such statements of strategic values, into whose transmission and reinforcement they put as much effort through training, discussion and behaviour as into any system of accounting or planning.

Secondly, these value statements need to be translated into clear, meaningful and achieveable operational standards, relating to quality, service and related behaviours: and much effort needs to be devoted to maintaining and improving these standards. The standards are 'owned' by those responsible for delivering them, not imposed as a control mechanism for finding fault or imposing blame. Problems are in common ownership, not attributable to scapegoats.

Thirdly, the importance of these values (hopefully long term) and standards (short term) requires continual reinforcement in symbolic terms which serve to signal their critical importance and speak to the affective side of human nature. Capacity to 'manage symbolically' is not enough - after all, Hitler excelled in this respect.

Finally, the moral basis of co-operative endeavour needs continuous assertion - values such as integrity (personal), trust and openness (interpersonal), consistency (behavioural) and clarity (task): for these qualities enable organisations to confront real issues of behaviour and of business rather than through the impersonal but apparently rational language of bureaucratic control. However, the existence of such qualities is made evident in behaviour - just as an organisation's strategy is visibly and regularly delivered by the behaviour of its humblest employees, whether in service or manufacturing. An executive preaching the virtues of cultural change, but denying them in his or her own behaviour, will soon destroy the basis of his or her own rhetoric.

In sum, organisations can be transformed, both as a result of outside pressures (the economic model) and through self-transformation. For natural monopolies, the private/public dimension seems neutral with respect to the potential for transformation, but the existence of one kind of change (privatisation) may serve to legitimate and facilitate a deeper transformation. For many organisations, however rooted in bureaucracy and with a massive technical system imperative, such change will be particularly difficult and if achieved (as with all organisations), will require continuous nurturing.

REFERENCES

Allaire, Y. and M.E. Firsirotu (1984) Theories of organizational culture. Organizational Studies, 5 (3), 193-226

Deal, T.E. and A.A. Kennedy (1982) Corporate cultures. Addison Wesley

DeLamarter, R.T. (1986) Big Blue: IBM's use and abuse of power. Macmillan, London

Douglas, M. (1978) Cultural bias. Occasional Paper, Royal Anthropological Institute, 35

Hatch, J. (1987) Privatisation and the consumer. Privatisation Paper no.4, Templeton College, Oxford; Chapter 4 in this volume

Heath, J. (1987) BAA Plc. Privatisation Paper no.2, Templeton College, Oxford; see Chapter 11 in this volume.

Leach, E. (1982) Social Anthropology. Fontana

Levi-Strauss, C. (1976) Tristes tropiques. Penguin

Ouchi, W. (1981) Theory Z. Addison Wesley

Pascale, G.T. (1985) The paradox of 'corporate culture'. Reconciling ourselves to socialisation. California Management Review, Winter

Peters, T.J. (1980) Leadership: sad facts and silver linings. McKinsey Quarterly, Spring

Rickard, J. (1987) Privatisation in the transport sector. Privatisation Paper no.3, Templeton College, Oxford; chapter 12, this volume

Schein, E. (1984) Coming to a new awareness of organisational culture. Sloan Management Review, Winter

Townsend, R. (1970) Up the organisation. Coronet

Woodward, S.N. (1985) Management - the ghost in the machine. London Business School Journal, Autumn

_____ (1986) Performance indicators and management performance in nationalised industries. Public Administration, Autumn

Part II

The Processes

7

The Financial Processes of Privatisation

Gerry Grimstone*

Privatisations are unlike any other financial transactions. In order to understand the financial processes of privatisation, it is necessary to establish the objectives which underlie most privatisation programmes and then to attempt to reconcile these objectives with techniques available in the market. Both objectives and techniques vary from country to country, and market to market, and what is appropriate in one environment will not necessarily be appropriate elsewhere. I intend to focus on objectives and techniques that have been used in the United Kingdom, many of which have subsequently been adopted for use elsewhere. In that over £25 billion worth of shares have been sold by the British Government, over 600,000 workers have been moved to the private sector, and the proportion of people who own shares in Britain has more than trebled, the British programme has clearly been a success in terms of implementation. Its success in terms of increasing the efficient utilisation of national assets will take longer to judge.

THE PROGRAMME'S OBJECTIVES

The original rationale for the British privatisation programme was primarily economic. Nationalisation in Britain had not been a success. Despite the high hopes of its originators, criticisms were continually voiced about the low return on the capital employed in the nationalised

* Schroders, London. This chapter is drawn in part from material published by the author in <u>Contemporary Record</u> (Spring 1987) and elsewhere.

industries, their record on prices, productivity and man-power costs, and about the low level of customer satisfaction which they provided. It can be argued that these shortcomings resulted from deficiencies in control techniques rather than being an endemic feature of state ownership. Whatever the truth of this contention, the British political and administrative system seemed powerless to bring about the necessary changes within the public sector. Privatisation was heralded by the incoming Conservative Government in 1979 as being the only way of bringing lasting improvements in economic performance.

Having noted that the primary objective of the programme in its early days was economic efficiency, the political success of the programme was helped by the realisation that a privatisation programme could fulfil other objectives than purely that of increasing efficiency. Indeed, increasing efficiency did not necessarily have to be the main priority, a discovery which was to create tensions later.

As presently organised, the British programme, in common with other programmes elsewhere, has the following key objectives:

(a) to increase efficiency through competition, de-regulation, or other means;

(b) to raise finance which can be used to fund other expenditure priorities, to reduce borrowing, to reduce taxation, or any combination of these;

(c) to encourage employees to own shares in the company in which they work;

(d) to boost the level of share ownership in the general economy;

(e) to strengthen the capital market; and

(f) to gain domestic and international prestige.

Judged by these objectives, the UK Programme has clearly been successful. Some 17 major companies and a number of smaller enterprises have been sold. Millions of new investors have been introduced to the stock market through the programme and there has been a high level of employee participation. One in five of the adult population of the UK is now a shareholder compared with one in ten in France and one in 20 in Japan. The performance of privatised companies has improved and, for example, the profits of British Aerospace have trebled, those of Cable & Wireless are up sevenfold, Amersham International's have doubled, Jaguar's are up by one-third, and the National Freight Consortium's have increased seven-fold. The combination of freedom from statutory and bureaucratic constraints, strong balance sheets, progressive elimination of internal inefficiencies, and generally favourable economic conditions has done wonders for the companies concerned.

IT TAKES TWO TO TANGO

Establishing the objectives of a privatisation programme is of little use if they cannot be put into effect. It is occasionally forgotten by those attempting to administer a privatisation programme that, unlike nationalisation, privatisation is a two-way process. Governments may want to sell a company but someone else must also want to buy it if the transaction is to be brought to a successful conclusion. Wishful thinking is rarely enough.

Methods of sale in the British privatisation programme have been determined by the programme's overall objectives and by practicalities. Because of the desire to spread ownership widely, public offerings of shares are the preferred choice if they can be achieved. Failing this - and a public offering is a severe test for a company - employee buy-outs have been welcomed provided that the funds are available and the company's cash flow can support the necessary leverage. The most difficult sales to bring to a popular conclusion are sales to corporate purchasers, particularly if overseas buyers are involved. The politics of privatisation is such that domestic investors normally have to be given preference, although minority sales overseas can be an important factor in bringing an otherwise domestic sale to a successful conclusion.

In practice, therefore, a hierarchy of political desirability can be established which coincides, fortuitously, with the level of capital market sophistication that is necessary to bring the sales to a conclusion. The hierarchy can be demonstrated diagnostically as illustrated in Figure 7.1. The public offering represents the acme of privatisation achievement: for countries with undeveloped capital markets, overseas trade sales may be the only option even if undesirable politically.

Figure 7.1: The hierarchy of political desirability regarding privatisation

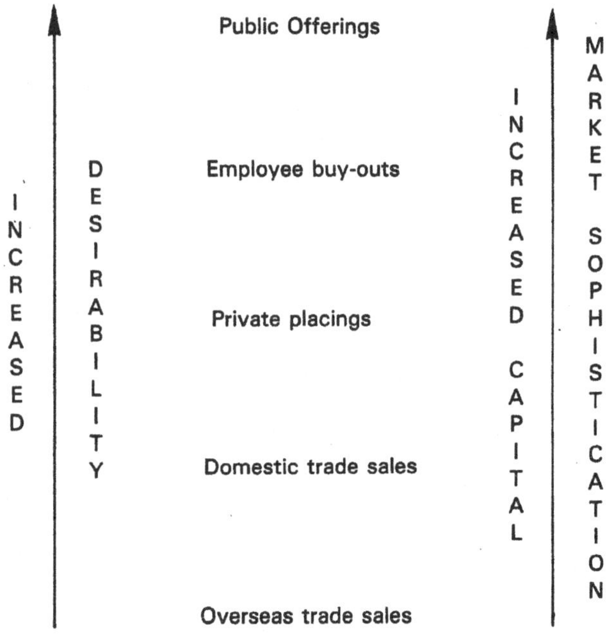

THE PRICE IS RIGHT?

Having determined in outline terms the method of sale and its structure, those conducting the privatisation will, at some point, need to advise the vendor on likely proceeds and, in due course, unless a competititve auction is held, to set a price. A competitive auction will mean that a demonstrably fair market price is obtained but this is not always as clear-cut as might be expected. Bidders, as well as naming a price, will often hedge it around with various conditions which may or may not be easy to value. If the management of the company concerned is itself particip-ating in the bidding process, the prospective bidder might be concerned that the management has an unfair advantage and thus may not want to bid. If the management bids but is unsuccessful, the result might be demoralisation and a damaged business. In some cases, management teams taking part in a competitive auction are given a defined price preference (say, 5 per cent), and this may cause a non-management prospective bidder to wonder whether the time and expense of making a bid are really worthwhile.

Pricing a privatisation of shares is never easy, especially if there are no market analogues already in existence. Coventional pricing techniques in the London market normally involve the establishment of likely earnings (for example, the profit attributable to future shareholders), and applying a multiple to these earnings based on a review of analogues tempered by a judgement of likely investor perceptions. Traditionally, there is an understanding that a well-judged flotation will go to an immediate after-market premium of between 10 and 15 per cent. Where no analogues are available, a certain amount of imaginative thinking will be needed. Provided a reasonably secure stream of dividends can be identified, a yield-based valuation can sometimes provide a useful insight. Techniques such as the Capital Asset Pricing Model or the Dividend Discount Model are rarely robust enought to be of any use, disappointing though this might be to business school graduates.

With a conventional offer for sale on the London Stock Exchange, the price is fixed at the beginning of the offer period and investors thus know what price they will pay for the shares if any are obtained. If with the benefit of hindsight the price set proves to be wrong, the vendor (or the underwriters) will suffer. In contrast, the tender offer allows the market to set the price. A minimum tender price is laid down and investors tender for shares at that or whatever higher price they would be prepared to pay. The striking price, which is generally the common price paid by all investors at which the vendor decides to clear the offer, is then determined in the light of the subscriptions. In order to get a bandwagon going, which is an essential feature of a successful tender, the minimun tender price has to be set low enough to attract the market and this price will generally be lower than would be achieved in a fixed price offer. The tender will be underwritten at the minimum tender price and this is, of course, good news for the underwriters. If the tender is successful, higher eventual proceeds might be obtained for the vendor but at some penalty to the after-market.

The problem with a tender are that it requires the prospective investor to make a judgement not just about whether or not he or she wishes to buy the shares but also what price should be paid. This added complexity tends to discourage amateur investors and the method is not therefore suited for shares which are intended to have a wide popular appeal. The apparent accuracy in pricing which results also tends to deflate the performance of shares in the after-market and this discourages speculative buying. Although this may appear desirable, a certain amount of excitement and market interest is always necessary as boring sales are rarely successful.

It may be rational for a vendor conducting a series of sales to seek to maximise advantage over a period of time rather than in relation to individual sales. In practice, if a government is planning a series of sales, it is unlikely to be in its interest to price a privatisation issue to the last penny if by so doing the risks of the offer failing are materially increased. The single offer will be achieved in these circumstances: the rest are likely to suffer disproportionately.

A PROPER UNDERWRITING RISK?

One of the marginal consequences of the recent British Petroleum (BP) sale, apart from securing for the Treasury a guaranteed stream of privatisation revenue over the next three financial years, is that it has brought to the fore the role of the underwriter in the London market - a role which in the past has not been well understood by vendors and even by some underwriters themselves.

The underwriting process in London generally works as follows. An issuing house, or group of houses (the lead underwriters) enters into a binding agreement to acquire, in certain circumstances, a number of shares at a given price. Then, the brokers to the issue, on behalf of the bank, lay off that risk to a greater or lesser extent by passing it on to a group of so-called 'sub-underwriters' who are prospective long-term holders of the shares (for example, pension fund managers). The issuing house then offers the shares to investors; if the shares are not taken up they pass to the sub-underwriters. In a typical private sector transaction, the lead underwriter is paid a commission of 0.5 per cent, the broker 0.25 per cent, and the sub-underwriter 1.25 per cent.

The stated reasons for underwriting have always been that it guarantees proceeds for the vendor and provides confidence to the market in that a reputable sponsor has not only put his name but his capital at risk. The Committee of Public Accounts of the House of Commons has, in the past, not always found these reasons convincing. The Committee's Seventeenth Report in the 1983-4 Session, having reviewed the sales of Britoil and Associated British Ports, concluded:

Underwriting

In our view the main benefit of underwriting a new issue is the assurance that, should the market be overestimated, as it clearly turned out to be for Britoil, the Exchequer will receive immediately the proceeds of the share price. However, the transfer of a substantial proportion of the issue to the hands of underwriters is not the same thing as an effective transfer to the private sector with a wide spread of ownership, and we note the high cost of underwriting. We trust therefore that the need for underwriting new issues will be kept under review particularly in cases where the price is set at a level intended to offer a firm prospect of full take-up.

With regard to sales of shares in companies which are already traded on the market, where it appears that the objectives have as much to do with financing the Public Sector Borrowing Requirement as with transfer of ownership and control to the private sector, it seems to us that the recent practice of using underwritten tender offers may be wasteful. We suggest that other selling methods, reflecting the wide experience of the Treasury and the Bank of England in managing the marketing of Government stock, should be considered as a more economical means of meeting Government objectives.

The Public Accounts Committee (PAC) returned to this theme in its Third Report of the 1985-6 Session when it considered the sale of British Telecom (BT). Having stated that it was not convinced that the extent of risk justified the rates agreed for placing commissions, it said:

We would emphasise that our previous recommend-ations should continue to be borne in mind in future sales; in particular it will be important on each occasion for a careful assessment to be made of the appropriate method of sale and of the need for underwriting.

The PAC's comments on the BP sale will no doubt contain further revealing insights.

The British Government has been successful in driving down underwriting commission rates for privatisation in the London market to a level at which a dispassionate observer would conclude that the transactions were effectively risk-free and thus not worth underwriting. As part of this process, the 1985 sale of Cable & Wireless shares, conducted for the government by Schroders, introduced the first-ever underwriting competition to the London market. The price of the shares on offer was set by the government, and lead underwriters were invited to bid to underwrite the offer at whatever commission they considered appropriate. At the time, this was seen as an extremely radical development and led to the lead underwriters' commission being reduced to 0.2625 per cent, which was the lowest ever achieved.

Having held one competition, the government understandably got a taste for more. The circle of banks invited to participate was progressively widened and some banks thought that bidding low for what they thought was a risk-free transaction was a cheap way of acquiring the prestige that seemed to be associated with having their name on the front page of the prospectus. The eventual consequence of this driving down of rates was that the commission paid to the lead underwriters for the BP sale amounted to the princely sum of £18,000 per £100 million pounds of risk that was insured. No wonder, perhaps, when the world's biggest-ever share sale coincided with the world's biggest-ever slump in share prices, that some houses squealed that this was not 'a proper underwriting risk' and sought to have the underwriting agreement terminated. If it had been, future underwriting of privatisation issues would clearly not have been justifiable, and the City of London's reputation as a financial centre would have been damaged.

The imprudent behaviour of some houses on the BP sale in assuming a greater risk than they were prepared to stand by raises the question as to whether the vendor and its advisers were prudent in adopting the offer structure that they did. It also brought to the fore the inherent conflict that exists between a merchant bank acting both as adviser to the government and as lead underwriter. The overseas offers could have been decoupled from the UK offer and the vendor could have insisted that the foreign branches in the USA, Canada, and Japan were more widely syndicated than they were. In addition by making the partly paid BP shares that were on offer so attractive in terms of yield and payment terms compared with the fully-paid shares already in the market, an element of instability was built into the structure. A rational market would value the partly paid shares more highly than the fully paid shares and it was always therefore likely that the price of the existing shares would drop below those which were on offer. The unsophisticated investor could well have taken this as a sign of incipient failure and stayed on the sidelines even if world stockmarkets had not been in turmoil. As it was, the completion of the sale was a triumph of confidence over uncertainty. Whether or not it leads to fundamental changes in the way that British privatisations are conducted remains to be seen.

ACHIEVING SUCCESS

What makes a successful privatisation is not easy to define. An after-market premium is a good thing provided that it is not too large. Millions of shareholders are desirable provided that their applications are not so sealed-down in terms of shares distributed per person as to be meaningless. Overseas sales are welcomed if they make the domestic offering 'successful'.

In practice, demand for privatised equity can be categorised as follows:

(a) employees' demand;

(b) domestic retail demand (i.e. from the general public);

(c) domestic institutional demand; and

(d) overseas institutional demand.

Unless the domestic institutions (e.g. pension funds and insurance companies) are keen to participate, the sale is unlikely to be achievable. Yet if their participation is too great, the political benefits of spreading ownership amongst employees and the general public will be lost. The ideal is an offer structure which segments the sale into defined portions and attempts to keep an element of unsatisfied demand in each portion but particularly amongst the domestic institutions (who are the most likely buyers in the after-market if left short of sales). 'Sid' may like shares but what he wants are shares which go to a premium. The right answer is complicated by the fact that the only demand which matters is that which manifests itself in applications for the shares which are to be sold.

Even using sophisticated market research techniques, this demand is very hard to predict in advance and thus an offer structure is needed which is flexible enough in its allocation across segments to cope with changes in the anticipated demand. We developed a method of doing this called 'flexible clawback' which involves allocating shares provisionally to institutions at the beginning of the offer period, thus creating a perceived shortage, promoting demand in the retail sector, then 'clawing back' the shares that had been provisionally placed with institutions, depending on the demand that materialises in the retail sector, in order to reallocate them to the retail sector.

Another recent innovation has been the 'partial tender' whereby shares are offered at a fixed price to the retail sector but with a margin tendered to institutions who bid, and pay, whatever price they choose provided it is at or above the fixed retail price. This technique both promotes wider share ownership (through making the retail offer as simple as possible) and increases marginal proceeds for the vendor (albeit with some effect on the immediate after-market).

CAPITAL MARKET EFFECTS

Privatisations are an order of magnitude greater than previously contemplated transactions and this has led to profound capital market effects. Two main positive impacts can be distinguished:

(1) privatisation can lead to a widening of the capital market by introducing new investors, both domestic and international; and

(2) privatisation can lead to a deepening of the market by introducing mature companies with a strong market position.

Both these effects, which are interrelated, are clearly advantageous.

As an illustration of the first effect, privatisation in the United Kingdom has clearly led to personal savings being switched into the stock market from other forms of investment. The sale of BT in 1984 was the first privatisation anywhere in the world specifically designed to have widespread popular appeal. Prior to then, there were many who doubted that the British general public could be taught to buy shares via privatisation. The proportion of shares owned by the general public was decreasing and attracting even 50,000 people into a privatisation offering was reckoned to be good going. Yet the British Telecom sale attracted around 2.2 million applicants, of whom around half had never before owned shares.

Just how was this done? The BT sale was five times larger than any sale that had previously been attempted and was the first to be marketed on a wide scale to the general public. It had been clear for some time that existing share-selling techniques were not capable of creating a new breed of shareowners. Stockbrokers were generally happiest when selling shares to their existing clients and, in consequence, if shares were to be sold widely, new distribution channels needed to be created. The vendor would have to go over the heads of the normal intermediaries both by motivating a more lively sales force than traditional stockbrokers and by selling direct to prospective shareholders. No vendor was more suited than the government to take on the challenge.

Why was it so popular? BT combined features of both a utility and a high-technology business which made it ideally suited to inexperienced shareholders. The sale was advertised widely in both the press and television, and generous commissions were paid to financial intermediaries. Small shareholders were, at the government's expense, given the added attraction of a 'one for ten' free loyalty bonus issue of shares if they held their shares for more than three years or, alternatively, were given discounts off their telephone bills. The sale captured the public's imagination, proved with the benefit of hindsight to be significantly under-priced, and was both a popular and political success. It marked the emergence of popular capitalism in the UK and showed that the largest privatisations, if properly handled, could be successfully absorbed by the capital market. Prior to BT, to raise £500 million in a single transaction was reckoned to be good going. The BT sale raised nearly £4,000 million, paid by instalments over a three-year period.

I said earlier that privatisation can deepen as well as widen a country's capital market. This arises because it is often a country's dominant businesses that were previously nationalised and brought into state ownership. They were brought into the state sector because of their position in the economy, their strategic importance, or their size and market dominance. It is these very characteristics which, on privatisation, enable them to give depth to a stock market and to provide ballast to what may have otherwise been an unduly speculative environment.

The experience of Britain and other countries is that privatisation - contrary to the original expectations of economists and others - can create its own market capacity. There are a number of reasons for this. Firstly, the equity that is being sold is normally of good quality and represents an attractive investment opportunity. Purchasers gain comfort from the fact that the vendor is a government and have learnt by experience that governments are risk-averse when it comes to privatisations. Success is valued highly, which is no wonder given privatisation's invariably high profile.

Secondly, a government that is raising finance by selling equities will borrow less for a given public sector financial deficit than it would do otherwise. A government's total demand on the capital market may therefore be unchanged by a privatisation programme. The equity of utilities that hold a dominant market share either via operating a natural monopoly or otherwise, can closely resemble debt in its financial characteristics and thus may be accommodated in that portion of an investor's portfolio previously reserved for fixed income securities.

Thirdly - and this point is often overlooked - even a single privatisation may create a company that is a material component of a stock market's index. Those investors who attempt to match their portfolios to the main constituents of a country's capital market must buy privatised equity if they are to maintain their relative position. Some privatised equity - for example, that of a national electricity or telecommunications equity - also gives good exposure to the totality of economic development in a particular country and this may be valued by an investor.

Fourthly, it should be remembered that governments which are selling equity become interested in the operations of the equity market and, implicitly or explicitly, take steps to strengthen the market. Traditionally, of course, governments only operated in the debt market, whereas the equity market tended to be left to market practitioners. This is now no longer the case in countries which are pursuing successful privatisation policies. It is also true that the same political philosophy which produces privatisation is also likely to encourage market liberalisation and deregulation. Privatisation and the growth of London as an international financial centre have gone hand in hand.

Despite the large proceeds raised from privatisation sales in Britain in the last five years, the total net issues of ordinary shares in London have reached record levels. It is clear that despite the heavy demands that privatisation has placed on the London market, private issuers have not suffered. New capital-raising has reached record levels. There has been no crowding-out of private investment by government sales and this is important if the overall success of a privatisation policy is to be maximised.

In order to achieve capital market benefits, a sophisticated marketing programme must be created to maximise interest from all classes of investors. This will normally be extremely cost-effective. Not only can such a campaign benefit proceeds and the commercial image of the company that is being sold, but it can also provide an opportunity to project a country's general economic development and financial status. Many countries would like to have a privatisation programme; few can assemble sufficient determination, expertise, and credibility to achieve one.

PRIVATISATIONS ARE NOT JUST FINANCIAL TRANSACTIONS

I said at the beginning of this chapter that privatisations were unlike all other financial transactions. The differences arise because of size, political sensitivities, investor interest, and the complexity of privatisation's objectives. In summary, I believe that the United Kingdom privatisation programme has been successful because the critical participants in the programme were identified early on and dealt with in the most satisfactory fashion. Key groups normally include the following:

(a) the general public as taxpayers, customers and voters;

(b) the employees of the firm being privatised;

(c) the management of the firm being privatised;

(d) prospective investors;

(e) commentators; and

(f) opponents of privatisation

Fair pricing which balances the needs of the taxpayer and the investor, voucher offers for customers, free shares for employees (not least to negate trade union opposition), retaining the privatised company's corporate structure, widespread distribution of shares, full disclosure of information, and careful attention to detail may all be necessary if a successful sale is to be achieved.

In political terms, few policies can claim the benefit of privatisation and be so attractively presented in terms of privatisation's ability to increase industrial efficiency, raise money, boost ownership amongst employees and the wider general public, and carry domestic as well as international prestige. Provided the relevant interested groups are clearly identified at an early stage, and are satisfied, everybody seems to win.

CONCLUSIONS

What lessons should be learnt from all this? Firstly, privatisations are not merely financial transactions, and opportunities will be lost if they are treated as such. Secondly, the case for the programme must be argued effectively and enthusiastically. Thirdly, involving employees and the general public to the greatest possible extent not only helps provide market capacity, but it can also create popular success. This is, of course, only the beginning of the process, however: for privatisation to be a long-term phenomenon, not just the sales but the companies which are created must be successful. Only time will tell the extent to which this is achieved.

8

Preparing for Privatisation:
The Financial Aspects

H. J. Hyman*

The UK experience of privatisation has shown that a wide range of businesses can be transferred from the public to the private sector. Although the time taken from the initial decision to privatise to the final sale of the enterprise can vary enormously, an established pattern has emerged in the preparatory processes necessary to achieve a successful privatisation. In view of the complexity of these financial transactions, the financial adviser is involved in all stages of this process, from the initial strategic decisions to the final detailed arrangements as to the type and method of sale. I would like to draw on my own experience of a number of privatisations in order to illustrate how individual businesses are prepared for private ownership.

At the outset of the privatisation process, there are a number of strategic decisions that need to be made which will determine the ultimate form the sale will take. These might include government fund-raising requirements, the timing of the sale, or wider political objectives such as extending share ownership or expanding capital markets. These decisions will determine the type of sale that is appropriate, ranging from a public share issue to a management buy-out or a trade sale.

After a strategic decision has been taken, an enterprise will undergo an often extensive process of preparation for life in the private sector. This will involve creating an appropriate legal form for the enterprise and creating a track record to attract investors. As the final form of the enterprise will often differ considerably from the form in

* Director, Privatisation Services Department, Price Waterhouse, London

119

which it operated in the public sector, this can be a protracted process and will involve financial restructuring to make the business self-sufficient and commercially viable. As a final stage of the process, a valuation will need to be placed on the business and appropriate selling techniques developed to enable a successful privatisation.

I intend to focus on the financial aspects of this preparatory process. What follows is based on the UK experience of privatisation, although the patterns and principles involved are equally applicable elsewhere. I will consider briefly the strategic aspects of the process where immediate fund-raising requirements have to be ranked with other objectives in determining the form the sale will take. Most of my discussion will, however, be concentrated on the financial aspects of preparing for privatisation, in particular the changes in capital structure and funding to allow financial self-sufficiency and the various ways this has been achieved. I will also examine the preparation involved in enabling a public enterprise to achieve accounting comparability with the private sector, including changes in accounting policies and reporting.

STRATEGIC CONSIDERATIONS

The general objectives and philosophies of privatisation fall largely outside the scope of this chapter. However, in order to understand the financial decisions that are taken as part of the privatisation process, such as the funds to be raised or the form that the privatisation is to take, it is useful to consider the principal objectives underlying the policy of privatisation.

The principal objectives of privatisation can be summarised as:

(a) A perception that the efficiency of the industry could be improved by transition to the private sector. Efficiency would be achieved by better motivation of management and employees, the forces of competition and the ability of management to run the business free from government interference.

(b) A means of raising funds for the Exchequer. Thus, for example, the British Gas flotation alone, including new debt created, raised some £7.7

billion. The British Telecom (BT) flotation raised £2.6 billion net of the pension liabilities kept by the government. The importance of privatisation as a fund-raising exercise therefore has a significant impact on the strategic decision of the form and timing of the sale.

(c) The desire to widen share ownership. Between 1979 and 1984 the primary objective of many of the privatisations had been to raise funds in accordance with an underlying philosophy to reduce the number of public corporations. The BT flotation emphasised the objective of widening share ownership. In 1979 it was estimated that the number of adults directly owning shares was some 4.5 per cent of the population, compared with 7 per cent in 1958. A recent survey commissioned by the Treasury and the Stock Exchange shows that some 8.5 million people in the UK, or almost 20 per cent of the adult population, now own shares.

The strategic decision-making process will need to determine how these various objectives are satisfied. The eventual form that privatisation is to take will be significantly affected not only by the nature of the enterprise itself but also by the relative significance of each of these strategic objectives. It is unlikely that any form of privatisation will satisfy all of these objectives - for example, a public flotation, which requires a long-term preparation of the business for sale may conflict with the government's immediate objective of raising funds. A type of privatisation that is easier to achieve in the short term, such as a trade sale, would not satisfy the objective of widening share ownership. Balancing these objectives is therefore an important part of the process in deciding what form privatisation should take.

TYPE OF SALE

There are a number of ways in which privatisation can be achieved. The main options are:

(1) a public flotation on the Stock Exchange, either by a fixed price, or by a tender offer with a minimum price;

121

(2) a management/employee buy-out;

(3) a placing with a group of investors; or

(4) a trade sale, in which a company is sold to a single person or a consortium.

Public flotation

The public sale of assets has been the most usual method of sale. This can take two forms. In an offer for sale, the shares in question are offered to the general public at a fixed price which is determined in advance of the sale. In a tender offer, the price is fixed in response to the applications themselves and a minimum tender price is stated. Once the applications themselves are received, the price is determined. Other factors may come into play, such as any preferential treatment given to small individual shareholders and to the workers and customers of the companies sold.

The advantage of a tender offer is that there is the possibility of raising the issue price to a higher level than might otherwise have been achieved with a fixed price offer. However, a tender has a disadvantage in that it is often too sophisticated for the small investor at whom the offer is aimed. The British Airports Authority (BAA) flotation therefore involved the innovative device of offering part of the shares at a fixed price and part as a tender, with the minimum tender price equal to the fixed price.

Whether a share issue is at a fixed price or a tender, both methods have the disadvantage that the company will need an established commercial track record prior to sale. This will often involve significant long-term preparation of the company with the result that such privatisations need to be planned many years ahead.

Management buy-out

An alternative to a public flotation is the option of a management buy-out. This method has the advantages of causing minimum disruption to the company and speed of sale. Another advantage of this type of sale is that a management buy-out will require significantly less disclosure than in a public flotation, reducing the amount of preparatory work prior to sale. In order for a management buy-out to be successful, three key conditions will need to be met, namely:

(1) management must have experience, competence and commitment;

(2) the company must have a strong cash flow from which interest payments can be met; and also

(3) a solid asset base to secure borrowing.

In many cases, however, this option is not appropriate and is best suited to smaller privatisations. A fine example of a successful management buy-out was the sale of the Vickers Shipbuilding and Engineering Limited subsidiary of British Shipbuilders to management and employees, one of the largest UK management buy-outs to date. It has also worked successfully in the case of a number of National Bus Company subsidiaries and the National Freight Corporation. In the case of the latter, considerable financial restructuring was required before the buy-out could progress.

Placing

A placing is a useful option in those cases in which the timing of the sale is an important objective. Part of a company could be placed with institutions (i.e. sold to clients of the sponsoring bank) in order to satisfy short-term fund-raising requirements, with the possibility of a public issue at a later date. However, if the entire issue were to be taken up in this way, the objective of wider share ownership would not be satisfied and might be considered politically unacceptable.

Trade sale

Another option for privatisation is a trade sale to a UK or overseas company. This is often the quickest route to privatisation, as the enterprise will not necessarily need to demonstrate a commercial track-record. Potential purchasers will take other factors into account, such as buying up the enterprise's market share, if it operates in a competitive environment, or the opportunity of providing a unique product or service. The business to be privatised may be particularly attractive to overseas purchasers who can use it as an opportunity to enter an otherwise closed UK market.

In these situations, purchasers are much more likely to consider the value of the enterprise's assets and its potential for future profits rather than its historical record in the public sector. Trade sales therefore have the advantage of speed, although offsetting this, they do not fulfil some of the other objectives of privatisation such as wider share ownership. In certain circumstances, a trade sale of a public enterprise, especially to an overseas buyer, can lead to political problems, as was evidenced by the proposed sale of Land Rover to General Motors in 1986.

THE PROCESS OF PREPARATION

In conjunction with the decisions that need to be taken as to the type of sale, a number of decisions will also need to be taken concerning the specific assets to be transferred to the private sector, the structure of the new organisation, and the legal form that this transfer will take. This part of the privatisation process will involve considerable preparation to create an entity that can be self-sufficient and operate in the private sector free from any remaining dependence on its ties with the public sector. I have considered these under the headings of organisational changes and legal changes.

Organisational changes

In some cases the form of privatisation has been fairly easy to determine. In the case of Amersham International and Cable & Wireless, for example, there already existed a Companies Act-type of organisation in public hands. Privatisation in this case was largely a matter of transferring a public sector enterprise to the private sector in a broadly similar form. In other cases, however, the enterprises to be privatised are often not in a form which enables them to be readily privatised. In these cases it is usually necessary to identify the specific assets that are appropriate for privatisation and to create an appropriate legal entity into which the assets to be sold can be transferred.

The process of identifying the appropriate parts of the business that are suitable for privatisation will often involve the break-up of an existing public sector organisation. The privatisation of Britoil, for example, involved the separation of the Exploration and Production assets of the British National Oil Corporation (BNOC) from the remainder of the Corporation. The remaining business of BNOC was retained in the public sector (until its abolition) in order to maintain government influence and to regulate trading of North Sea oil. Other examples of instances in which it has been appropriate to break up existing public sector organisations include the British Shipbuilders' warship yards and the National Bus Company subsidiaries. A similar debate is currently in progress regarding the privatisation of the water industry, as the form that the privatised industry should take may differ from its current structure.

In many cases, public sector organisations have complex interrelationships with other government functions which make it difficult to transfer the enterprise to the private sector in its existing form. Thus, for example, many organisations have social or 'public good' obligations which could not be performed profitability in a commercial environment. This problem can be resolved in two ways. One way of dealing with the situation is to remove the 'public good' duties prior to privatisation, as has been done in the case of the water industry with the creation of the National Rivers Authority, which will own and be responsible for the upkeep of the rivers. This move leaves the Water Authorities with only the commercial activities of water supply and sewerage treatment.

A second possible solution is to introduce regulation of the industry after privatisation: for example, it was made a condition of BT's licence that it maintain call boxes in rural areas, even though these might be inappropriate. The regulatory body established on privatisation would then ensure that this licence term had been complied with.

Many public sector organisations will also have complex financial links with government. These might include government subsidies, property owned with or shared by other government departments, or a dependence on other public sector organisations for business and income.

The Financial Aspects

Legal changes

After all the structural decisions have been finalised, legislation must be drawn up to allow the industry to be sold, to vest its assets and business in one or more public limited companies (PLC) and to define the rights and responsibilities of those PLCs. The shares in the new company would initially be owned by the government but would be in a form which would enable them to be subsequently sold to the public.

The constitution of a nationalised industry is contained in legislation which is specific to that industry. In the private sector the constitution of a company is contained in its Memorandum and Articles of Association, drawn up under the Companies Act 1985. The critical difference is that a public sector entity can only change its constitution through Parliament; in the private sector it can be changed with the approval of shareholders.

In some privatisations certain provisions in the Articles of Association were considered so fundamental to the national interest that they were entrenched by the creation of a so-called 'Special Share'. This Special Share is held by government and the special shareholder's permission is required for those provisions to be changed. Details of the principal restrictions entrenched by the Special Share are included in Appendix 1 of this chapter.

FINANCIAL PREPARATIONS

Once an appropriate structure and legal form has been created for the enterprise, it will be necessary to ensure that the company is financially prepared for the transition to the private sector. This will involve a period of financial preparation and may involve some element of restructuring prior to sale. The most important aspects are:

(a) creating a commercial track record;

(b) capital restructuring prior to sale;

(c) accounting adjustments to achieve comparability with the private sector;

(d) quality of accounting information; and

(e) pension arrangements.

126

Creating a commercial track record

Whether a public sector organisation is to be privatised by means of a public share sale or a trade sale, it will be important to demonstrate to potential investors the commercial record of the business. As already discussed, this may pose some practical problems if the enterprise did not operate in its restructured form - for example, if it formed part of a larger organisation or if parts of the business had been removed.

This will often involve significant changes to the business and in some cases will involve turning a loss-making enterprise into a profit-making one. Thus, for example, British Airways made a loss of £541 million in the year to 31 March 1982, and this had been converted to a profit of £181 million by 31 March 1986. Another interesting example is British Steel which is due to be privatised in 1988. Once regarded as one of the black spots of British industry, British Steel has turned a net loss of £1,784 million in 1979-80 into a net profit of £178 million in 1986-7. The Corporation has been able to discard government support for the first time and is now able to fund its own spending needs, including a £269 million capital expenditure programme.

The creation of a commercially sound track record has often involved a significant degree of rationalisation of the enterprise. Thus, for example, the 1982 loss reported by British Airways includes some £429 million of rationalisation provisions. At British Steel considerable rationalisation is also taking place and the work-force of the UK's largest manufacturing employer has fallen from 200,000 a decade ago to just over 50,000 today. The result is a streamlined industry built to compete in the private sector.

Many privatised industries have also made changes at board level in preparation for privatisation. In the case of British Airways, the Chairman, Chief Executive and Chief Financial Officer all arrived in anticipation of privatisation. BT also made significant board changes in the run up to privatisation, with half of its board in 1984 (immediately prior to flotation) being new compared with the previous year and an overall expansion of the Board from eleven members in 1983 to 15 in 1987. In addition, the National Bus Company had a whole range of boards to strengthen for their new independent position, or in some cases to create them from scratch.

The Financial Aspects

The quality of management will be significant not only in ensuring that the enterprise has an appropriate track record prior to sale, but also that it generates confidence and credibility with City institutions and helps ensure the success of the sale.

Capital restructuring prior to sale

Perhaps the most significant aspect of financial preparation is ensuring that the new enterprise has an appropriate capital structure for operating in the private sector. The level of capital will need to be adequate to ensure that the business is financially self-sufficient and to ensure that the level of funds is sufficient to allow future investment. In this context, the mixture of equity capital and debt will be significant. Too high a level of debt will drain the resources of the privatised entity, and too low a level might throw doubt on the company's ability to generate cash. A decision has therefore to be taken as to the amount of government debt that is to be retained in the company or, alternatively, if this is to be converted to equity capital or written off.

There are a number of significant factors that will affect the decision as to the most appropriate capital structure for the company. These include:

(a) the amount of funds required by the government;

(b) the amount of capital required by the company for its investment needs; and

(c) the appropriate mixture of equity and debt.

The amount of funds required by government will obviously be an important consideration. Having said this, there are a number of ways in which the net receipts for government can remain unchanged while creating a variety of possible capital structures for the company. To take a simple example, a company may be funded primarily by government loans prior to privatisation. On privatisation, the government can either write off the loans receivable from the company, thereby increasing its net assets and its selling price, or it can leave them in the company. In either case, the net proceeds receivable by the government will remain the same, ceteris paribus, but the capital structure of the new company can be significantly different.

In the above example, government proceeds remained unaltered but the capital structure of the company was changed. As part of the privatisation process it may be necessary to increase or decrease the capital base of the company, affecting the absolute proceeds received by government. An increase or decrease in the capital base may be necessary to bring the funding of the company in line with its business requirements. If a company is under-capitalised, the business will operate within tight restraints and this could lead to problems with cash flow or funding investment projects. If a company is over-capitalised, this can lead to inefficiencies and poor investment decisions as the pressure on management for efficiency will be reduced.

Extra capital can be raised for the company (rather than the government) in one of two ways. Firstly, the company can make a rights issue to the single shareholder, the government, who can then sell the shares on to the public. In the second case, the company can issue shares directly to the public at the same time as the government sale. The advantage of the second method is one of presentation in that it gives an impression of providing its own finance even if the company is only using the funds to repay government debt. The difference is merely present-ational, as the overall effect is the same. Thus,the precise form that the privatisation will take will therefore depend on the immediate cash requirements of the government and the capital required by the company for its operational needs.

In addition to the total amount of capital in the new company, the mixture between equity and debt will also be significant. The capital mix will affect the company's profitability and, to an extent, the value placed on the company by investors. Profitability will be affected because of the effect of interest payments on debt on earnings. The value of the company will be affected because of the valuation techniques used by market. One form of valuation takes account of the company's net assets; however, in the case of many nationalised industries this type of valuation is not appropriate because of the practical problems in arriving at an accurate value (consider, for example, the problems involved in valuing a telephone network or a sewerage system).

The most usual form of valuation is therefore the use of an earnings multiple in order to determine the price (the PE ratio). To the extent that earnings are likely to be depressed

129

by too high a level of debt, the total value placed on the company is likely to fall. However, the total value placed on the company will depend not only on the expected level of future earnings but also on the choice of PE ratio which is determined by investors' perception of risk. In this context it is interesting to note that the total value placed on the company can fall if the level of debt is too low, as investors may consider that this throws doubt on the ability of the company to generate cash and therefore the size of the multiple used will fall.

Depending on the relationship between interest rates and the PE ratio, additional debt could increase or decrease total government proceeds. The amount of debt to be created will therefore need careful calculation if proceeds are to be maximised. An example of the effect of the level of debt and the PE ratio on proceeds is shown in Appendix 2 to this chapter.

The new capital structure of the company is therefore important in determining the amount of the proceeds immediately available to government and the adequacy of funds available to the company. The mix of equity and debt will be significant in determining the absolute amount of the proceeds. It is useful to consider some examples of how this has happened in practice in order to illustrate these points.

British Telecom

Table 8.1: BT's balance sheets before and after privatisation

| | £ million | |
	Before	After
Government loans	(2,790)	-
Unsecured loan stock	-	(2,706)
Other net assets	8,740	8,696
Totals	5,950	5,990
Ordinary shares	-	1,500
Preference shares	-	750
Long term liabilities	1,250	-
Reserves	4,700	3,740
Totals	5,950	5,990

As the balance sheets in Table 8.1 indicate, the equity of the company was increased by £1.3 billion and the debt/equity ratio reduced from 60 to 48 per cent as the mix of equity and debt was significantly altered. It was decided to maintain government debt within the company, although this was largely converted to unsecured loan stock, rather than convert it to equity or write it off. Another interesting feature of the BT flotation concerns the decision not to transfer the long-term pension liability of £1,250 million from the Corporation to the new company. This was principally because of uncertainties over the extent of the liability (caused by a shortfall in the pension fund) and the practical problems to which this would give rise in floating the company.

British Gas

Table 8.2: British Gas's balance sheets before and after privatisation

	£ million	
	Before	After
Government debt	(217)	(2,500)
Other net assets	7,684	7,681
Totals	7,467	5,181
Share capital	-	1,038
Reserves	7,467	4,143
Totals	7,467	5,181

British Gas is an example of how net assets can be reduced prior to privatisation. As a profitable and cash-rich company, the introduction of debt was intended as a financial discipline. The mix of debt and equity was established at a level similar to that of BT with a debt to equity ratio of 0.48. This is also a good example of the use of debt to maximise proceeds, as discussed above.

British Aerospace

The mixture of equity and debt can also be changed by the use of part of the proceeds from the issue for the purposes of the company. In the case of the British Aerospace (BAe)

issues additional cash was raised for the company by the issue of new shares direct to the public. As these shares were issued by the company to the public rather than sold by government, additional cash is raised which was used to eliminate government debt. British Aerospace raised £100 million by this means in the first issue and £188 million in the second issue.

Associated British Ports/National Freight Corporation

Where the level of debt to equity prior to privatisation is too high, adjustments will need to be made to reduce the level of debt so that this is not a burden on the new company. In the case of Associated British Ports (sold by means of a public flotation), £81 million was written off prior to sale and in the case of the National Freight Corporation, £100 million of debt was written off to improve the capital structure.

Accounting adjustments

In addition to the adjustments to the enterprise's capital structure, other financial adjustments are often necessary in order to effect the transition to the private sector. Most types of privatisation will require the preparation of a prospectus which will contain an accountant's report on the historical accounting information.

In making their report to be included in the prospectus for the flotation, the reporting accountants are required to make any adjustments to the existing accounts as are in their opinion appropriate for the purpose of the report and to state that all adjustments considered necessary have been made, or, where appropriate, that no adjustments were considered necessary. There are generally two situations that necessitate adjustments to profits or to balance-sheet items. Firstly, adjustments are necessary where there has been a material change in accounting policies applied during the period of the report, or acceptable accounting principles have not been applied. Secondly, where material facts have come to light relating to events or transactions which occurred in a prior period, the accounting effect of which could not be determined with reasonable certainty, the reported results will be restated.

The purpose of these adjustments is to provide potential investors with consistent information prepared in accordance with generally accepted accounting practice. This will be presented in a five-year table of results to show the development of the enterprise over that period.

Examples of the principal adjustments that have been made in privatisations to date are discussed below.

Accounting convention

In many cases accounts of nationalised industries, despite a wealth of detail, are not directly comparable with those of private sector companies. A major difference between the accounts of nationalised industries and private sector companies is that most nationalised industries prepare accounts under the current-cost convention as opposesd to the historic-cost convention which is used in the private sector. This difference has been dealt with in a number of ways in practice:

(a) In the case of BT the accountant's report was prepared under the historic-cost convention, although current-cost information for the last two years prior to privatisation was included as a separate section.

(b) Both British Gas and BAA presented prospectuses showing the historic-cost and current-cost information side by side in the prospectuses.

As a result of the failure of the Accounting Standards Committee (the body responsible for determining accounting practice in the private sector) to reach agreement over the appropriate form that current cost accounts should take, very few private sector companies publish current cost information. It is interesting to note in this context that BT has now dropped current-cost information from its annual accounts.

Asset lives and depreciation

Another frequent adjustment on privatisation is to asset lives to bring them into line with estimates more common in the private sector. The BT prospectus explained the change in lives of some assets by saying that 'the shortening of asset lives took place in the exceptional circumstances of change from a statutory corporation to a public limited company operating in a new regulatory environment'. The effect of this adjustment was to decrease profit by £130 million over the five-year period as a result of extra depreciation. In the case of British Gas, asset lives were extended, resulting in a write-back of depreciation of £151 million for 1982, £156 million for 1983 and £181 million for 1984. As a result of this change in policy British Gas was also able to release deferred taxation of £170 million over the three-year period.

BT also changed its accounting policy regarding supplementary depreciation that had been charged in the accounts to provide for the replacement costs of certain fixed assets. This practice was not consistent with generally accepted accounting practice in the private sector and the amounts of between £361 million and £626 million from 1980 to 1983 were added back to profit in the accountant's report.

Capitalisation policies

In addition to the changes made to asset lives and the corresponding depreciation effect, changes are sometimes necessary to the capitalisation policies followed by nationalised industries. In the case of BT, irrecoverable costs of installing connections to customers' premises and expenditure on telephones, both of which had previously been capitalised, were written off in the prospectus at a total cost of £196 million.

Change in operations

Where a significant change in operations has occurred, the five-year table will be adjusted in order to show comparable information. This was the case in the British Gas accountant's report, in which the profits relating to the British Gas oil exploration arm at Wytch Farm, which had been disposed of in 1983 and 1984, were excluded.

Quality of accounting information

In some cases, the preparation of the five-year table for the accountant's report has proved a problem because of the limited availability of information for earlier years. This has occurred because of the primitive nature of the accounting systems at some nationalised industries and the consequent difficulty in obtaining information.

Many of the nationalised industries were poor at providing good-quality management information about their businesses. Prior to 1981, for example, BT operated on a cash basis and had only a limited idea of the true cost of providing any of its services as a whole, let alone to any one customer. It is interesting to note in this context that the BT's regulator, Brian Carsberg, had originally been called in as an advisor to the government on BT's accounting system and is a professor of accounting. It would however be an exaggeration to argue that the reforms introduced into BT's accounting practices led to anything approaching the type of information that would normally be necessary for an ordinary private sector company requiring listing on the Stock Exchange. This is demonstrated by the disclaimer contained in the BT prospectus referring to the years 1980 and 1981:

> As a result of industrial action which disrupted normal accounting procedures for billing, estimates were used to a significant extent in preparing the financial information set out in this report in respect of the year ended 31 March 1980 and it has not been possible to determine that there has been a proper allocation of results between the years ended 31 March 1980 and 1981. Conventional fixed asset accounting procedures have been progress- ively introduced over the period covered by our report, but were absent to a significant extent in respect of the two years ended 31 March 1981... Because of the significance of these uncertainties, we are unable to form an opinion on whether the financial information... gives a true and fair view of the profit and source and application of funds for the years ended 31 March 1980 and 1981.

Pension arrangements

Another area in which changes may need to be made as part of the financial preparation for privatisation is that of pensions. The status of the company's pension scheme and the obligations of the company in respect of any shortfall will need to be established at an early stage. This has been dealt with in various ways. In the case of BT, as already discussed, a liability of £1,250 million relating to a shortfall in the pension fund was not transferred to the public limited company created for privatisation. In another case, the government injected £47 million into the National Freight

Company's pension fund before the company was sold to management.

Where a public sector organisation is to be fragmented as part of the privatisation process, a decision will also need to be taken as to how the existing pension arrangements are to be maintained. There are basically three possibilities, all of which have been used in practice:

(1) Either the employees of the newly privatised company can remain in the existing scheme even though they are no longer employed by the public sector organisation. This was the case with the British Shipbuilders' warship yards, where employees of the individual privatised companies were allowed to remain within the existing British Shipbuilders' pension scheme.

(2) Or the pension fund could be divided between the various companies to be privatised, as was the case with the National Bus Company subsidiaries.

(3) Or a new scheme could be created on or prior to privatisation. British Airways, for example, closed the existing 'Airways Pension Scheme' to new entrants on 31 March 1984 as the level of benefits of the scheme was considered unduly high compared with private sector companies. A new scheme, the 'New Airways Pension Scheme', was created for new entrants, providing a lower level of benefits.

In view of the significance of pension costs to the company the choice of which route to take will be an important financial decision prior to privatisation.

LIFE AFTER PRIVATISATION

Finally, it is worth noting that new performance standards will be applied to the company after its transition to the private sector. The company will be accountable to a whole range of new shareholders instead of to a single shareholder as before. The company's performance will be related to bottom-line profit rather than government financing limits and the achievement of these profits will be important in maintaining the company's share price in the market and its future fund-raising abilities. Investors will judge the newly privatised company in accordance with established investment criteria such as earnings per share and the price/earnings ratio.

CONCLUSION

I have attempted to present an outline of the financial aspects involved in privatising a public sector organisation. In particular I hope to have provided an understanding of:

(a) the considerations to be taken into account when determining what form privatisation should take;

(b) the means by which a structure and legal form is created for a public sector organisation prior to privatisation;

(c) the need for a commercial track record;

(d) how a capital structure is determined; and

(e) the adjustments necessary to accounting policies and bases to achieve comparability with the private sector.

As I hope you will now be aware, the financial preparation for Privatisation can involve a number of complex decisions at a strategic and a detailed level. The basic steps required, however, now form part of an established pattern. Anticipation of these requirements and thorough planning for each step is the key to a smooth and successful privatisation.

APPENDIX 1: Principal restrictions entrenched by special share

Restriction on foreign ownership to 15 per cent	BAe, RR
British Chief Executive	BAe, BT, C & W, RR
Voting control restricted to 15 per cent	Amersham, BG, BT, Jaguar, C & W, RR, Britoil (50 per cent), Enterprise (50 per cent), BAA
Prevention of winding-up	Amersham, Britoil, C & W, Enterprise, Jaguar, RR, BAA
Restriction on asset disposals over 25 per cent	Amersham, C & W, Jaguar, RR

Note: Abbreviations are expanded in the Abbreviations List at the front of the volume.

APPENDIX 2: Effect of debt on total proceeds

PE multiple	10	20
Interest rate (%)	5	10
Profit before interest and tax	1,000	1,000
Tax at 35 per cent	(350)	(350)
Profit after tax	60	650
	x10	x20
Proceeds	6,500	13,000
Create debt	2,000	2,000
Profit before interest and tax	1,000	1,000
Interest	(100)	(200)
	900	800
Tax at 35 per cent	(315)	(280)
Profit after tax	585	520
	x10	x20
Proceeds before debt	5,850	10,400
Add debt	2,000	2,000
Proceeds including debt	7,850	12,400

Effect of debt on proceeds:	increase	decrease

9

Managing Operations and the Relevance of Privatisation

David Chambers*

EFFECTIVE WORKING MODELS

This chapter suggests that in the early 1980s, and almost by accident, the UK at last found the elusive key to effective management and control of public enterprise. In this period a number of public enterprises in the UK showed that they could reconstruct themselves and transform both their productivity and the quality of their products and services.

What happened in the UK at this time carries very important lessons for other economies now striving to infuse their PE sectors with a new dynamism and a preoccupation with productivity and quality. Indeed, the UK experience demonstrates effective ways both to restructure public industries and to modify the nature of interventions by their supervising ministries. The analogies extend from the programme of perestroika and the reduction in Gosplan's scope, through the revitalisation of the PE sector in newly industrialising countries.

It should be added that by an irony which future historians will hugely relish, this renaissance within Britain's PE sector took place just as many of the industries were being prepared for sale to the private sector. In the time capsule of two or three years before privatisation, each industry in turn showed that it is possible for managers and other employees, ministry officials and government ministers to act in concert to maximise the value of the industry to its owners, the nation's public. After three decades of often tortured debate about the control and management of nationalised industries, at last in this brief period, the UK

* Professor, London Business School.

did show that it is possible to get the relationships right. Hence, the experience of each industry in this time capsule is of great interest not just in itself, but also as an exemplary demonstration of how the governance of a PE can be effectively conducted, in a mixed, competitive market economy.

THE MANAGEMENT OF OPERATIONS

Reconstruction in the UK's PE sector will be considered here from the perspective of how an enterprise manages its operations. In the context of the great debates over public versus private ownership this may seem like a lowly vantage point. Most discussions of the better control and management of PEs focus on higher-level variables, external to the enterprise: financial pressure, constraints on transactions, and changes in market structure. Discusssion centres on how to put pressure on the PE so that it will achieve productive efficiencies, and not on how these efficiencies are to be achieved.

At the same time quality, delivery, performance, productivity, customer service - the dominant concerns of the operations manager - are the topics most often cited when the public is asked to comment on PE performance. It is often argued that the advantage from the PE form of organisation in increasing public accountability for these industries has come at too high a cost in poor quality, poor delivery performance, poor service and poor productivity. The criticisms recently voiced by the Soviet leader Mr Gorbachev have also been heard in most other countries with a significant PE sector. For whatever reason, good operations management appears to have eluded many PEs: hence, there is good reason to look directly at the management of operations, and at how this has changed, in the industries under review.

A second reason for choosing 'the management of operations' as a frame for analysing the changes in UK PEs in this period is that the better conduct of operations became a major preoccupation in the early 1980s in many countries besides the UK and in many other sectors besides those in public ownership. Quality, delivery, service and productivity had long occupied the lives of works managers and their teams. Over quite a short period of time these topics also came to occupy a great share of boardroom and media time. Commentators whose interest in productivity had not gone further than aggregate measures or inter-company comparisons of outcomes, developed a new interest in the activities by means of which the outcomes are delivered: training, flexible working, process and product design, delegation, and good housekeeping.

Two related factors probably account for this promotion of shop-floor issues to a high place in managements' agenda: firstly, that many more firms had begun to measure themselves against international competition, and secondly that for many firms it came as a severe shock to find that the standards of productive efficiency in the best international firms were so much higher than in their own. There are many well-documented examples of firms which revised their estimation of production possibilities sharply upward in this period. As it happened, most of the exemplary, standard-setting companies were Japanese, and many firms found that they were being outperformed by Japanese companies on every important dimension: cost, quality, delivery, quality, service, and by very wide margins. To match (if not to beat) the Japanese became a rallying-cry in many company reconstructions, and while the best international production practice was not always found in Japan, it was a convenient shorthand to refer to a linked set of 'Japanese' production practices.

What are the main features of the Japanese approach? From a wealth of recent literature, a few main themes may be picked out:

(a) An emphasis on work flow. Endless effort is devoted to smoothing the production flow. Where production is by batch manufacture, the goal is to eliminate discontinuities so that batches can be made to behave like continuous flows. This is achieved, for example, by whittling away at set-up times and by eliminating the need for in-process inventories.

(b) Devolved responsibility for product quality: each department and within the department each worker takes responsibility for the quality of work done. Poor quality is eliminated during the production process, rather than being detected by final inspection.

(c) A highly trained work-force with flexible skills.

(d) Stable and long-term relations with suppliers, so

that both the smooth flow of work and the total control of quality will extend back into the supplier's factory.

(e) In sum: a perspective which puts the production process at the centre with the other functions in supporting roles. This leads to many devices for preserving the integrity and regularity of production flow in the face of external fluctuations and buffetings. The Japanese assign a very high implicit cost to disruption of the production process.

These topics occupy a central place in contemporary discussion of how best to regain viability and competitiveness for firms operating in international markets. They can also be brought centre-stage in the policy debates over management and control of PEs.

CASE EXAMPLES

This section takes one example, the case of Jaguar Cars Ltd, as an illustration of work in progress. Table 9.1 categorises a number of actions at Jaguar whose effect was to increase the coherence and manageability of the operating unit. (Similar tables and narratives for other recently privatised PEs are at various stages of completion and will be presented in a future paper.)

Jaguar Cars Ltd

In 1980 Jaguar's sales had fallen to about half their historic peak. Its largest export market, that to the US, had collapsed. Delivery lead times to dealers were unpredictable and dealers were demoralised and ill-organised. Industrial relations at the company's three plants in Birmingham and Coventry were tense, productivity was very low and small groups of militants were bypassing the trade unions to lead a series of unofficial strikes.

In the ensuing three years the company transformed itself. Jaguar's subsequent privatisation, when the equity shares of Jaguar PLC were floated on the London Stock Exchange, took place in August 1984. The turn-around in Jaguar's fortunes preceded its privatisation. The financial

143

Table 9.1: Changes aimed at increasing the potential market value of UK PEs

<u>Jaguar Cars</u>

1. <u>Changes in operating practice</u>

Much greater emphasis on quality	Task-forces, targets, re-allocated responsibilities
Significant extensions of flexible working practice	Associated with re-equipment
Selection within work-force exercised by management	Associated with overall reductions and a generous severance-payment plan
Tighter manning standards	Output per employee increased by c. 250 per cent (Table 9.3)
Increased investment in new plant and equipment	Major injection of funds
Internal 'electioneering' by leadership	Personal contact, videos, briefing sessions

2. <u>Greater autonomy for the operating unit</u>

- for production operations	Taking sole responsibility for previously shared facilities
- for personnel and finance functions	Control pulled back to Jaguar
- for marketing and sales	Taking sole responsibility for export dealer network
- for terms and conditions of employment	BL's grading structure still applied

Table 9.1 cont.

3. Re-defining operating relationships across the enterprise's boundaries

- with suppliers
- with sales agents or dealers

Supplier involvement; penalty clauses for defects.
Number of domestic dealers halved; new standards and discount structure defined.

4. Re-balancing the rights and obligations of different stakeholders groups

- employees

- gave up: skill demarcations and veto on reductions in work-force
- gained (for survivors) enhanced job security (with little difference in pay)
  (for leavers) relatively good severance terms

- consumers

- gained from greatly increased attention to quality reliability and customer service; and from systematic surveys of customer reactions

- taxpayers and general public

- gained from staunching public subsidies
- gained from securing of long-term jobs
- gained from export sales

- government

- gave up (or refrained from exercising) methods of influence which had been used in the past: on investment, market interventions, regional policy, domestic purchase, executive remuneration, product prices
- gained: as for taxpayers and general public (see above)

record is shown in Table 9.2.

Table 9.2: Jaguar's financial record

	Years ended 31 December					
	1980 £m	1981 £m	1982 £m	1983 £m	1984 £m	1985 £m
Turnover	166.4	195.2	305.6	472.6	634.1	746.5
Operating Profit/(Loss)	(44.3)	(30.9)	10.1	51.1	91.5	121.3
Interest	(3.0)	(0.8)	(0.5)	(1.1)	-	-
Profit/(Loss before taxation)	(47.3)	(37.7)	9.6	50.0	91.5	121.3
	1.3	-	(0.1)	(0.5)	(34.4)	(33.7)
Profit/(Loss) after taxation before extraordinary items	(46.0)	(31.7)	9.5	49.5	57.1	87.6

Sources: Annual Reports, Prospectus.

The preconditions and framework for this recovery were established in 1978-80 under the direction of Michael Edwardes, who had accepted a three-year posting as Chairman of British Leyland (BL) with a relatively free hand to take the action necessary to save the Group's better businesses. In early 1980 Edwardes appointed John Egan as Chief Executive of Jaguar. Egan took up his post in April 1980. Appropriately, he arrived on a day when a strike about job grading had brought production to a halt. Egan's actions in the months that followed were directed to:

- re-establishing control, against a heritage of demoralisation and under-achievement; and
- re-establishing the company as a separate and coherent entity, i.e. disentangling it from the Group and defining organisational boundaries.

A condition agreed between Edwardes and Egan was that control over its personnel and finance should be given back to Jaguar, and new Directors of these two functions joined the company shortly after Egan. Before the task of reconstruction could begin, Egan first needed to get the work-force back at work. The strike of April 1980 was over a new grading structure, general to all BL employees. Both the grading system and BL's related productivity bonus system were judged by Jaguar workers to favour BL's high-volume plants at the expense of the smaller and specialised operations. Egan immediately met the shop stewards, with the clear message that BL's grading structure could not be altered by Jaguar management, that he would undertake to use the BL appeals procedure in hard cases, that he was fully committed to Jaguar's recovery, but that BL would only continue to support Jaguar if the employees demonstrated their own commitment. Four days later the workforce voted at a mass meeting to return to work.

The drive for quality

Egan immediately instituted a change in product strategy. Before his arrival, the effort in Jaguar's engineering departments had focused on developing the new model (the XJ40) to replace the existing series. Their emphasis was on technological leadership and innovation and little attention was being given to product and process improvements for the existing series. Egan insisted that the first priority must be to improve product quality. If faults in design and production were not corrected, they would recur when the new model came to be produced. A comprehensive drive for product quality would be the fundamental strategy for recovery. Egan drove home this message by arranging for customer comment to be brought forcefully to the attention of all management and work-force. Product quality acted as a key for opening up in turn each of the company's main problem areas: the motivation and commitment of employees, the organisation and control of supplies, and management of the dealer network. The message was taken up and repeated in many different forms, in presentation, internal news sheets, regular memoranda, press releases, and later in the company videos. Egan believed that successes scored in the separate problem areas would be mutually reinforcing.

In order to engage all employees in issues of quality

147

improvement, Jaguar introduced Quality Circles, modelled on Japanese experience. By the end-1983 Jaguar had some 60 circles, each with around a dozen members (i.e. about 10 per cent of the work-force), in areas ranging from cylinder block and cylinder head production to engine assembly and re-conditioning. Over the period 1980-3, the numbers of quality inspectors in the company declined from 677 to 360, reflecting the view that quality must be built in, not inspected in, and that responsibility for quality inspection on the line rested with the production supervisors.

Many of Jaguar's quality problems were attributable to the failure of components from external suppliers. In Egan's initial survey of product faults, some 60 per cent had been due to substandard components. The company embarked on a systematic programme of supplier involvement, going far beyond the conventional exchange of specifications. Suppliers were educated in the realities of the relevant production processes in Jaguar. The company introduced a penalty clause in its most critical contracts, which was triggered if the component failure rate exceeded 1.5 per cent. The penalty covered full replacement costs including labour and handling.

Production operations

Jaguar's operations took place in three plants: Assembly and Engine Building in Coventry, and Body and Paint Work in Birmingham. Historically, the Birmingham works had been the main site of the independent body supplier, Pressed Steel, with Jaguar, Rover and BMC among its customers and at its peak, a work-force of 10,000. In 1967 Pressed Steel merged with BMC and by 1980 the Birmingham works had become a problem site with ageing plant, poor layout and a work-force which had shrunk to 1,800, of whom 1,400 worked on Jaguar car bodies. Morale was low and militants had gained the ascendancy in the union branches. Manpower allocations were subject to concurrence by shop stewards on a daily basis and job demarcations were rigid.

Many of Jaguar's problems could be traced to this plant, and Egan recognised it as a nettle that had to be grasped. Firstly, Jaguar took over full responsibility for its operation. Egan then brought in outside consultants to undertake a fundamental analysis of all operations in all three Jaguar plants. They had the remit of defining those areas fundamental to the production process, where there need be few redundancies, and discretionary areas where numbers could be sharply reduced. The result was a 30 per cent reduction in the work-force, across all three plants (see Table 9.3).

Table 9.3: Output and manpower at Jaguar, 1980-5

	Cars produced	Numbers employed
1980	13,800	10,500
1981	14,600	7,067
1982	22,100	7,849
1983	28,100	8,700
1984	33,500	9,500
1985	38,500	10,200

The programme of redundancies went hand in hand with an active publicity campaign to drum home the message that the company's fight for survival was an uphill one. Relatively generous redundancy payments were offered and most redundancies were voluntary. Moreover, most of those regarded by the management as 'trouble-makers' left, or were induced to leave, in this period, leaving behind a much more committed work-force.

From the moment of Egan's arrival, the flow of information to the work-force and management increased by an order of magnitude. He quickly made himself known on the shop-floor of each plant. He introduced the use of regular videos (normally four a year) shown to the work-force in groups of about 400 with the whole work-force covered in the space of one to two days. Senior managers attended these meetings to answer questions. One of the early videos included an interview with one of Jaguar's largest dealers, covering the problems he faced in explaining quality defects to irate customers. Weekly performance briefs were circulated for each plant, covering plant efficiency, quality and special problems, together with current sales information. A monthly management bulletin covered new developments in each plant, cost performance and bonus earnings, with a constant emphasis on market performance of the end-product and with a commentary from Egan.

Egan set himself a programme in this period like that of a candidate in an election campaign, taking every possible opportunity to explain and project his politics and to win a broader and broader base of support.

The Dealer network

Until 1982, Jaguar's sales in the UK were through 300 outlets, each with separate showroom and service provision for Jaguar. Egan and his colleagues believed that standards were very uneven across the network, and in 1982 they initiated a campaign to weed out inadequate outlets. This brought the total number down to 150. The novel device of a Franchise Development Fund was introduced, under which Jaguar cut its discount to dealers by 3.5 per cent, and used the Fund to make bonus payments to dealers offering 'exceptionally high quality service' (in terms which were carefully spelled out). The aim was to get rid of those dealers who achieved their sales through price discounting rather than by investing and maintaining excellent after-sales service.

Jaguar's export sales were managed by the BL European and Overseas Sales Organisation, and one of the main planks in Egan's programme was to regain control of its own export outlets. Sales in West Germany had been through Austin Rover dealers. Jaguar took the view that this made as little sense as if Mercedes were to use Lada dealers for its UK sales. In the US, there appeared to be too many outlets, with low individual turnover and variable standards of service. During 1982, Jaguar negotiated the transfer back of full responsibility for its own export sales, and proceeded to reduce dealer numbers in all its main overseas markets.

New technologies and Government support

The design of Jaguar's XJ40 range (launched in 1985) took advantage of the huge strides in production technologies which had happened in the previous decade. The designers paid much more attention to manufacturing considerations. Thus, the saloon which the XJ40 replaced had 560 separate body pieces; for the XJ40 the number was just 330.

A fully automated line was intalled to make the cylinder block for Jaguar's new aluminium alloy engine, the AJ6. Jaguar collaborated with Dainichi Sykes to build automated manufacturing systems around robots imported from the Japanese company Dainichi Kiko. This ambitious programme of re-equipment was in turn made possible through substantial grants from the government. Jaguar absorbed some £100 million of the total £2 billion of government support to BL. The transformations in its technology and manufacturing systems, and the potential for greatly increased output, depended critically on this once-for-all injection of funds.

Government influence

In the 30 years after 1950, successive UK governments used many different devices to influence the car industry. These included:

(a) Intervention in the domestic car market through varying the terms for consumer credit. At different points in this period, the minimum required deposit as a percentage of the purchase price varied from 15 to 50 per cent. These interventions related mainly to governments' balance-of-payments policies.

(b) Directions or incentives concerning location of new plant. These related to governments' regional policies.

(c) Directions on prices These related to governments' anti-inflation policies.

(d) Directions on the remuneration of public enterprise executives, and of other employees. These related again to governments' anti-inflation policies, and specifically to their incomes policy.

(e) Directions or incentives relating to the purchase of certain components from domestic suppliers. These related both to governments' balance-of-payments and employment policies.

(f) Investment approval procedures. These, applied across the public sector, represented governments' commitment (after excluding numerous special cases) to economic principles of allocative efficiency.

In the period of Jaguar's recovery, government refrained from exercising these powers. In the case of investment approval procedures, this was possible because Edwardes could in effect act as plenipotentiary. He was in a position to assess the strategic case for investing £100m in re-equipping Jaguar in the light of his assessment of the risks, both in labour relations and in markets.

Considered from an operations perspective, the list of devices by which successive governments chose to influence the car industry give very little weight to the factors this chapter has labelled as 'Japanese': smooth work-flows; insulation of the production process as far as possible from external instabilities; operating flexibility; a strategic view of capital investment. During the period of Jaguar's recovery, and no doubt influenced by Edwardes, government followed a self-denying ordinance in not using this industry as an instrument for its current macroeconomic policies.

CONCLUDING COMMENT

In this chapter, reconstruction of UK PEs in the early 1980s has been attributed to two causes:

(1) A new preoccupation with how any enterprise manages its operations. This might be termed the 'Japanese' effect.
(2) A new awareness of the PE as a going concern which has, potentially, a <u>valuation</u>.

What would it be worth if it were floated on the stock market? Moreover, and significantly, how is this potential valuation affected when government imposes or removes some constraint on the PE's operation? In the past, the somewhat metaphysical concept of potential market valuation has not figured prominently in public debate. 'Potential market valuation' deserves to become a central concept in the management and control of PEs. The long-overdue attention directed in the early 1980s to the <u>valuation</u> of PEs might be termed the 'privatisation' effect.

10

Contracting-Out: Managerial Strategy or Political Dogma?

Ceri Thomas*

INTRODUCTION

Contracting-out is both part of and wider than the issue of privatisation. While privatisation is primarily a question of the transfer of ownership from public (or state) hands to private shareholders (corporate, institutional or individual), contracting-out focuses more on the question of 'Who manages?'.

The contracting-out of certain ancillary functions has been common to enterprises both public and private. All companies employ auditors and accuntants to check their accounts and reports: until the era of desk-top publishing, most organisations contracted out any printing and design work to outside specialists; maintenance and cleaning of buildings are traditionally 'contract' jobs in the private sector and many parts of the public sector too. It is therefore wrong to think of contracting-out as either new or as synonymous with privatisation.

On the other hand, contracting-out has assumed a particular significance in the years of industrial restructuring since the mid-1970s. Organisations have increasingly asked themselves: 'What business are we in?' and 'What are we here to do?'. The answers to those questions usually point to activities which are at best 'support', 'ancillary' or even 'marginal' to their primary function and 'mission'. Add to that the perceived overhead that an accumulation of marginal activities may build up, the tendency for such activities to assume more than a proportionate or justified share of management time and

* Senior Consultant, Percom Ltd.

any perceived labour inflexibilities associated with such work, and it is not surprising that managements persuade themselves that such work could be handled better by a 'contract for service' than by 'contracts of service'.

For some organisations, the employment protection legislation of the 1970s allegedly served only to increase the attraction of the contracting option. Large manufacturing organisations have actively contracted-out many trades that, while traditionally part of the company work-force, were at best support functions. Such a choice is not always prompted by a desire to increase 'efficiency'. In many cases, the requirement simply to reduce numbers was the prime motivation for contracting - that is, the motive was primarily to play a numbers game rather than increase efficiency or reduce unit costs.

Central government initiatives in the early 1980s were arguably more about reducing the head count than carefully designed to increase efficiency. Large multi-divisional companies also sought manpower reductions for their local sites by, for example, establishing 5 per cent annual target reductions in full-time or permanent workers. Contracting-out may meet a central management requirement without necessarily tackling problems of inefficiency and manpower utilisation - it may be primarily a manpower displacement programme. The transfer of workload from the NHS to local authorities via the policy of 'Care in the Community' is another well-known case of labour displacement (without meeting the normal definition of contracting-out).

Contained within the rationale for contracting-out, however, is the fact that while an activity might be performed and managed by agents outside the organisation they are nevertheless accountable to it for the satisfactory performance of the work. Indeed, it may be easier for an organisation to focus on 'performance' - effectiveness, efficiency, economy - when work is undertaken in discrete chunks by outsiders. The work has to be clearly specified in quantitative and qualitative terms, and (ideally) the appropriate central overhead allocated and charged out fairly and accurately to that activity (so that the client organisation does not retain a redundant management capacity post-contract). Managements may succeed in regaining control of work in just this way.

While contracting-out may be a logical extension of a process of work specifications, performance measurement and cost allocation, it is not the only one - indeed, the increasing use of cost centre analysis at local levels is symptomatic of a general decentralisation of certain management functions closer to the point of production (while maintaining central control through sophisticated management information systems and performance measures, manpower budgets, profit targets, etc.).

Central to most contracting exercises, however, is the notion of 'choice' - i.e. the client may choose:

(a) to put a contract to tender;

(b) to cancel a contract (if improperly or inadequately performed);

(c) to retain/undertake the work in house; and

(d) to select contractors according to the client's own criteria, and so on.

In essence, the client organisation seeks to maximise its bargaining power by trawling the widest possible market. It will attempt to retain this bargaining power during the course of the contract. The control over the performance of the contract which this bargaining power implies is indeed one of the prime motives for contracting-out in the first place, especially where management control of in-house work is perceived to be inadequate.

In well-established fields of contracting activity, such choice arguably sustains an effective market for services. Difficulties occur where only a small number of contractors operate in the field. This very fact may suggest why the client has carried out the work in-house anyway. As we will discuss later, certain activities simply do not carry the potential for profit-maximising that private contractors require to operate successfully. Some work may, for example, be so specialised and particular to a firm's needs that it is not worth another firm creating a capacity to meet the need (by sinking capital into the project, and so on) - there are insufficient economies of scale to he had. In some recent research in a chemicals organisation, it was found that while the client company wished to contract out the laundering of heavily soiled industrial overalls, no private contractor would take on the work (or at a price at which the client would make a saving).

There are many fields, however, where contracting-out has formed part of a broader strategy aimed at achieving labour flexibility. The so-called 'flexible firm' uncovered by Atkinson (1985) and the Institute of Manpower Studies incorporates contracting-out into a wider model of labour flexibility (including temporary, part-time, seasonal workers). Accordingly, such companies have core and peripheral labour forces - an extension of the earlier models of labour market segmentation.

While most of this chapter deals with contracting-out in the public sector, particularly local government manual jobs, it is clear that the phenomenon is not confined to any sector or stratum of the labour force. Many networking schemes in high-tech industries begin from the partial contracting-out of certain functions to set up individuals or groups as separate enterprises (Rank Xerox spawned many enterprises in just this way - i.e. Networking + Contracting-Out = New Separate Enterprises). General practitioners act as contractors to the NHS, not employees, for their own traditionally preferred reasons; and the rapid increase in a range of consultancy services in professional fields testifies to the attraction of contracting-out to a variety of organisations and occupations.

In a period of rapid technological change, moreover, when product life cycles are shortening and when product markets themselves are changing rapidly, it makes sense for organisations to consider contracting for services to organisations who have specialist expertise, have built entry barriers and who have absorbed many of the innovation and development costs. Increasingly, skill shortages in the labour market (especially in certain growth areas) reinforce the attraction of contracts for service (at fixed rates) than contracts of service (at escalating or unforseeable rates).

The difficulty for client organisations, however, may be that their very inability to undertake such specialist activities in-house makes them vulnerable. They may not be capable of assessing, controlling or enforcing the required standards of work. While contracts for services imply that a given output is contractually binding, client organisations regularly report the need for skills in managing the contractor. While certain management tasks are removed by the contract, therefore, others are created. In highly secure or potentially hazardous environments it is especially important that contracting staff behave according to standards laid down for all other staff; know site regulations, health and safety procedures and so on. In other words, the fragmentation of the work force into contracting groups does not remove the need for 'site' policies to be followed. (Such issues in connection with subcontracting have been noted by the UK Health and Safety Executive, 1987.)

The rest of this chapter concentrates on the particular experiences of contracting-out in the UK public services, especially in the light of 1987-8 legislation requiring local authorities (independent employers in the UK) to subject key services to competitive tender. The contrast between the local government experience and the 'normal' contracting out process is stark and two-fold. Firstly, the important factor of 'choice' - whether to put the tender up for competition or not and under what framework? - is either highly constrained or removed from local authorities. Indeed past experience has shown that, given the choice, authorities are reluctant to contract out. Secondly, the services to be contracted-out cannot be said to be 'ancillary', but rather are central to the delivery of services which local authorities exist to provide. The jobs affected are likely to equate to almost half the local authority employment in the UK.

The government's reasons for making competitive tendering compulsory, rather than voluntary, may be contrasted with the normal commercial reasons discussed earlier. The government's central belief is that there is little in the public sector that could not be performed better and more efficiently in the private sector. The primary intention is therefore not to improve managerial control or to focus on the central objectives of the organisation, but to strip away substantial elements of the public organisation, leaving the local authority as an administrative rump. The final section of this chapter, moreover, emphasises that this rump will have substantially reduced revenue-raising powers (via the abolition of the rates) and operate in an environment in which strategic resources (such as schools) may be permanently taken out of local authority control by a group of highly motivated parents or loss-leading contractors.

COMPULSORY TENDERING AND LOCAL GOVERNMENT

Legislation passing through Parliament in late 1987 was set to compel local authorities to put six key services out to competitive tender. This built on the experience of an earlier Act (1980) which imposed new commercial obligations on local authority (building) direct labour organisations (DLOs). The services to be 'contracted-out' under the 1987-8 legislation were:

- refuse collection;
- school meals and other catering;
- maintenance of parks, gardens and grounds;
- vehicle maintenance and repair;
- cleaning of offices and other buildings; and
- other cleaning (including street cleaning).

(The government had also proposed the inclusion of sport and leisure management).

While the most publicly visible service is probably refuse collection, this only accounts for about 30,000 of the half a million or so jobs affected. By far the majority are in the school cleaning and meals service, where there are well over 350,000 jobs - mainly part-time. Thus, the government's proposals are on a vast scale, likely to affect 1 in 20 of the country's total work-force directly.

In addition to requiring local authorities to put their largest areas of manual employment out to tender, the government will also control the process in a number of ways:

(a) advertising of work to be contracted-out;
(b) specifying a rate of return for in-house tenders (previously set at 5 per cent), i.e. as if a private contractor would build such a profit element into a competitive tender;
(c) phasing the tendering period over $2\frac{1}{2}$ years (April 1989 to October 1991) to allow contractors to schedule their tendering programme and to develop expertise in areas not previously undertaken in the private sector (notably ground maintenance, parks and gardens, and so on);
(d) controlling the manner in which the tender process operates (i.e. ensuring that the local authority does nothing to inhibit competition); and
(e) retaining powers to specify other services for contracting-out.

In general, it is clear that the government's experience of its earlier 1980 legislation has enabled it to provide a much tighter legal framework and to limit local authorities' opportunities to frustrate its underlying objectives. The requirements of the tendering process will offer dissatisfied contractors the chance to quiz local authorities on the reasons for their decisions and to challenge them if they appear to have been 'unreasonable'.

A particular target for the legislation has been 'contract compliance' - the practice of requiring contractors to meet certain employment and/or non-commercial obligations. This has a long history in both the UK and the USA. In the UK, Fair Wages Resolutions (FWRs) represented government attempts to prevent workers being exploited by contractors in the course of carrying out government work. The Resolutions, the first of which was passed in 1981, had been developed by local authorities for their own contracts. Thus, while the Conservative government abolished the FWR for central government contracts (and renounced the International Labour Organisation convention 94 to do so) in 1983, it still had no power to outlaw the use of similar clauses by local authorities. The new contracting-out legislation provides such powers.

The new legislation also outlaws the inclusion of non-commercial matters in the consideration of tenders (e.g. a company's contacts with South Africa, the nuclear industry, and so on). The only significant exception to this rule of 'non-interference' is the responsibility that local authorities retain for promoting racial equity and harmony in their local areas and this may involve contractors in, for example, employing an ethnically 'balanced' work-force. 'Quotas', however, fall outside UK legislation.

In the USA, by contrast, contractors are normally required to meet certain ethnic, sex and disabled workers quotas to secure and retain public work. The nature of litigation, the size of penalties and the importance of public contracts all combine in the USA to ensure that 'contract compliance' is a powerful strategy available to the state in regulating private sector employment practices.

PRACTICAL MANAGEMENT CONCERNS

While the espoused intention of the local government legislation is to promote competition, a primary objective of contracting organisations, inside or outside the 'client' organisation, is to minimise this competition. To use the terminology of Porter (1985) and others, competitive advantage may be gained in a variety of ways: raising barriers to entry (to competitors); building switching costs (for clients); and changing the basis of competition (e.g. by transforming a service which may be price-sensitive into one which is not).

In practice, as we will report below, the type of services involved in the main contracting-out programmes in the National Health Service and local government are not always conducive to these strategies. However, nonetheless, the first management obligation arising from contracting-out is a clear separation of the role of 'Client' and potential 'Contractor' within the organisation (e.g. local authority), to remove any potential conflicts of interest.

The issues facing management can then be summarised as follows:

Client

(1) Specification of contracts (involving decisions about whether to specify tasks and inputs or results and outputs: certain work like hospital cleaning is difficult and expensive to monitor in output terms, so contracts are often framed as 'tasks'; in contrast, refuse collection, which is easily monitored, may be framed in output or results terms).

(2) Assessment of tenders and appraisal of potential contractors (for example, financial solvency, feasibility of tender to meet specifications, and so on).

(3) Awarding contracts (recording reasons/giving explanations as required and justifying these decisions to auditors, and so on).

(4) Monitoring - some contracts are easily monitored, often with the help of the public (e.g. refuse collection), while others are more difficult (where the work is qualitatively rather than quantitatively assessed - cleaning, catering, and so on). Monitoring also includes the administration of penalty clauses etc., where a contractor partially or wholly fails to carry out the terms of the contract.

(5) Retaining essential controls (for example, health and safety, other remaining legal liabilities).

(6) Safeguarding or creating public service orientation

amongst contractors' staffs.

(7) Maintaining credible employee relations policies across the organisation (including the contracting and non-contracting elements).

(8) Sustaining an organisational strategy in a turbulent environment. (As outlined in the final section of this chapter, local authorities are being required to plan their contracting-out at a time when their control over strategic activities - notably, the provision of educational services -is under threat via government proposals on 'opting out', 'financial delegation' and 'Community Charge'.

Internal contractors (Direct Labour/Service Organisations) (DL/SOs)

(1) Building Competitive Advantage (pre-tender) by, for example, establishing standards that the client wants/needs/regards as standard, but which cannot easily be met by competition.

(2) Establishing a data base (personnel/tasks/output, etc.) to support well-informed decisions on work-force restructuring and so on, pre- and post-contract.

(3) Preparing a competitive tender.

(4) Gaining the commitment of the existing work-force.

(5) Restructuring work-force/managing redeployment; work-force reduction, and so on.

(6) Renegotiating terms and conditions (e.g. bonus schemes on the basis of competitive tender - 'tender-led bonus schemes').

(7) Establishing methods of producing the specified rate of return on assets (without jeopardising efficiency by, for example, cutting assets artificially to raise 'profitability').

(8) Managing change (role separation into client/ contractor; culture change to support competition; job/task/work-force flexibility, and so on).

(9) Attacking central overheads (to ensure that the DSO does not carry unnecessary central overheads within central departments).

Outside contractors will have their own management concerns and priorities, prominent amongst which will be the likely profitability of the contract. The experience of this in public services is less than totally reassuring for the contractors. The Audit Commission (February 1987) referred to the 'unhappy examples' of Brengreen Holdings (now part of BET) and Pritchard Services (now part of the Hawley Group): share-price performance on the London Stock Exchange was not encouraging (1982-6). The Commission sounded some warnings about the whole process:

> Privatisation will not necessarily secure competitiveness. It would be unwise to assume that the private sector is necessarily able to provide a comparable service at lower cost than every local DLO. And privatising a service in total could result in replacement of a public monopoly with a private one, unless authorities retain an in-house capability to ensure contractors remain cost competitive.

There are also what the Commission describes as 'good strategic reasons' for the unattractiveness of local authority work to contractors in many situations:

(a) the contractor will be under continual competitive pressure, and 'entry barriers' to new competitors in most of the services will be kept low;

(b) any performance failures are likely to reverberate around the local government system, affecting other prospective tenders;

(c) there may be special local management and/or capital requirements which many contractors simply could not supply (within forseeable time-scales); and

(d) the services are not, in the main, high 'value-added', their whole thrust being towards cost-minimisation, limiting prospective profit margins.

The Institute of Fiscal Studies (IFS) and the London Business School, in a 1987 study which found considerable savings from the contracting-out of cleaning services in the NHS, also identified what it termed the 'winner's curse'. The Institute concluded that many contracts were won on the basis of 'information failings', probably resulting in loss-making to the companies concerned or reduced service standards. Over a period, however, this was redressed and savings moderated:

> Interpreted in this way it can be concluded that the
> information failings have been remedied, at least
> partially, by the experience gained in these early
> contracts. Recent bids have risen to a more
> realistic level and appear to be converging toward
> the level of savings associated with in-house
> contracts. (Domberger et al., 1987.)

Clearly, the same findings could be used to conclude, firstly,
that contractors deliberately overstate the potential for
savings and operate a loss-leader policy to take possession
of the contracts; and secondly, that once the contract has
been won, prices are raised in subsequent tenders and
savings to the client eroded (the client's bargaining position
itself having been eroded by the loss or diminution of its in-
house work-force).

Sources are divided about both the extent and success
of contracting-out in the public services to date. Few now
deny that some savings have been made. The IFS estimated
the savings in the NHS at around 20 per cent, where
tendering had been used (either via the service going outside
or being retained by an in-house work-force).

PULSE (the pro-contracting-out pressure group) has
claimed annual savings in UK local government of around
£20m, a tiny fraction of local authority spending or around
£3 billion on the 'named services'. 'Political decisions by
local authorities to take private services back in-house have
caused the first recorded decrease in the savings made by
local authorities in contracting-out their services to the
private sector' (Public Service Review, 1987). Such a
voluntary shift away from contracting-out by local
authorities was also noted by the Local Government
Chronicle (LGC) Survey, and demonstrated that, without
legislation, the government's wishes could well have been
thwarted by elected local councils.

> The fourth LGC privatisation survey has identified
> only 36 councils (out of 500 or so) handing delivery
> of services over to private enterprise in the past
> year. The number of councils contracting services
> out has fallen sharply since the last survey from
> more than 16% to 10% of the total responding.
> The small scale of council privatisation is

further emphasised by the total value of the contracts put out to the private sector: less than £120 million compared with total local authority current spending of about £34 billion a year. The amount councils reported saving by contracting out was less than £1.5 million.

More than two-thirds of the number of councils reporting privatisation said they had done the opposite and brought services previously contracted out back in house. Of these 27, there were 13 Labour controlled, 7 Conservative and 2 Alliance. (Local Government Chronicle, 1987.)

In the NHS, the trend towards privatisation in at least some services has been equally halting. The NHS laundry service, for example, was reported by the Association of British Laundry, Cleaning and rental Services to have changed hands only marginally. The market share held by contractors has remained at around the 10-11 per cent level which prevailed <u>before</u> competitive tendering in 1983. Moreover, 19 of the 207 contracts had been terminated before completion, eight because of poor quality work (Committee of Public Accounts, 1987).

The conflicting evidence about contracting-out in UK public services therefore seems to point to:

(1) some savings, but possibly at a lower level than in the early days;
(2) client resistance to widespread extension of contracting-out;
(3) increased in-house capacity to compete and even to win back contracts; and
(4) perception on the part of some contracting organisations and associations that competition has not been altogether fair.

However, the prospects for contracting-out seem far brighter in the post-1987 climate and following the passing of the local government legislation. Against this, two remaining points bear consideration: the concentration of the contracting industry's ownership; and the effects on work-forces of contracting-out.

Firstly, UK experience indicates that it is clearly unrealistic to expect public monopolies to be replaced by a diverse market of small, locally owned, competing entrepreneurs. In practice, the industry is highly concentrated in two or three major multinational groups. Some 60 per cent of refuse and cleaning services and 50 per cent of NHS cleaning services contracts go to just two commercial groups: BET (including Brengreen, Exclusive, HAT, Initial) and the Hawley Group (including Pritchards and Crothalls, Taskmaster, Provincial, Mediclean) (The Guardian, 13 November 1986). Many other groups have either pulled out because of the problems involved in providing the services to specification, or have been taken over by the larger groups. Of the 46 companies in the Contract Cleaning and Maintenance Association only a few have won contracts and fewer than ten continue to compete for tenders. Some major companies like Blue Arrow pulled out altogether.

The second important issue is the effect on work-forces. The secretary of the General Municipal and Boilermakers Union (GMB) described contracting out thus:

I believe the process of compulsory tendering decided by the government is immoral in all its aspects. It does things to people which should never be done by any employer, by any government.

First, it entirely deprives ancillary workers of job security - that is a terrible thing to do, particularly for people who joined the service because of that one thing it offered them - it did not offer them good pay, nor good conditions and offered them a pretty horrible job in many instances - but it did offer job security. So the government has taken away the one aspect that people valued. It puts people in the position of having to bargain for their existing job - it's a demoralising and alienating experience - which is not fully appreciated by people until it's applied to them or people who are important to them.

There are very few people who would like to see their own job advertised in the newspapers in the knowledge that if someone applied with presentable, not even good, paper qualifications, with no need to produce a track record, but who was prepared to do the job at a lower rate of pay, then the job would pass from the existing holder to the new holder. Very few people in this country would accept that. But that is an exact analogy for what is happening.

Contracting-Out

(John Edmonds at a Templeton College, Oxford seminar, 24 February 1986.)

While in most cases work-forces have accepted the transfer of work, there have been examples of outright resistance. The contracting-out of services at Barking Hospital, east London, was accompanied by twelve months of 24-hour picketing by the members of the National Union of Public Employees (NUPE) who worked there. There was a 17-month dispute at Addenbrooke's Hospital, Cambridge, when contractors 'scrapped or cut holiday, pension, bonus and sick pay entitlement, and reduced most full-time workers to part-time status with consequent loss of income and employment rights' (Brindle, 1986).

While the contracting industry would dispute that its conditions are generally lower than those it has replaced, it seems evident that most savings have been made at the expense of the total pay-bill - whether this means fewer jobs (with perhaps higher pay for those remaining), lower pensions, poor sick pay provisions or lower hourly pay rates.

The industrial relations history and climate in public services and local government in particular, contributed to contracting-out becoming a clear political objective for the Conservative Government. Equally the legislation was an overt threat to the public service unions like NUPE and the GMB themselves whose membership numbers have weathered the storms of the recession better than many other, private sector-based trade unions.

Public sector unions were not the sole target of the legislation, however. Equally under fire was the principle of national bargaining by local authorities as employers. These national agreements were seen by central government both as barriers to market forces and political obstacles in themselves, symbolising local authority autonomy and collectivism.

Whilst in 1987 local authorities were generally still holding to the principle of national bargaining with trade unions, the scope of the bargaining and the local autonomy provided by the agreements was very much under review. The national agreement for manual workers (i.e. those most affected by the contracing-out legislation) was revised in 1987 in order to remove many of the prescriptions held by individual local authorities to be handicaps during the tendering process. (Outside contractors were no longer bound by the respective national agreement, as they had been under previous legislation and fair-wages clauses). The new agreement provided for the negotiation of working conditions at local level which had previously been a national level preserve. Items such as the length of the working week or the number of annual hours or seasonal working could be negotiated at local level to suit the need to win contracts for in-house work-forces.

As the legislation drew nearer, local authority managements were therefore being confronted with both new local autonomy (as far as wages and conditions were concerned) and new legal requirements on a vast scale. The degree to which they would be capable of meeting these challenges was highly variable. Some authorities had already experienced contracting out (Wandsworth, Southend, Merton), while others had steadfastly kept jobs in-house. For the vast majority, however, the years 1988-91 promised managerial challenges at levels which many of them had never experienced.

1987: A NEW CLIMATE

While the 1987 election victory for the Thatcher administration was the third, and might for that reason be seen as representing 'continuity', it provided a new mandate for change.

The compulsory tendering of ancillary services in the National Health Service was administered in 1983 via HC(83)18. Building organisations within local government had been brought under a competitive 'regime' by the 1980 Local Government Planning and Land Act, but this was not of central importance to most local authority activities or jobs. These initiatives were either within the government's own orbit as employer or of fairly limited significance (in terms of jobs and services).

A third emphatic election victory provided Mrs Thatcher with a new opportunity (and she would argue a mandate) to tackle perhaps the final, outstanding base of political opposition - local government itself. Previous legislation sought to control the expenditure of local authorities, 'capped' their ability to raise revenue, abolished 'supplementary rates' and provided mechanisms for treating individual authorities individually, rather than collectively. Proposals before Parliament in 1987-8 included:

- the abolition of the local authority domestic and industrial rating system, to be replaced by a system of Community Charges (or 'Poll Tax') and fixed industrial rates;
- the provisions of 'opting-out' choices for schools to leave local authority control and to be supported directly from Whitehall;
- the removal of polytechnic colleges from local education authority control; and
- the imposition of a national curriculum and regular, national testing of children at several stages in their school career.

These fundamental changes in the local government financial and service environment overshadowed the extension of compulsory tendering in local government; yet the Local Government Bill, which was due to receive the Royal Assent in 1988 and due to be phased in in April 1989, provided for the vast majority of manual jobs within local government to be put out to tender and potentially to move around one million jobs from the public (heavily unionised) to the private (little unionised) services sector.

It is possible to identify in the period up to 1987 a local authority strategy of financial and political time-buying - in the expectation of Mrs Thatcher losing power (either through the Conservatives losing the election, or their winning so marginally that a different complexion of Conservatives would assume the leadership). This strategy took the form of, for example, creative accounting to circumvent financial controls, lease-back arrangements to facilitate expenditure, and so on. The abolition of the Greater London Council and six metropolitan county councils (all Labour-controlled) did little to dent Labour confidence that 1987 would see Mrs Thatcher removed from power. Local elections of 1985 and 1986 had bolstered this belief. The Conservatives lost control of the Association of County Councils for the first time in living memory; Sir Keith Joseph, Mrs Thatcher's philosophical guru, retired from the education fray having, to many, won most of the arguments but lost the battles. His departure, however, was soon to be followed by the demise of collective bargaining for teachers (at least in the short term). Thus, over half a million people were effectively denied by government the right to negotiate their pay and conditions. Their negotiating forum was replaced in the short-term by an 'advisory' body of government appointees, while a longer-term solution was sought. This apparently draconian step again served to foster a sense of righteous indignation amongst political opponents and to support the view that the great British public would cry 'foul' at the next electoral opportunity.

Such faith proved ill-founded. The time-buying strategy failed and many of the unpalatable questions that Labour had postponed now re-emerged. Local authorities would not be 'baled-out' as some had gambled they would be. Trade unions would not be re-invited to seats at the top table as they had hoped. In effect, those who went to the cupboard looking for new strategies of resistance found it bare - not least because the post 1987 Labour leadership (including some leading trade unionists) now declared the time right for a radical re-examination of fundamental Labour policies.

Implicit in such a review was the whole question of the relationship between Labour and the trade unions: was it now politically damaging to both? Explicit in the review was the question of public ownership, the role of the state in industrial strategy, the importance of the private sector in sustaining a competitive environment, and so on. Political opposition to private involvement in many parts of the public sector could no longer be guaranteed from the Left. Greater concern was being expressed for identifying those parts of the welfare state which should, in all circumstances, remain under the direct control of elected bodies (local or central government) than for blanket opposition to all forms of contracting-out. Labour, in effect, was beginning to accept the popularity of many forms of private ownership and enterprise.

A combination of economic, political and social trends had therefore created a climate in 1987 in which large-scale contracting-out of up to one million local authority jobs could proceed or at least lead to a radical restructuring of working practices to fend off private competition. Attitudes were reported by trade unionists like Jack Dromey of the T&GWU to have undergone a 'sea change' since the 1983 general election, with manual workers anxious to improve services to keep them in-house (The Financial Times, 31 January 1987).

Legislation had twice been shelved - in 1985 and 1986 - allegedly because the moment was not opportune or, as Secretary of State Ridley argued, because insufficient parliamentary time had been available. The delay provided the government with more time to study possible loopholes and close them; and, coming so soon after the election, provided it with both a stronger mandate and more time to phase in the measures to suit itself, the private sector contractors and last (and probably least) the local authority managers who would have to manage the whole process.

The scale of change in employee relations in the local authority sector in the years 1987-91 (the years of full implementation of contracting-out) promised to be vast. The threats to large general unions like the GMB and NUPE were fundamental, given the new obstacles to organisation they would face in the contracting industries.

For local authorities, their traditional aims to be 'good employers' and to place 'equity' alongside economy, efficiency and effectiveness as organisational watchwords were beginning to look like increasingly distant goals or expensive luxuries to be jettisoned.

REFERENCES

Atkinson, J. (1985) Flexibility: planning for an uncertain future. Manpower Policy and Practice (Institute of Manpower Studies), Summer

Audit Commission (1987) Competitiveness and contracting out of local authorities' services. Occasional Paper, 3, (February)

Brindle, D. (1986) A chastening experience. Local government manpower. LACSAB (December)

Committee of Public Accounts (1987) Minutes of evidence. HMSO, London, 4 November

Domberger, S., S. Meadowcroft and D. Thompson (1987) The impact of competitive tendering on the costs of hospital domestic services. Fiscal Studies (Institute of Fiscal Studies), November

Health and Safety Executive (1987) Annual Report

Labour Research (1987) Local councils - caring or tender. Labour Research Department, September

Local Government Chronicle (1987) Finance and local government (Supplement). 3 July

Porter, M.E. (1985) Competitive advantage: creating and sustaining superior performance

Public Service Review (1987) 12 (Public Service Research Centre)

Part III

The Sectors

11

Privatisation: The Case of BAA PLC

John B. Heath*

INTRODUCTION

The purpose of this chapter is to report on the privatisation of what is now BAA PLC, to raise some key issues and to respond to some of the questions which Professor Ramanadham put at the end of his paper (see Chapter 1).

THE TIMETABLE

The sequence of events in privatising the former British Airports Authority (which owned and managed seven airports in the UK) was as follows:

June 1983	<u>Conservative government</u> re-elected, and in the Queen's Speech the government declared its intention that 'as many as possible of Britain's airports shall become private sector companies';
August 1983	<u>First Memorandum on Privatisation</u> submitted by the British Airports Authority to the Secretary of State for Transport, at the government's request;
December 1983	<u>House of Commons Transport Committee</u> announces its intention 'to undertake an enquiry into the organisation, financing and control of airports in the United Kingdom';

---

* Formerly Professor at the London Business School and Member, British Airports Authority.

173

June 1984	Second Memorandum on Privatisation submitted by the Authority to the Secretary of State for Transport;
July 1984	Transport Committee Report published on 'The organisation, financing and control of airports in the United Kingdom' (3 volumes);
June 1985	White Paper on Airports Policy (Cmnd 9542) published (this was largely to do with government decisions on the Inspector's Report on the Airports Inquiries following the planning application by the BAA to develop Stansted Airport, but it also contained a number of important policy decisions on privatisation);
January 1986	Airports Bill introduced into the House of Commons;
July 1986	Airports Act 1986 receives the Royal Assent 8 July; 31 July, separate airport companies began operations;
August 1986	All the property, rights and liabilities of the former British Airports Authority, which included its shares in the separate airport companies, vested in BAA PLC (Vesting Day, 1 August);
November 1986	Permits issued to BAA airports to levy airport charges, and the price regulation formula announced;
11 June 1987	General election: Conservatives re-elected;
22 June 1987	Pathfinder Prospectus published;
8 July 1987	Impact Day: Share price of 245 pence announced; full Prospectus issued;
16 July 1987	100 per cent of the ordinary shares in BAA PLC offered for sale (partly paid) to the public, 75 per cent at the fixed price and a maximum 25 per cent by open tender. Shares also available to employees on special terms.
28 July 1987	Trading in BAA PLC shares commenced on the London Stock Exchange

RESOURCES

The time that elapsed between the government's announcement of its intention to privatise the British Airports Authority to the flotation of BAA PLC was some four years. The 'critical path' - the minimum feasible time - was, however, nearer 16 months. This assumes six months for the government to decide exactly what it wanted, that there were unlimited resources and no hindrances. This remarkable difference was due to several factors:

(1) the enquiry by the Transport Select Committee, which took seven months;

(2) other state enterprises having priority over the BAA in the government's privatisation programme;

(3) 'no go' periods, including time periods laid down in the 1986 Act, holidays, periods when Parliament was not sitting, Budgets;

(4) some scarcity in critical resources.

In the 16 month 'critical path' nearly one half was 'time determined', largely due to parliamentary procedures. From the introduction of the Airports Bill to Royal Assent was almost six months, though the Act was fairly complex, with 85 Sections and six Schedules, some 97 pages in all, and there were no significant delays (the equivalent period for British Telecom was $9\frac{1}{2}$ months). Moreover, following Royal Assent, the Order bringing the provisions of the Act into force and establishing the detailed regulatory scheme had to lay before Parliament for 40 sitting days (subject to Negative Resolution). The Prospectus could not be finalised and printed until the regulatory scheme was defined and in force. Furthermore, the Draft Prospectus had to be published over 1 month ahead of the listing of the company on the Stock Exchange. The other 8-9 months were a mixture of 'time-determined' and 'resource determined' activities. Policy had to be decided and the Airports Policy White Paper then had to be turned into a Bill. A period of six months was assumed, which was the actual time between the White Paper and the publication of the Bill. While this period was determined in part by the number of parliamentary draftsmen (in fact, there was a severe shortage of such persons), the main delay was caused by the need to resolve some basic questions of policy. Indeed, some had not been decided before the Bill was published. The Act emerged about twice the size of the Bill as first presented to Parliament, and the government was still adding clauses during the third reading in the House of Lords. With a less complex form of regulation, privatisation could have been achieved much more quickly.

So the 16 months is partly an estimate, based on assumptions. In another country with different government systems and parliamentary procedures, the 'critical path' might be either longer or shorter. In fact, the BAA conducted formal Critical Path Analyses for planning and for internal resource allocation, which proved to be most valuable. In particular they could readily answer questions such as 'could you be ready by...?' or 'how long would you need for...?' or 'what if...were delayed?'

REGULATION

Airports are 'natural' monopolies. Even around a big city like London or New York, where there are several airports, in practice the scope for genuine competition between airports - as distinct from competition between airlines, which can be intense - is extremely limited, especially where the proportion of international traffic is high (Heathrow is the world's largest international airport, and Gatwick is now the world's second largest). Moreover, market entry for aiport competitors is always a matter for governents and is in no sense 'free'.

The monopoly issue was seen to be crucial right from the start, and it was probably the single most important factor. There were several points.

(a) Given its strong monopoly position (73 per cent of the UK market overall, and much higher in some specific locations), should the BAA be subject to special economic regulation; and if so, of what kind?

(b) Should the government take special powers to regulate airport operations in any way (on top of the technical regulation concerned with safety already undertaken by the Civil Aviation Authority (CAA), which was not an issue), including, for example, the distribution of traffic between London's airports, limitations on air transport movements, and the allocation of capacity (landing take-off 'slots') at peak times?

Economic regulation also turned out to be, at the highest level, a question of organisational structure. The two were interdependent.

The BAA's initial proposal (Transport Committee, British Airports Authority evidence, 20 March 1984) was that the Associated British Ports model should be followed. In 1982 Associated British Ports Holdings PLC was set up, and its shares were subsequently sold to the public. This company was given the powers of a Holding Company over Associated British Ports (formerly the British Transport Docks Board), a statutory corporation described as a 'body corporate and a public authority'. The Transport Act 1981 laid down the powers and duties of Associated British Ports, this being in effect a form of regulation, though with wider powers and more freedom than possessed by the former Transport Docks Board.

The British Airports Authority also had statutory duties under the 1965 (and subseqently the 1975) Airports Act, and they could likewise have been adapted to the private sector, with a PLC holding company and perhaps two subsidiary statutory corporations, one for the three South-east airports (Heathrow, Gatwick and Stanstead) and one for the four Scottish airports (Glasgow, Edinburgh, Prestwick and Aberdeen), where the problems were very different. It was argued that in these circumstances no additional economic regulation of a special kind would be necessary.

Another possibility was for the government to retain overall control through a majority shareholding and for the company to contract out the management of each airport - and perhaps of each terminal separately at Heathrow and Gatwick - to private sector contractors on a competitive basis. Both the Transport Committee and the government looked carefully at this option.

A further set of possibilities was to sell off the BAA as a single group, or to sell the South-east and the Scottish airports as two airport groups, or to sell each of the seven airports individually, or some combination of these, with or without a special regulatory regime. Again, these options were closely examined.

Not surprisingly, of these latter options the BAA strongly preferred the first: sale as a single unit (after all, it had developed a highly successful airports group and the last ditch would be to preside over its dissolution), while the most outspoken protagonists for competition argued for the opposite extreme - selling each airport separately. It was argued that this second solution would also minimise the need for special regulation. The Transport Select Committee devoted much time to this.

In the end, the Secretary of State decided to sell the BAA as a single group, and in the June 1985 White Paper he gave the following reasons:

(a) On the proposal to float seven independent airport companies -
* 'The volume of business switching from one airport to another within a group to enjoy lower landing charges or better service standards is, on past experience, very small.'
* 'If the airports were separated, the prospects and profitability of each individual airport would be very largely dependent on decisions made by government.'
* 'Separate ownership would introduce undesirable rigidity into the administration of government policy for route licensing and traffic distribution, and for airport development.'

(b) On the two-group solution (South-east and Scottish airports) -
* 'Separation would do nothing to increase competition'
* It could 'jeopardise the efficiency gains that have been achieved at the Scottish airports... because they benefit from the services supplied centrally by BAA Headquarters...and both sets of airports benefit from the interchange on staff'.
* 'It is questionable whether the Scottish airports as a separate group could attract adequate quality of management staff to take on the new activities.'
* 'There would certainly be a delay before the (Scottish) airports as a wholly separate enterprise would be attractive to investors, and this would deny...the benefits of early privatisation.'

(c) On the single group solution -
* 'The BAA has been consistently profitable.'
* 'Privatising BAA as a whole will retain maximum flexibility in the administration of government

aviation policies.'
* 'It can be implemented speedily.'
* 'The new BAA PLC will be able to expand into non-airport activities from which the BAA as a nationalised industry has been excluded.'
* It will result in a substantial number of advantages, BUT -
* 'The new BAA PLC will need to be regulated to ensure that it does not abuse its monopoly position.'

Thus, there was then the question of the form of economic regulation which should be adopted. Early in 1984 the BAA and its consultants had sent a team to the United States and Canada to examine their public utility regulation, and had studied the options. In January 1986 (following the White Paper) the government employed a firm of economic consultants to examine the options and to make recommendations. The outcome was a unanimous rejection of 'rate of return' regulation, at least as practised in the United States. The main reasons were the immense burden of administration which was inevitably involved, and the fact that price increases were restricted by the regulators in boom times and by the market in depression so that the enterprises always lost out, and incentives were blunted. There was also a tendency to overinvest. In the UK some version of 'RPI - X' to regulate prices and charges was preferred; but what should this formula be applied to?

The BAA has two sorts of customers: nearly 200 airlines (though about 50 of them contribute over 90 per cent of landing-fee revenue), and some 55 million passengers. In broad terms, just over one half of the BAA's income comes from landing fees but almost all of the (historic-cost) profits come from commercial revenues, mostly from passengers. One key issue, therefore, was whether economic regulation should apply just to landing fees or to the total; and if the latter, would this not stifle any incentive to innovate and to earn more per passenger - the results of inventiveness and effort merely being to reduce landing fees still further?

The outcome was that -

(1) Only 'airport charges' (landing, passenger and aircraft parking charges paid by aircraft operators) at 'designated airports', currently the South-east airports as a whole, and at Heathrow and Gatwick

      separately, would be subject to the RPI - X 'price conditions'. The 'X' was set at 1, and the formula remitted 75 per cent of any increase in security costs which resulted from government requirements (and the reverse for any decrease). These 'price conditions' would be reviewed every five years by the Monopolies and Mergers Commission (MMC), following a reference by the CAA.

(2)   'Operational activities' would also be subject to investigation by the MMC as part of the 'price conditions' reference every five years. These are activities 'which are carried on wholly or mainly for the benefit of users of the airport' or 'the revenues of which are wholly or mainly attributable to payments by such users'. Thus, both airport charges and most of the commercial activities would be subject to MMC scrutiny, on 'public interest' criteria.

(3)   'Trading conditions' may be imposed at any time by the CAA and apply to all airports. They relate to 'relevant activities', which are in effect a subset of 'operational activities', and include the landing, parking or taking-off of aircraft, the servicing of aircraft and the handling of passengers or their baggage, and of cargo. 'Trading conditions' seek to remedy or prevent unreasonable discrimination, the unfair exploitation of a bargaining position, any unreasonable limitation of third party opportunities at airports, and predatory pricing.

(4)   'Accounts conditions' also apply to all airports. They require the disclosure of certain information in the statutory accounts of each airport company, including details of any subsidies furnished to the airport operator from any source, and the aggregate income and expenditure attributable to both 'airport charges' and to 'operational activities'.

That is not the end of the regulatory story. The government has retained powers in the 1986 Act to limit the number of Air Transport Movements (ATMs) at any airport with substantial spare capacity, and an annual limit of 78,000 movements has been set at Stansted. The Secretary of State can also make rules to distribute air traffic between two or more airports serving the same area in the UK, and under this provision intercontinental flights in

Scotland are required to operate only at Prestwick and not at either of the other Lowland airports at Glasgow or Edinburgh. Under certain conditions he can also allocate between airlines the times at which aircraft may land or take off at airports (aircraft 'slots'). At present these are arranged by Scheduling Committees of airlines.

The Secretary of State also has powers in relation to airports under certain other legislation. He can, for example, require the operator of an airport designated under the Civil Aviation Act 1982 to take action to limit aircraft noise during take-off or landing and he can restrict (and has done so at Heathrow and Gatwick) the number and type of aircraft movements at night. He can also require airports to give noise insulation grants, and has done so at Heathrow and Gatwick.

There are of course detailed provisions relating to each of these matters which include complaints procedures, consultation, the method of approval (in some cases parliamentary approval), references to the MMC under certain circumstances, enforcement, and so on: for details the reader should refer principally to the Airports Act 1986, to the various 'Permissions to Levy Airport Charges', and to the Civil Aviation Act 1982.

Three factors have to be understood to appreciate the reasoning behind some of these regulations. The first concerns the charging policy of the British Airports Authority. This was based on economic rather than accounting considerations, and involved marginal-cost pricing (as the various Nationalised Industry White Papers had required it to do). The two extremes were Stansted, where prices were based on short-run marginal cost because of massive spare capacity, and Heathrow, where peak-hour prices were based on the long-run marginal cost of new capacity because of severe congestion (it is demand in the peak which leads to the need for extra capacity). Thus, once the 1985 White Paper designated Stansted for a major expansion of traffic, airport charges had to move up sharply. The only way to accommodate this within the RPI - 1 price regulation was to give Stansted pricing freedom within the overall South-east framework (Stansted has only 0.5 million passengers compared with a South-east total of about 48.5 million, so a large increase in the amount per passenger recovered through airport charges at Stansted would be lost in the much larger total).

Furthermore, northern airports, in particular

Manchester, had long opposed the development of Stansted, fearing that it would starve them of traffic and of capital investment. Although these arguments were effectively countered by Graham Eyre QC in his massive Report on the 'Public Inquiries into the Development of Heathrow and Stansted Airports' (December 1984), the political pressures continued to be strong. One result was the disclosure provision concerning subsidy in the 'accounts conditions', another was the ATM limit on Stansted to prevent the airport's growth beyond about 8 million passengers per annum without the Secretary of State for Transport first laying an Order before Parliament.

The third factor arises from the government's international obligations relating to UK airports. In particular there is the Bermuda 2 Air Service Agreement between the British and the United States governments (July 1977) which specified, inter alia, that user charges at airports should be just and reasonable, that they should not exceed the full cost of providing appropriate airport facilities, and that they may provide for a reasonable rate of return on assets after depreciation. They should also be based on 'sound economic principles and on the generally accepted accounting practices within the territory of the appropriate contracting party'. These provisions were amplified by the Memorandum of Understanding and Settlement Agreement in April 1983 of the long-standing dispute with 17 foreign airlines, principally about the basis of airport charges (the airlines, led by Pan Am and TWA, argued that landing fees should be determined on an accounting cost basis while the BAA and the government argued for an economic basis), and specifically about the peak-hour charges at Heathrow. 'RPI - X' was of deep concern to them.

ORGANISATIONAL CHANGE

In preparation for privatisation, very early on the BAA set about considering what internal organisational changes were needed to be able to respond effectively to the opportunities and challenges of the private sector. A very wide range of options was considered. The principal changes which did take place were:

(1) setting up the BAA PLC as a company;
(2) setting up each individual airport as a limited

company, also with a holding company for the four Scottish airports, all wholly owned by BAA PLC;

(3) converting the former Head Office of some 680 people at Gatwick into (a) Group Services (later called British Airports Services Ltd) of some 630 people, and (b) a Corporate Office in London, of some 50 people; and

(4) setting up Business Development Departments in each airport.

On (1), the BAA has followed in the footsteps of British Telecom in being at one time - until 1965 - a government department with all its employees Civil Servants, then a public corporation (the British Airports Authority 1965-86, then a PLC with all of the shares owned by the Secretary of State on behalf of the Crown, and finally a company fully owned in the private sector: please note that the initials do not stand for British Airports Authority PLC; they are simply what they say, BAA PLC). Accompanying the new name there was also a new corporate logo (proposed by outside consultants), and other corporate image changes will follow.

Setting up each airport as a limited company (in accordance with the White Paper policy but also as a part of the BAA's own strategy) was very significant. The attitudes of the BAA have moved a long way from the days when people called 'Airport Commandants' ran these airports. Then they were called 'Airport Directors', now each airport in the South-east has its own Chairman and Managing Director in a combined post, and a small board. In Scotland each airport has a Managing Director, and the Chairman of all four airports is the Managing Director of Scottish Airports Ltd.

Because it was also decided to delegate as much responsibility as possible to airport chairmen and managing directors, because no one had been used to working in this way, and because no Head Office had been replaced by Group Services and the Corporate Office (see also below), it was thought desirable to write down clearly and explicitly what matters were reserved to the Corporate Office and to the PLC board for decision, and what were the duties and the scope of authority of the airport boards. This proved very useful in the new circumstances: accountabilities were clear, and people knew where they stood and who was responsible for what.

In July 1985 the BAA initiated a study on all of the

options for organisational change in anticipation of privatisation. Interviews amongst senior management revealed, amongst other things, that it was time to change the balance of authority between Head Office and the airports, which had now grown to large businesses and had well-trained and experienced airport directors in charge. In October the board approved the setting up of a small top-level working party of three persons to investigate one proposal in depth - that the existing Head Office should be totally re-structured. In January they reported back to the Board, and on 1 April 1986 the proposed changes came into effect.

Instead of it being unclear exactly who was in charge on a day-to-day basis (on many matters Head Office thought that they were), what had been decided was to split the former Head Office into two - and thereby to break the bureaucracy. The largest part was to supply central services to the airports on a repayment basis - hence the title 'Group Services'. A 'code of practice' was drawn up to regulate this emerging internal competition. On 1 April 1987 - one year on - the BAA's airports could buy these services from Group Services (on that date the name was changed to British Airports Services Ltd, BASL), undertake them internally, or buy them externally from third parties. BASL was also encouraged to sell its services elsewhere in the UK and abroad.

The one-year period was for transition, and so that Group Services could discover what their individual services actually cost (hitherto Head Office costs were a standard percentage overhead charge to the airports), develop competitive charging and contractual policies, set up their own marketing department to find out what the airports really wanted and what opportunities existed abroad, and thus to discover how to manage themselves as a business.

The change was dramatic and the effects were entirely positive (though not without much agony on the way). The reasons for its success were:

(a) the total commitment of the Chairman to make it a success;
(b) the thoroughness of the investigation;
(c) the general agreement of most senior management - indeed, many said that such a change was long overdue;
(d) the appointment of one of the three persons who

did the original investigation as the first Corporate Director Group Services (he was Personnel Director at the time, and formerly the no.2 at Heathrow Airport). He is now Chairman and Managing Director of BASL; and

(e)   the appointment to the BASL Board of Directors of the constituent parts of the company - the Director Engineering Services, the Director Commercial Services, the Director Business Services, the Director Personnel Services and the Director Financial Services, and the highly positive responses from their staff.

The remaining part of Head Office was formed into a small Corporate Office, and relocated in London. It consists now of the Chairman, the Company Secretary, the Chief Executive, the Group Finance Director, the Company Solicitor, the Director Public Affairs, the Director Corporate Strategy and their staff. The Director of Safety and Security is also part of the Corporate Office though physically located alongside BASL at Gatwick. In addition, the privatisation teams temporarily had their home in the Corporate Office. When in London the board meets there.

The final major organisational change was the formation of a New Ventures Group, now under the Director Corporate Strategy, and subsequently of Business Development Departments in each of the airports responsible to their airport chairmen. Communication between these departments, and their co-ordination where necessary in the interests of BAA PLC, are achieved by the small group in the Corporate Office.

Since new ventures may be expected to spring from the skills, experience and other assets of the BAA, being rooted in what the organisation is good at, there is the question of the extent to which specific new ventures fall within the definitions of 'operational' or 'relevant' activities for regulatory purposes. These are matters which can only be decided on the circumstances of the individual case.

FLOTATION

Following the public application for shares, the allocations were: 375 million at the fixed price of 245 pence; 125 million at a minimum tender price of 282 pence; and 500

185

million Ordinary Shares in total, which will raise £1,284 million for the government (and nothing for the BAA PLC). The terms and conditions for the provision of shares to employees, Directors and pensioners are described below.

The fixed price issue was about eight times oversubscribed. The Secretary of State decided that all who requested 1,000 shares or less should be allocated 100 shares, and that all who asked for more than 1,000 shares should receive nothing. There were about 2.1 million persons in the first category and about 350,000 in the second. Each recipient of the 100 share allocation had to pay £100 down and £145 before 19 May 1988.

The tender part of the sale was oversubscribed by six times, and as a result all those who tendered above 282 pence received their full requests, those who tendered exactly 282 pence were scaled down and those who tendered below 282 pence were allocated nothing. Those applying for the tender offer were required to pay the full price tendered less the 145 pence per share which was due later.

Employees had three categories of special offer. Firstly there was a Free Offer to each eligible employee of 41 shares. Secondly, there was a Matching Offer under which the government gave employees two free shares for each one purchased at the fixed price, up to a maximum of 82 shares purchased by the employee. Thirdly, there was the Priority Offer to all Directors, employees and pensioners at the fixed price of a minimum of 150 shares and a maximum of 4,082 shares. Free shares obtained under the Free Offer and the Matching Offer were placed in the BAA Trust Company Ltd and are subject to some restrictions on dealing.

The general structure of this flotation was different from the two immediately previous public sales of government-held shares (see Table 11.1).

The Rolls Royce sale raised 6 per cent more cash than did the BAA sale, yet Rolls Royce issued 60 per cent more shares to do so. British Airways had a share price about one half of that in the BAA, with a 44 per cent larger number of shares available, to raise much less cash.

It would appear that the primary decision for the government was the number of shares which should be issued. Once 500 million was chosen, then on the basis of £80 million profit after tax for the year ended 31 March 1987, the pro forma earnings per share were 16.0 pence; and on a desired price/earnings ratio of about 15 (based on the average FT 500 index) the price per share worked out at 240 pence. The decision on the actual share price is left until the last minute (in the BAA case it was two days before Impact Day) and is assessed on the market conditions at the time and how well the flotation seems to be going.

Table 11.1: Comparative flotation structures of UK privatisation issues

Date	Company	Fixed/ tender price (pence)	Number of shares available (million)	Total market capitalisation (£ million)
Feb 1987	British Airways	125(F)	720.2	900.25
May 1987	Rolls Royce	170(F)	801.5	1,362.55
July 1987	BAA	245(F)	375.0	
		≥ 282(T)	125.0	
			500.0	Total 1,283.75

While choosing to sell a relatively small number of shares at a high price (around 240 pence per share rather than, say, the 125 pence of British Airways) provides for finer tuning of the share price if one wanted to stick to multiples of 5 pence, it did also seem to indicate that the government had the larger investor in mind. In the event, however, it appeared to be the cause of wider share ownership which won the day in terms of the subsequent allocation. While this avoided having a ballot, it did leave a significant number of frustrated would-be larger investors with nothing. (It also left the BAA with the requirement to administer an initial share register of 2.1 million persons, and many angry brokers who would not normally deal with such small amounts of cash.)

In relation to this sale and its background there are several other issues which should be mentioned. The first is a political point, the significance of which is difficult to assess. When the crucial last-minute decisions were being made there was a new Secretary of State in office (the third since the BAA privatisation was initiated), appointed following the June General Election. There also was the prospect of another five years of Conservative Government with many more privatisations planned. The BAA privatisation could have been seen as as time for experimentation -

the combined fixed price/tender offer was indeed an innovation, and the share number/price decisions were also a departure from previous practice.

The second point is that the time horizon of strategic planning in the BAA had to be very long, significantly longer than the City has been accustomed to. The reason is that, in the South-east at any rate, every major airport development will arouse the most bitter opposition from interested parties. The first White Paper - May 1967 - supporting the proposed major development of Stansted Airport followed a Public Inquiry which started in October 1965. The White Paper which gave the final go-ahead, albeit with a very limited development in the first instance, was dated June 1985. The first phase of the development is expected to be complete in 1991. While this time-scale is exceptional, all major developments have had to face Public Inquiries, and this will continue to be so. A minimum 15-year planning horizon is quite normal. This meant that the BAA could not be regarded as just another company: the City had to be educated.

Furthermore, the fact that BAA privatisation aroused such political controversy from so many quarters - those who wished to see the BAA airports sold individually, those who still wished to stop any development at Stansted, and those airlines who still wished to see a different price regime at Heathrow - meant that public relations had to play a key part in educating and influencing the City, and public and parliamentary opinion. Moreover, the 'road shows', the advertising and Share Stands at every BAA airport constituted a significant activity. Public Affairs in the Corporate Office became a key department. Although the government sold all of the ordinary shares, it retained one 'Special Share'. Of the 42 sales of government shares in the last 10 years this was only the 11th occasion when there was a Special Share.

While that Share attaches no voting rights to its owner, normally the Secretary of State for Transport on behalf of the Crown, it does give him the right to attend and speak at shareholder general meetings. It also gives him some powers, requiring his consent prior to the voluntary winding up, disposal or relaxation of control of a 'designated airport', and in relation to certain changes in the Articles of Association, in particular that which prohibits any person from having ordinary shares which would give him or her more than 15 per cent of the votes at a general meeting.

Finally, there was an important issue about the appropriate accounting base for the BAA. The Company argued that a Current-cost Accounting (CCA) basis for its main accounts was appropriate - as indeed as a nationalised industry had been the government's requirement. The BAA is unusually capital-intensive (its net assets on 31 March 1987 were £1,138 million on a CCA basis, yet the Company employs only 7,478 people - over £152,000 net assets per employee). In these circumstances it is clearly important to be valuing these assets on a replacement-cost basis. On an historic-cost basis, too, little would be set aside for depreciation and replacement, and the true value of the BAA would be distorted.

The government's arguments for presenting the main accounts on an historic-cost basis when privatised were that the City was used to this form of presentation and would be confused by CCA, and that there is no form of CCA accounts on which the accounting profession agree. No doubt also because the profits looked much larger there was the possibility of raising more money.

In the event the Company's accounts are now presented in full on a CCA basis and in an abbreviated form on an historical-cost basis. (The difference is marked. On a CCA basis net assets on 31 March 1987 were £1,138 million and on an historical-cost basis on the same date were £694 million, so the argument was not a trivial one. In addition, CCA profits in that year were £38 million and on historical cost were £78 million.)

GENERAL CONCLUSIONS AND LESSONS

Airport privatisation is likely to pose particular problems for most governments. A principal international airport may be seen as a strategic asset both economically and militarily. It may be a major gateway for trade and tourism and itself be a major earner of foreign exchange. It can be a gateway for less desirable traffic involving criminal and subversive persons and activities. It may occupy vast tracts of land, usually near to centres of population, and its operations may create major noise and surface traffic problems. Governments are involved in air traffic right agreements with other governments and many such agreements are very sensitive politically. For all of these reasons most governments would be unwilling to allow the control of such assets to fall into foreign hands or to be influenced by undesirable elements. They would also wish to ensure that the economic power which most airports possess through their monopoly position would be used responsibly and to national advantage.

It is evident from the BAA example, however, that privatisation need not involve a government in surrendering all of its special powers in relation to an airport. Not only can the legislation giving effect to privatisation retain many such powers, but the device of a Special Share can also be used. The important implication is that such powers would have to be brought into the open and be written down. It is also evident that there are ways of regulating a private sector monopoly to ensure that it does not act in ways contrary to the public interest. Experience will be needed to test the efficacy of the methods chosen for the BAA.

However, for a country without an institution experienced in economic regulation, such as the MMC in the UK, and without a trustworthy and efficient private sector, privatisation of the kind introduced for the BAA would not be recommended. There are, nevertheless, several other ways of introducing a private sector element into airports without a government surrendering its overall control. Thus, for example, only a minority of shares need be sold, with the government retaining majority control. A government owner could contract out its airport management for a limited period, specifying performance criteria which the successful contractor must meet. It could use the Associated British Ports device of a statutory corporation within a holding company.

Thus, the form of BAA privatisation should not be taken as a blueprint model. There were special circumstances which led the UK government to adopt this particular approach, some highly political; but the UK experience, in examining the options, developing the arguments and managing the process, could be of great value to foreign governments.

The process of privatisation may be spread over a very long period, which can create problems, even though the 'fair weather' critical path would be much shorter. The build-up of staff enthusiasm has to be carefully controlled, for if it peaks too soon with further delays there will be much disappointment and frustration. In addition, it is crucial to have commitment and dedication at the top, with a clear vision of where the organisation should be heading, to sustain it through the slack periods, the frustrations of delay and the uncertainties of political controversy.

The transition from being Civil Servants in a government department, no doubt with certain career expectations, to being employees in a public corporation, and then to being in a company fully in the private sector, all in 20 years, requires a great deal from the staff: attitudes have to change; new skills have to be learnt; new training programmes have to be devised and implemented. New people will join the organisation who come with a very different background and experience from those longer serving members of staff, and they are likely to occupy senior positions. Radically new forms of organisation may be introduced. Trade unionists may be torn between the traditional attitudes of their officials opposing privatisation, and the wishes of their individual members who know a good thing when they see it (98 per cent of BAA employees became shareholders in the company).

Good communication between managers and staff throughout the whole process of privatisation is therefore vital, with full information flowing in both directions, and with opportunities to voice doubts and grievances. To be successful, all of these changes have to be positively managed. Again, strong and effective leadership is crucial. Good planning of the privatisation process is also essential. There are so many issues to be considered and decisions to be taken in such a wide variety of fields that without a firm hand on planning and progressing, much time and money could be wasted. The effort required - especially from the top executives - should not be underestimated.

The prospect of privatising the BAA was clearly the trigger for internal change of many kinds. Their full consequences will, however, only become apparent with time and experience, but the prospects look favourable. It was the government's privatisation as an act of political choice, it was the Secretary of State's sale of the shares, but it was the future of the BAA in the private sector which was at stake. The BAA had always to balance its own long-term interests as a business against the shorter-term interests of the government - to privatise the BAA in a politically acceptable form and to raise as much cash as possible. This required a high level of political awareness by the BAA, courage, determination - and first rate teams on both sides. The success of the venture was due in large measure to the presence of these conditions.

The Case of BAA PLC

APPENDIX: BAA financial performance 1983-7

1.   Consolidated (current cost) profit & loss accounts

	Note	1983	1984	1985	1986	1987
				As at 31 March		
				£ million		
Revenues	1	280	316	362	396	439
Operating costs		(252)	(269)	(292)	(313)	(348)
Operating profit	2,3	28	47	70	83	91
Net interest	4	(1)	(3)	(6)	(7)	(7)
Gearing adjustment		3	4	8	8	6
Profit on ordinary activities before taxation		30	48	72	84	90
Taxation	5	(6)	(11)	(22)	(36)	(44)
Profit on ordinary activities after taxation		24	37	50	48	46
Extraordinary items	6	–	(48)	–	(3)	(2)
Profit/(Loss) for the year after extra-ordinary items		24	(11)	50	45	44
Pro forma earnings per share	7	4.8p	7.4p	10.0p	9.6p	9.2p

Source: BAA PLC Prospectus, July 1987

2. Consolidated (historical cost) profit & loss accounts

	Note	1983	1984	1985	1986	1987
				£ million		
Revenues	1	280	316	362	396	439
Operating costs		(208)	(229)	(252)	(267)	(308)
Operating profit	2,3	72	87	110	129	131
Net interest	4	(1)	(3)	(6)	(7)	(7)
Profit on ordinary activities before taxation		71	84	104	122	124
Taxation	5	(6)	(11)	(22)	(36)	(44)
Profit on ordinary activities after taxation		65	73	82	86	80
Extraordinary items	6	-	(48)	-	(3)	(2)
Profit for the year after extra-ordinary items		65	25	82	83	78
Pro forma earnings per share	7	13.0p	14.6p	16.4p	17.2p	16.0p

As at 31 March

Source: BAA PLC Prospectus, July 1987

The Case of BAA PLC

3. Consolidated (current cost) balance sheets

	Note	1983	1984	1985	1986	1987
				£ million		
Fixed Assets						
Tangible Assets	8	968	1,046	1,179	1,325	1,400
Current Assets						
Debtors	9	36	31	36	39	44
Cash at bank and in hand		1	1	1	1	-
		37	32	37	40	44
Creditors:						
Due within one year	10	(72)	(90)	(126)	(150)	(132)
Net Current Liabilities		(35)	(58)	(89)	(110)	(88)
Total Assets Less Current Liabilities		933	988	1,090	1,215	1,312
Creditors:						
Due after more than one year	11	(53)	(48)	(43)	(39)	(79)
Provision for Liabilities and Charges	12	(2)	(67)	(84)	(96)	(95)
Net Assets		878	873	963	1,080	1,138
Capital and Reserves						
Called up share capital	13	-	-	-	-	-
Reserves	14	878	873	963	1,080	1,138
		878	873	963	1,080	1,138

As at 31 March

4. Consolidated (historical cost) balance sheets

	Note	As at 31 March				
		1983	1984	1985	1986	1987
		£ million				
Fixed Assets						
Tangible Assets	8	446	554	679	791	956
Current Assets						
Debtors	9	36	31	36	39	44
Cash at bank and in hand		1	1	1	1	–
		37	32	37	40	44
Creditors:						
Due within one year	10	(72)	(90)	(126)	(150)	(132)
Net Current Liabilities		(35)	(58)	(89)	(110)	(88)
Total Assets Less Current Liabilities		411	496	590	681	868
Creditors:						
Due after more than one year	11	(53)	(48)	(43)	(39)	(79)
Provision for Liabilities and Charges	12	(2)	(67)	(84)	(96)	(95)
Net Assets		356	381	463	546	694
Capital and Reserves						
Called up share capital	13	–	–	–	–	–
Reserves	14	356	381	463	546	694
		356	381	463	546	694

12

Privatisation in the Transport Sector

John Rickard*

The Department of Transport's responsibility covers land transport (including railways and buses), air travel and shipping. The Department's privatisation programme is or has been concerned with the following enterprises:

- National Freight Corporation
- Associated British Ports
- British Airways
- British Airports Authority
- British Rail
- National Bus Company.

In this, a summary paper, brief references will firstly be made to British Airways (BA), the British Airports Authority (BAA) and British Rail (BR) and then the greater part of the chapter will be devoted to buses where the issue of competition and efficiency continues to evoke some interesting questions.

The BAA was privatised in July 1987, and BA earlier in the same year. The National Bus Company (NBC) has been split up and today 45 companies out of a total of 73 have

* John Rickard is the Chief Economic Adviser at the Department of Transport but this chapter is written by him in a personal capacity and does not necessarily reflect the views of the Department. He is, nevertheless, grateful to his colleagues who provided material and comments. This chapter is subject to Crown copyright.

been sold. BR remains within the public sector though Sealink and some hotels have been hived off. The proceeds to date to the Exchequer are listed in the accompanying table (see Table 12.1).

Table 12.1: UK privatisation proceeds

National Freight Company	1982	£7m
British Rail Hotels	1983	£30m[a]
Associated British Ports	1983-4	£34m
Sealink	1984	£66m[a]
British Airways	1987	£892m
British Airports Authority	1987	in excess of £1,000m
National Bus Company	to September 1987	n.a

Note: a. Proceeds retained by British Rail, though with subsequent adjustments to the borrowing limits.

For further details on National Bus Company and National Freight Company, see Appendix 3.

The government's policy objectives from privatisation fall into the following categories:

1. Supply side benefits of greater efficiency. These could be achieved by:
   (a) introducing greater competition;
   (b) giving managements more freedom, e.g. liberating them from public sector controls and forcing them to raise capital in the market place;
   (c) making managements answerable to shareholders.
2. Widening share ownership, providing scope for employees' share ownership and reducing the role of the state (these are largely political objectives).
3. Securing proceeds for the government.

The government's objectives have been documented in a

useful series of papers <u>Privatisation and regulation - the UK experience</u>, edited by J. Kay, C. Mayer and D. Thompson (Oxford University Press, 1986). A central theme has been the conflict between, on the one hand, the breaking up of a public enterprise to foster greater competition in the market compared with, on the other hand, maintaining the enterprise in tact to benefit from various scale economies. In the latter case it is necessary to rely on regulation to avoid monopoly abuse.

The Department of Transport's contribution to these objectives has been varied. The total level of proceeds is significant, though not on the scale of British Telecom or British Gas. The privatisation of BA and the BAA did not lead to greater competition although the government reviewed the structure of the airline industry before proceeding with the sale; while the BAA might be described as a regulated 'quasi-monopoly'. It is with buses, however, that major changes have been made to the structure of the industry, allowing wherever possible market forces to be dominant, and the full effects of which have yet to be assessed.

BRITISH AIRWAYS

Although one of the earliest candidates for privatisation, BA did not initially have the financial strength or efficiency to lead to a successful sale. Indeed, in 1982 and 1983 it was technically insolvent, and was only able to continue trading with the benefit of a government guarantee. Rather than transfer the company in that state to the private sector the government itself appointed new management to take the steps necessary to prepare the company for sale. These steps included the abandoning of unprofitable routes, the sale or scrapping of some 20 aircraft and a reduction of around 20,000 in the number of staff employed. These measures, combined with a positive step approach to marketing, turned BA into a commercially successful company.

However, before proceeding with the privatisation, the governent asked the Civil Aviation Authority (CAA) (which licenses operators and regulates the industry) to review the structure of the UK civil airline industry (see Appendix 1 for the recommendations) because of fears that, once freed from government control, BA would abuse its dominant position to the detriment of the government's objective of securing a sound and competitive multi-airline industry. The CAA recommended a substantial restructuring of the industry, including a compulsory transfer of routes from BA to other airlines, for which the government would have needed to take special powers. The government concluded, however, that the independent airlines should have opportunities to grow and prosper, given fair competition, without any forced reduction in the size of BA. However, there was a voluntary exchange of routes between BA and British Caledonian designed to strengthen the latter; and BA agreed to provide up to £450,000 per route to help other independent airlines with the development costs of starting up to 15 new routes.

Recently, the proposed merger between BA and British Caledonian has raised major questions about the structure of the industry and the government's objectives for competition within it. The issues are at the time of writing being examined by the Monopolies and Mergers Commission (MMC).

THE BRITISH AIRPORTS AUTHORITY

The BAA exercises considerable monopoly power through its ownership of the three London airports and was privatised in that form. The government thought long and hard about whether efficiency benefits could be achieved in the most natural way - by restructuring the industry in order to introduce competition. One option was to break up the BAA and sell off its seven airports separately, but we did not think that effective competition would be created in this way. Within the London system, for example, Heathrow is very much the dominant airport because it is larger than the others, and therefore able to offer more interlining connections for airlines, and it is nearer to central London. The White Paper on airports policy (published in June 1985) explained quite fully, but in general terms, why it was difficult to create competition between airports:

- airport charges are a relatively small part of an airline's total costs;

- Heathrow will continue to have a dominant position as a traffic hub; and

199

- for administrative reasons, the distribution of traffic between airports will remain the responsibility of the government.

The expected efficiency gains should arise in terms of a sharpening of management attitudes, free from direct bureaucratic interference. Nevertheless, some government controls still apply. The Department, operating through the CAA, remains responsible for traffic regulation and safety, in particular the distribution of traffic. The government also imposes a price restraint on Heathrow and Gatwick individually and on the three airports collectively using the now familiar formula of 'RPI - X'. This applies to airport charges (landing, parking and taking-off) and the CAA has powers of direction on the structure of charges with appeal to the MMC. 'X' in the formula was set by the Secretary of State so as to:

(a) prevent overcharging and provide assurance to airport users on the level of charges they are likely to face over the next five years;

(b) encourage a high level of efficiency and productivity in the operation and development of the airports; and

(c) provide for a level of charges sufficient to renumerate investments in additional airport capacity in time to meet demand, having regard to the need to attract funds to finance an extensive capital programme.

BRITISH RAIL

There are at present no plans to bring about the comprehensive privatisation of the core activities of BR. This is partly because rail services (as is the case in most parts of the world) depend upon substantial levels of government subsidy which make it difficult to create genuine situations of risk for a private sector operator, independent of government guarantees and controls. In addition, railway networks are by their nature interdependent and it is therefore difficult to single out individual lines and services for privatisation. There have been proposals to create a track authority which might be responsible for the infrastructure and allow private sector companies to operate trains; but there are major problems with this, not least the difficulty of arranging for the right contractual relationship between the operator and the track authority which allows for the interdependence between infrastructure and operating decisions and their costs. BR has considered several proposals in the past such as the Slough-Windsor and Southend-Frenchurch Street lines but no acceptable formula for privatisation was found which offered efficiency gains. However, the Department does not rule out the possibility of future opportunities for private operations, perhaps on a franchising basis subject to strict conditions on quality of service.

In the meantime, limited progress has been achieved with peripheral activities: for example Sealink, hovercraft and hotels have been sold along with £500m of surplus property. The sale of British Transport Advertising to a management group was announced in July of this year. The Board allows competition for station catering sites, the supply of prepared food for trains and trolley catering and is likely to convert Travellers Fare (currently part of BR) to company status as a preliminary to eventual sale. The private sector is playing an increasing role in supplying railway equipment and rolling stock by tender, reducing the former dependence on British Rail Engineering Limited.

BUSES

Because of the considerable potential in the bus industry, the Department took a clear and determined policy decision that competition was to be the primary means of creating greater efficiency and that privatisation would be associated with a major structural change in the industry. The steps were as follows:

(a) deregulation of express coaches, 1980;

(b) bus deregulation outside London, 1985;

(c) the NBC to be broken up and its 70 subsidiaries to be sold separately;

(d) local authority bus operations to be transferred to arms-length companies;

(e) subsidies to be paid for specific services (where social benefits arise) rather than, as previously, to maintain a network of bus services; and

(f)   bus companies were to make competitive tenders to operate the subsidised services.

London was excluded but, as discussed below, is likely to follow the rest of the country shortly.

The above steps were taken in the light of a thorough examination of the bus industry, much of the findings of which were published in the White Paper Buses, Cmnd 9300, July 1984; (see Appendix 2 for the government's proposals). It was concluded that increased competition offered the best prospect of reversing the secular decline of bus travel, the pressures for increasing subsidies, and rising costs and organisation inefficiencies. There was evidence that private sector operators had lower unit costs than public sector counterparts and that a large proportion of government subsidies were 'leaking' into excess capacity and high labour costs. It was also hoped that deregulation would improve allocative efficiency by matching services more closely to demand and by allowing the growth of new types of service run by new types of vehicles, notably a shift towards smaller and more efficient buses.

It was recognised that some problems might arise from the erosion of cross-subsidy which had enabled services which were not commercially viable to continue to the benefit of:

(a)   rural passengers at the expense of urban passengers;

(b)   passengers on low-density routes at the expense of passengers on high-density routes; and

(c)   those living in less accessible urban areas.

Checks and balances were subsequently devised to enable local authorities to provide subsidised services to counter any adverse social consequences.

The Transport Act 1985 deregulated the bus industry and, outside London, bus operators are now free to run services wherever they wish subject to prior notification and certain safety requirements. The Department's Transport and Road Research Laboratory is monitoring the effects and preliminary conclusions are as follows:

(a) bus mileage has been maintained across the country as a whole;

(b) the total levels of service have remained about the same though their structure has changed;

(c) new operators have entered the market and the proportion of services operated by private companies (excluding privatised NBC subsidiaries) has increased; and

(d) local authorities have managed to maintain previous service levels in general while at the same time reducing subsidy levels: over 83 per cent of all services are now run commerically.

All NBC operations are to be privatised by January 1989. In preparing for the disposal of subsidiaries the NBC has been given the objective of promoting sustained and fair competition by enabling the companies to compete against each other. Thus, earlier proposals to divide the NBC into three or four large regional groups were rejected, and some of the larger companies were themselves split into a number of new subsidiaries. New balance sheets have been created so that each subsidiary could operate as an independent, commercially viable company without cross-subsidy from within the NBC. A further feature of the Department's policy has been to encourage management buy-outs by allowing limited discounts.

The Act also required local authorities with bus undertakings to form public transport companies, limited by shares registered under the Companies Act 1985. Some 53 public transport companies were formed in Great Britain by 26 October 1986, of which 42 are in England, 7 in Wales and 4 in Scotland. Seven of these companies are under the control of the Passenger Transport Authorities (PTAs), the rest under the control of district councils. These companies are now trading. They vary considerably in size, the smallest having less than 40 vehicles and predicted turnovers of only a few hundred thousand pounds, and the largest being companies like Greater Manchester Buses which operates about 2,000 vehicles with a predicted turnover of over £100 million.

There has been some speculation in the Press that plans to break up the public transport companies, formed from the old PTE bus operations in the Metropolitan areas, are being urgently studied by the government. Certainly, there are powers in the Transport Act 1985 for the division of an initial bus company but there are no immediate plans to introduce changes to the bus companies run by the PTAs.

The Transport Act 1985, which abolished road service licensing for local bus services in England, Wales and Scotland, exempted Greater London from deregulation for the time being. The government made it clear that the exemption was a temporary one, designed to allow the recently established London Regional Transport (LRT) time to achieve improved efficiency and a reduced subsidy requirement before imposing a further major change in the way public transport is provided in London.

Since 1985 LRT has operated a programme of competitive tendering for services in particular areas. Route tendering has been less successful in encouraging competition, innovation and reducing overall subsidy costs because it gives overriding importance to the planning function in the establishment of the route network rather than letting operators respond freely to the market forces and provide what passengers want. The government feels that only full deregulation in London will allow services to develop in response to the market.

CONCLUSIONS

Economists, as a professional group, are mainly interested in improving efficiency and privatisation creates opportunities for testing the effectiveness of market forces. The privatisation of BA and the BAA has resulted in fiscal benefits though with little change to the structure of the markets. It ramains the government's intention to achieve greater competition by the liberalisation of the airline industry in due course. With buses, however, the Department of Transport undertook major organisational reform of the industry prior to full privatisation - perhaps the most dramatic of any industry in the government's privatisation programme. Such changes provide an exciting test of theories of competitive and contestible markets though the full effects have yet to be assessed.

APPENDIX 1: The Civil Aviation Authority's review

11. The Government plans to privatise British Airways early in 1985. It has a dominant position in the industry, because of its size and its operating base at Heathrow, the world's busiest international airport. British Airways has in recent years made substantial improvements in its efficiency and financial performance. Over the last ten years, the independent airlines have accounted for a growing share of the industry's available output. But they fear that a more efficient and more competitive British Airways could overwhelm them. These fears would need to be recognised even if British Airways were to remain in the public sector.

12. The Government is concerned to establish as free a market as possible in civil air transport but one in which a multi-airline industry can survive and prosper. It is not part of Government policy to protect the inefficient. But all Britain's airlines have a right to expect a market which is not only competitive - and one in which competition is fair - but also allows them to operate in a stable regulatory environment. It was to ensure this and to meet the concerns of the independent airlines that the Secretary of State for Transport asked the Civil Aviation Authority to review the implications of privatising British Airways for competition and the sound development of the industry. The Government is grateful both to the Authority for its detailed and thorough work and to the many interests - airlines and others - who contributed their ideas.

13. The main conclusions and recommendations of the Authority's report were:
   (1) There should be some reduction in the relative size of British Airways so that other airlines have adequate opportunity to develop and prosper including at least one airline fit to replace British Airways on any major intercontinental route should the need arise. Additional competition by British airlines on intercontinental routes should be licensed wherever possible.
   (2) Intercontinental routes to Saudi Arabia and Harare should be transferred from British Airways at Heathrow to British Caledonian at Gatwick.
   (3) The Authority, acting within existing policies and powers, will seek to increase the range and market penetration of European scheduled services from Gatwick.

(4) British Airways' scheduled service routes from Gatwick should be taken over by other British airlines.

(5) British Airways' European routes from provincial airports should be taken over by other British airlines.

(6) The Government should take specific powers to give effect to the reallocation of routes in recommendations (2), (4) and (5) above. These powers should then lapse.

(7) The Government should look again at the possibility of increasing available capacity at Heathrow and Gatwick.

(8) Provision should be made for access to Heathrow for competing services on those British Airways' domestic trunk routes where direct competition does not already exist, if necessary by reducing British Airways' frequencies.

(9) The Authority would favour a strengthening of its air transport licensing powers in order to promote the sound development of a competitive British airline industry and deal with anti-competitive behaviour.

(10) The Authority does not propose any immediate restriction on British Airways' or British Airtours' charter operations but, given a strengthening of its powers, will not hesitate to set a quantitative limit to their penetration of the holiday charter market if it is shown there is abuse of a dominant position.

(11) The Authority proposes to introduce, on a two-year experimental basis, an area facility allowing airlines to serve any domestic route other than those specifically excluded.

(12) The Authority proposes to cease regulating domestic air fares but will still require fares to be filed with it so that it can intervene to prevent predatory or monopoly pricing. It will consult the Channel Islands and Isle of Man before extending the new arrangements to them.

APPENDIX 2: The Government's proposals

2.1 The Government's proposals concern all aspects of public road transport in Great Britain. They are set out in the following chapters. While broadly the same problems and opportunities exist throughout the country, the position in and proposals for Scotland differ in some respects and are described in chapter 7. The annexes bring together factual material and technical analysis on the major issues. The proposals, in summary, are as follows:

2.2 Bus services will be freed from restriction on competition by abolishing road service licensing throughout Great Britain (except for the framework of controls in London which will be retained for the time being). (Chapter 4)

2.3 Supervision of the quality and safety standards of public service vehicles and operators will be maintained and tightened. Further resources will be provided for this. (Paragraphs 3.1 - 3.2 and 4.15)

2.4 Many essential bus routes are not and never will be viable and local authorities will be able to continue to subsidise services that would cease in the free market. But they will be required to seek competitive tenders for contracts to run bus services which they wish to subsidise. (Paragraphs 3.4 - 3.8)

2.5 Concessionary fare schemes will continue and all operators will be enabled to participate in them on an equitable basis. (Paragraphs 3.9 - 3.10)

2.6 The Government is determined to foster public transport in rural areas. Additional resources will be made available to help with problems in these areas. There will be a special innovation grant and a transitional grant for rural services. Wider use of services run by education, health and social services authorities, the Post Office and others will be explored. (Paragraphs 3.11 - 3.13)

2.7 The structure of the bus industry must be allowed to change to meet market needs. The National Bus Company will be reorganised into smaller free-standing parts which will then be transferred to the private sector. The Government will welcome bids from the employees. Passenger Transport Executives (PTEs) will be required to break down their operations into smaller units, which will become independent companies. Municipal bus operations will be incorporated into companies still owned by their district councils. After a suitable transitional period, both PTE and municipal companies will stand on their own feet. They will compete with other operators for passengers and for contracts to run subsidised services (Chapter 5)

2.8 Taxed and licensed hire cars will be allowed to carry passengers at separate fares in certain circumstances. It is also intended to begin a gradual relaxation of the restrictions on numbers of taxis which apply in some areas. The Government will be consulting the parties concerned on each of these proposals. (Chapter 6)

2.9 In Scotland, as elsewhere, quantity restrictions will be scrapped and quality controls strengthened. Special measures will be taken to improve services in rural areas. Subsidy will be subject to open tender and the structure of the municipal and PTE operations will be changed to improve efficiency and reduce costs. (Chapter 7)

2.10 The Government intends to bring a Bill before Parliament at the earliest opportunity and, subject to Parliamentary approval, to bring in the proposed changes without further delay.

Source: <u>Buses</u> (Cmnd 9300, HMSO, London, 1984).

APPENDIX 3a: National Bus Company - private sales

BUSINESS

National Bus Company is the major passenger transport operator of buses in the country. Under the Transport Act 1985 the company was restructured in order to achieve competition and in preparation for privatisation. Subsequently a number of subsidiary companies have been sold.

SUBSIDIARIES SOLD

Management buyouts

Devon General Limited - August 1986
Badgerline Limited - September 1986
Cheltenham and Gloucester Omnibus Company Limited -
    October 1986
The Southern Vectis Omnibus Company Limited -
    October 1986
The Maidstone and District Motor Services Limited -
    November 1986
Cambus Limited - December 1986
The Eastern National Omnibus Company Limited -
    December 1986
Midland Red Coaches Limited - December 1986
Midland Red (West) Limited - December 1986
Potteries Motor Traction Company Limited -
    December 1986
South Midland Limited - December 1986
Trent Motor Traction Company Limited - December 1986
The City of Oxford Motor Services Limited - January 1987
East Yorkshire Motor Services Limited - February 1987
Eastern Counties Omnibus Limited - February 1987
West Riding Automobile Company Limited - February 1987
The Yorkshire Traction Company Limited - February 1987
East Kent Road Car Company Limited - March 1987
Provincial Bus Company Limited - May 1987
Northern General Transport Company Limited - May 1987
National Welsh Omnibus Services Limited - May 1987
South Wales Transport Company Limited - May 1987
Brighton & Hove Bus & Coach Company Limited - May 1987
Wilts & Dorset Bus Company Limited - June 1987

Privatisation in the Transport Sector

Private sales to:

Frontsource Limited

Alder Valley Engineering Limited
Bristol Engineering Limited
Carlyle Works Limited
Eastern National Engineering Limited
H & D Distribution Limited
Kent Engineering (NBC) Limited
Southdown Engineering Services Limited
United Counties Engineering Limited
    - all February 1987

ATL (Holdings) Limited (Pleasurama Group)

National Holidays Limited - July 1986
NTE Coaches Limited - February 1987

Stagecoach Limited

Hampshire Bus Company Limited - April 1987
Pilgrim Coaches Limited - April 1987

Gurna Limited

Voyage National SA - July 1987

ADVISORS

Financial advisors to HM Government

Price Waterhouse

Financial advisors to the company

Barclays de Zoete Wedd Limited

Solicitors to the company

Slaughter and May

APPENDIX 3b: National Freight Company - private sale, February 1982

BUSINESS

National Freight is Britain's largest road freight business, providing standard and specialised distribution services.

SALE DETAILS

Vendor

Secretary of State for Transport

Purchaser

National Freight Consortium plc (a management consortium).

Share capital

£5 million.

Gross proceeds of sale

£7 million net; £54 million paid for National Freight Consortium Limited less £47 million paid into the under-funded pension scheme by HM Government.

Net assets sold

£93.3 million at 13 June 1981, after eliminating a provision for unfunded pension liabilities eventually settled by HM Government and after £100m of HM Government debt was written off.

Price/earnings ratio

1.6 times based on the net proceeds above and the estimated results for the year ended 3 October 1981.

Privatisation in the Transport Sector

Gearing ratio (debt/equity)

19% based on a pro forma balance sheet as at 13 June 1981, as adjusted for the pension liabilities settled by HM Government.

ADVISORS

Financial advisors to the consortium

Barclays Merchant Bank Limited

Financial advisors to HM Government

J Henry Schroder Wagg & Co Limited

Solicitors to the consortium and offer

Ashurst, Morris, Crisp & Co

Solicitors to the company

Freshfields

Resistrars

Lloyds Bank Limited

Source: Privatisation: facts (Price Waterhouse, London, 1987).

APPENDIX 4: BAA PLC, September 1987

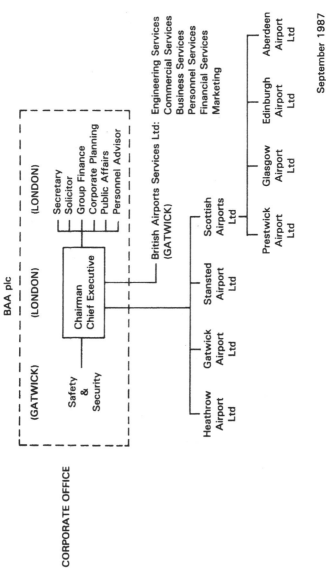

CORPORATE OFFICE

BAA plc

(GATWICK)   (LONDON)   (LONDON)

Safety & Security

Chairman
Chief Executive

Secretary
Solicitor
Group Finance
Corporate Planning
Public Affairs
Personnel Advisor

British Airports Services Ltd: Engineering Services
(GATWICK)   Commercial Services
     Business Services
     Personnel Services
     Financial Services
     Marketing

Heathrow Airport Ltd

Gatwick Airport Ltd

Stansted Airport Ltd

Scottish Airports Ltd

Prestwick Airport Ltd

Glasgow Airport Ltd

Edinburgh Airport Ltd

Aberdeen Airport Ltd

September 1987

APPENDIX 5: British Airports Authority, July 1986

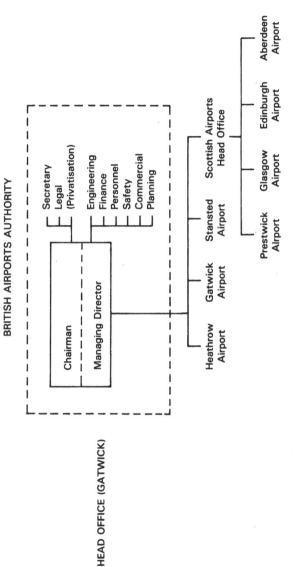

BRITISH AIRPORTS AUTHORITY

HEAD OFFICE (GATWICK)

Chairman

Managing Director

Secretary
Legal (Privatisation)
Engineering
Finance
Personnel
Safety
Commercial
Planning

Heathrow Airport
Gatwick Airport
Stansted Airport
Scottish Airports Head Office

Prestwick Airport
Glasgow Airport
Edinburgh Airport
Aberdeen Airport

July 1986

13

Privatisation in the Water Sector

W.R. Harper*

Privatisation of the water industry presents a combination of some of the most difficult questions and issues that have arisen to date in the government's programme of privatis- ation of public sector services. It involves the questions of monopoly regulation, of environmental and community protection, and of disaggregation of an existing public sector organisation. To provide a backcloth for issues for review and debate, it is helpful to outline the nature of the functions of the region of the water industry in England and Wales, and some of the changes in the nature of that industry and the public perception of it that have brought privatisation to the fore as an issue.

NATURE OF THE PRESENT ARRANGEMENTS

Water services in England and Wales are administered by ten regional water authorities and by 28 statutory water companies. (In Scotland different arrangements apply. River management functions are separated from the water utility functions, which remain largely in local government hands.) The statutory water companies are responsible for drinking water supplies in approximately one-third of England and Wales. They are statutory companies set up under parlimentary powers and cannot currently be regarded as normal Companies Act companies.

The ten regional water authorities administer a range of water-related functions. The bulk of their responsibilities relate to clean water supply, the operation of sewers and

---

* Managing Director, Thames Water

the treatment and disposal of water-borne wastes. These clean and dirty water functions account for around 90 per cent of turnover and activity, and for the vast bulk of their capital investment programmes.

In addition to these basic utility functions, the water authorities are also responsible for two important areas of regulation affecting water management:

(1) The control and licensing of water resources. This function involves planning the requirements of all water users for water over long time-periods and the licensing of access to both surface and underground water sources. The aim is to conserve from an environmental point of view the naturally available resource.

(2) The planning and management of natural water quality. This involves monitoring the present state of quality of surface and ground waters, forecasting future movements in condition, setting targets for quality in surface, ground and coastal waters, and then setting standards for discharges of effluent to the water courses aimed at securing these overall quality standards.

In both areas the water authorities are both regulator and major operator, since they take perhaps the largest part of water resources for their own supply purposes and they are the major dischargers of polluting material through their sewerage and sewage treatment function. This structuring of functions has been generally described as producing a combination of poacher and gamekeeper roles, has become the subject of increasing controversy and has been a major factor in the progress of the privatisation debate.

In addition to utility and regulatory functions, the water authorities also administer a number of services giving general community benefits, the largest of which is land drainage and flood protection. This involves management and improvement of the natural watercourses and coastal areas to avoid flooding protection. This service is currently financed largely by precept upon local authorities. There are also a number of smaller functions which include the management of fisheries, the maintenance and improvement of fish stocks in water courses. Navigation functions are exercised by only three water authorities, the largest one of which is on the River Thames. Water authorities also have a number of general conservation and recreation powers associated with their ownership and management of water space and their related amenities.

There has been a major shift in the way water services are regarded in the public sector. In the latter part of the nineteenth century they were very much seen as part of the major municipal local government development of that particular time, most obviously water supply and the development of the sewerage function. Since that time there had been little major change in the structure of the water management services, founded largely in local government, the only substantial changes being the creation of river boards to look after the river management functions and the land drainage function, and the increasing use of joint local authority boards for water supply and sewerage to serve areas not sensibly co-terminus with the smaller local government boundaries. In the early 1970s it became clear that the challenges facing water services were such that this patchwork of provision by local authorities, by river boards and by joint water boards cound not adequately respond to the problems likely to face the industry. These problems included increasingly scarce water resources, increasing pollution of the natural water environment, major asset deterioration problems in both water supply and sewerage services, and rising customer and environmental expections of the industry.

In 1974 the ten regional water authorities were formed. Their borders were drawn on hydrological boundaries, broadly the natural drainage boundaries of the river system. Whilst only Thames Water covers the catchment area of a single river, all the other water authorities encompass one or more natural river systems, and manage that river system in its totality from the abstraction of water from its natural source to the return of that water at the end of the drainage systems. These arrangements have largely been regarded as a technical, operational and scientific success. What were until recently seen to be less successful were the financial management regime of the industry, its management performance and its customer relations performance.

This developing perception of water authorities led to a change in its statutory structure in 1983, when the original local government-style boards of management were removed and much smaller nationalised industry-style boards introduced. This was done with the overt purpose of bringing a more commercial style of management to the water authorities, aimed largely at sharpening their managerial efficiency and their reaction to the needs of customers. To that end a number of new chairmen, board members and in some areas senior executives were brought into the industry to produce the new attitudes, thinking and expertise that was required to achieve this change of stance in the industry.

At the same time the government was also continuing to develop its financial policies, seeking over a period of years to reduce to zero the financing required to be provided to the industry by government. Through the medium of the National Loans Fund the government was providing several hundred million pounds of financing to the water industry and in the early 1980s it declared its intention of phasing out that net financing contribution to the industry. This was to be achieved by restraining costs and investment, but also by increasing profit targets with their attendant price increases. That policy has been implemented over a series of years, and has become increasingly controversial in its impact and implications. Whilst the industry in total is now at break-even point in financing terms, there is within the industry a wide scatter of achievement. At the time of writing (October 1987), the Thames Water Authority generates very substantial financing surpluses, in the current year of the order of a £100m, whereas other authorities, particularly those in the north of England where substantial pollution and asset dereliction problems occur, still remain dependent on loan financing from government in order to maintain capital investment programmes.

The creation of publicly owned water authorities which are now substantially profitable and which have deployed the changing managerial attitudes has naturally led on to a pressure to look at them very much in parallel with private sector concerns. The familar arguments about government interference in the running of commercially orientated public sector businesses have surfaced with the water authorities as the new managements came to grips with their task. It was a combination of these managerial attitudes and the financial situation of the industry which gave rise to a call both from the industry itself and from the government to examine the prospects of privatisation.

The government's first Discussion Papers on Privatisation came out during 1985. A White Paper on the future of the industry appeared in early 1986 which indicated that a large part of the functions of the regional water authorities were to be privatised, the exception set out at that stage being the land drainage and flood protection function. The original intention was that the privatisation would be pushed through at a fast pace in order to try to achieve the main legislation during 1986 and 1987, but it subsequently proved too technically and politically difficult a task. In the later part of 1986 the Secretary of State halted rapid progress towards privatisation and the matter remained at a much lower key until the recent general election. In preparing for that general election the present government had stated in outline terms its intention of approaching water privatisation in a different way. It signalled that it wished to separate out the regulatory and community functions from the basic utility functions of water supply and sewerage and to retain these functions in the public sector, privatising just the water supply and sewerage functions. The government had recently published a consultation document intended to explore with the industry and with interested groups more generally the implications of that particular split. What I will seek to do in this chapter is to examine some of the implications of that approach of the government, and then to explore the issues concerned with the privatisation of the utility functions.

DIVISION OF WATER AUTHORITY FUNCTIONS

The present package of water authority functions is managed and operated cohesively to obtain the benefits of interaction between the various water-related services. This management approach is described as integrated river basin management. It enables the water authorities to support the various objectives they have for their services by interrelating the management of the individual parts. Thus, for instance, there are clearly interactions between water resource management and management of the water supply function. In the Thames region the supply function is operated in support of its water resources strategies. Similarly, sewerage treatment operates closely with management of natural water quality, and again the methods of operation of the Authority's sewage treatment works contribute towards strategies for achieving water quality objectives. Indeed, all the services closely interact both in terms of overall, management strategies and in day-to-day operations where the administrative boundary lines are not necessarily sacrosanct in practical operational situations, and particularly where emergencies arise. The government's proposals now herald a division of these functions with the water supply and sewerage functions becoming the responsibility of water services public limited companies (WSPLCs) and the regulatory and river management functions becoming the responsibility of a new body to be called the National Rivers Authority (NRA).

The water authorities are much concerned about the loss of the operational benefits of integrated river basin management. On the other hand, in its consultation document the government has stated quite clearly that it believes the benefits of carrying the utility functions into the private sector will outweigh the losses arising from the disaggregation of water services functions. It is certainly clear that if the utility functions are to be carried into the private sector the poacher/gamekeeper combination of functions which has proved to be tolerable within public sector control is clearly not acceptable in political and public-interest terms and has been an important factor in the change of pattern of functions now proposed. Whilst some of the arguments concerning the need to keep the organisations in total are perhaps unique to water services, there are points being made in the water industry situation that are familiar ones when the approach to privatisation of a public sector concern is being discussed. The industry is clearly keen to keep together its package of functions and seeks to demonstrate its operational effectiveness and efficiency, and its commercial development potential. The management is also pointing out that the separation of functions will involve some significant administrative and management disruption, endangering not only the continued effective operation of the services to the public but perhaps delaying and disrupting the process of flotation. The government, on the other hand, is concerned that certain of the public-interest elements in the present function package can only be administered within the public sector and have acted accordingly. An important issue to be determined in the water industry over the next few years is the extent to which that disaggregation of functions is proved to be unavoidable and can be achieved against tight time-scales without any disruption of service and without producing adverse effects both internally and externally to delay the process of privatisation.

One approach to minimising the losses of integrated management and the disruption that may occur has been to examine the potential for contracting between the National River Authority and WSPLCs. Clearly, the WSPLCs could retain some of the operating capability they currently hold and could offer a contracting service to the NRA. The government has made it clear, however, that it could expect those services to be offered in competition with other private sector organisations capable of offering similar contracting services. Within the water industry there is now a considerable amount of effort being devoted to examining what would be the implications, for both the NRA and the WSPLCs, of contracting arrangements. The emerging consensus opinion is that the contracting could only be approached on a fully commmercial basis by both the NRA and the companies. Such arrangements would not be proper if they blurred accountabilities or sought merely to fudge issues of responsibility and resourcing in the interest of avoiding administrative and operational restructuring.

The other approach being advocated by some RWAs involves confining the NRA to a regulatory and supervisory role, and assigning operational management responsibilities to the WSPLCs on a long-licence basis. Such an approach does offer the prospect of keeping the essential public interest features of the industry in the public sector whilst retaining broad-based and integrated WSPLCs. For this to be achieved, however, complex legislative and relationship problems need to be solved, which will require innovative, and perhaps unprecedented, solutions. These issues are only now emerging as the result of the government's consultation exercise, and will be the subject of intense discussion and negotiation in the coming months.

ISSUES IN UTILITY PRIVATISATION

Monopoly regulation

The services of water supply, sewerage and sewage disposal are clearly monopoly services, and there is no prospect of creating any form of main stream alternative provision in order to secure the benefits of competition for the consumer and the public at large. The water industry privatisation cannot be about producing a competitive environment. It is the conversion of a public monopoly to a private regulated monopoly. The industry itself does not contest the need for effective regulation, and observing the experience of other privatised industries accepts that an effective regulatory machine will also serve the interests of the companies if it is seen to build confidence and produce the right relationship with the customer.

The regulatory framework that is being developed is based in broad terms on the packages that have emerged from the British Telecom and British Gas privatisations, in that the central points of control are price and standards of service.

(1) Price control - control of prices is likely to be based on the now familiar 'RPI - X' formula. A development of the formula is anticipated to take into account the increasing operating cost and investment burdens arising from the need in many parts of the industry to up-grade the performance of asset structures and to meet rising expectations of customer service and environmental quality. Major investment programmes for extending water treatment capability, sewage treatment works performance and coastal water quality have heavy financial impacts on the industry which would need to be recognised in the price control formula if investor confidence in the companies is to be maintained.

(2) Standards of service - the industry's basic standards of service in terms of drinking water quality and sewage treatment works performance are set by statute. Many aspects of other service performance are set by non-statutory indicators currently in use in the industry for its own internal management purposes and for discussion with government and with consumer groups. It is expected that these levels of service indicators will be sharpened and form the basis of dialogues with the Director-General on performance.

(3) Asset condition - a matter of concern both to the industry and to the public at large is the condition of fixed assets, particularly the underground assets, the water mains and sewers. In reality there is a wide range of asset conditions in the industry and the much publicised dereliction problem is not in fact as universal or as extreme as has been depicted in some of the popular press. However, the industry recognises this area of concern and has been devoting its time and resources in recent years to surveying formally and

understanding the performance of its system and to assessing the works necessary to bring it up to full effectiveness. It is acknowledged that asset condition will eventually reflect itself in performance of the organisation, but given long lead-times between deterioration of assets and loss of customer perceived performance, systems need to be developed to give assurance to regulators and to the public that the companies will maintain the stock of assets at an adequate level in the public interest.

(4) Insolvency - special provisions are being considered to guard against possible insolvency situations of the WSPLCs. Clearly, managements cannot be protected from the financial consequences of incompetence or mismanagement, but at the same time the consumers and public at large cannot be placed at risk from any collapse in the performance of the water services. To meet this conflict special insolvency provisions are being developed which would allow an insolvency administrator to take over operation of the company to ensure delivery of service, whilst the implications for management and shareholders were worked out and remedial steps put in place.

One of the features of concern in the water industry privatisation is the emergence of a proliferation of regulatory agencies. The Director-General has already been mentioned in connection with economic regulation and with the oversight of standards of performance as they relate to the customers. Government will maintain an interest in the performance of the industry both in terms of its primary standards of performance and the statutory involvement in the quality of its services. Her Majesty's Inspectorate of Pollution will also be involved in the performance of its waste-water treatments plants, and agencies such as the Monopolies and Mergers Commission and the Office of Fair Trading will have a locus in the activities of the organisation. The NRA could have regulatory and operational interfaces with the WSPLCs, and certain of the quality review functions are in the hands of local authorities. This presents both to the industry and to the public at large a complex of regulatory mechanisms with the real risk of overlap, duplication and confusion. This would not only affect the industry but the general public may feel and experience the lack of clarity in the roles and relationships.

ACCEPTABILITY OF WATER SERVICES AS UTILITIES

Whilst within the industry and in informed groups it is becoming common to talk of the water supply and sewerage functions as utilities, this perception is a recent one. In the not-too-distant past these services were seen as part of the local portfolio of community provisions funded from the local property tax from the rates. It is only in recent years that the utility nature of these services has become more pronounced - that the charge for the services has been increasingly distinguished from the rateable value charge, and with the nature of the financing, customer relations and performance control becoming more akin to the other more traditional utility services. Privatisation in fact takes this trend and extends it logically as a continuation of developments seen in recent years.

However, it has to be acknowledged that there remain deep-seated misunderstandings and misgivings about presenting these water services in this way. There are still large numbers of people, both lay and informed, who are concerned that the water supply services and the drainage services are not analogous to the utility functions. There is not yet a widespread acceptance that these services should necessarily be paid for by measurement rather than part of a tax base, and this is evidenced by the public concern about the industry's and the governments's proposals to extend the use of metering within the industry. I think there is little disagreement in informed circles with the view that water services like any other would benefit from being charged for on a measurement basis rather than any form of flat rate or taxation charge. Public health requirements can be looked after by the tariff structure and by social security measures, but the bulk of the demand for water services is now commercial, industrial or amenity-based, and should not carry any obligation to charge other than on a normal pricing basis. There are still many people who believe there is something wrong if such services are provided 'at a profit'.

RATIONALE FOR PRIVATISATION

If it is accepted that the water utility services are available for a price as in line with other services, then the issue of ownership in a sense becomes irrelevant. The primary issue at stake in such an environment is that of proper regulation of their monopoly activities. Inside and outside of the industry there is no challenge to the need effectively to regulate price, performance and the public interest elements of the activities of these organisations. What is now under debate is whether government ownership is the right, and indeed the only, form of achieving monopoly regulation. Much has been made (and need not be repeated here) of the problems arising from government control of, and involvement in, the management activities of industries operating on a trading basis. I think it is now fairly widely accepted that management should be free to manage against price and output targets, free from the interference of government. In the water industry it is particularly clear that the government's policies have been influenced by primarily financial interests that go beyond the interests of the consumers of the industry. In such circumstances privatisation will be a means of freeing the water industry and its consumers from having the industry operated as part of the wider set of mechanisms available for government to achieve their financial and broader policy objectives. It does offer the prospect of a sharper form of customer accountability, as well as opening up the potential for developing and diversifying devices on a commercial basis.

On the other hand, it has to be acknowledged that in public ownership the water services have been operated technically and operationally as a package in the public interest, using the ability to operate across the range of functions without concern for administrative boundary lines or financing complications. These benefits of public ownership will be lost if a division of functions occurs.

The debate on privatisation in the water industry contains, in my view, deeply political issues underlying some of the managerial, financial and legal problems. Water services, more than any other of the public sector industries, lie on the boundary line between the public and private sectors. A government committed to changing those boundary lines was certain to approach the water industry sooner or later, and to find it to be one of the most difficult and controversial areas.

14

The Regulation of a Privatised Electricity Supply Industry

George Yarrow*

GENERAL REMARKS

Regulatory issues in utility industries such as electricity supply are numerous, frequently complex, and generally (as yet) poorly understood in Britain. To date regulatory policy has focused heavily upon price-control formulae (e.g. RPI - X) for average prices of a basket of goods and/or services but, as the experience in telecommunications indicates, the apparent simplicity of this approach is illusory. Thus, issues that need to be tackled include the following: the prices that are to be regulated; the value of X; the base-year price levels and structures; the methods to be used in the construction of regulated price indices; the scope for relative price changes in the initial indexation period; whether to allow adjustments for certain changes in input costs; incentives for improved service quality (including security of supply); information disclosure requirements; the timing and methods of regulatory reviews; the criteria to be used in reviews; access terms (for example, to transmission and distribution facilities, power pools, and so on; and controls on anti-competitive conduct.

While many of the above issues appear to involve relatively technical matters, the decisions taken will nevertheless have substantial implications for economic behaviour. The following list sets out some of the things that can go wrong if mistakes are made:

* Hertford College, Oxford

- scope of regulation: cross-subsidisation; incentives for predatory and anti-competitive pricing; higher entry barriers;
- the value of X, base-level prices, and tariff rebalancing: allocative inefficiency; deficient service quality; sub-optimal investment;
- index construction: allocative inefficiency; predatory and anticompetitive pricing; higher entry barriers;
- service quality: deficient service standards; lower security of supply;
- information disclosure: anti-competitive behaviour; poor incentives for internal efficiency;
- review decisions: poor incentives for internal efficiency; higher discount rates and underinvestment;
- access terms and conduct regulation: higher entry barriers; and
- detailed analysis of these and other regulatory problems is contained in Vickers and Yarrow (1988).

In the electricity supply industry (ESI) the situation is further complicated by the technology of the industry which, apart from exhibiting natural monopoly characteristics in transmission and distribution, also leads to a number of 'externalities' associated with the integrated supply network. It is doubtful, therefore, that all transactions can efficiently be organised by means of arm's-length contractual relationships. Thus, for example, it is important to beware of slipping into the trap of assuming that simply increasing the number of generating companies will automatically lead to the establishment of effective competition in wholesale (bulk) markets. Without strong regulation, the outcome might simply be explicit or implicit collusion, and the creation of an unregulated cartel would probably be the worst possible outcome. In the short- to medium-term at least, whatever decisions are taken about the future structure of the industry, regulation of wholesale markets will be as much needed as regulation of retail markets, and this is a further complicating factor for policy-makers.

Regulation of a Privatised Electricity Supply Industry

In what follows, I will consider only one or two aspects of regulatory policy for the ESI, but it will be useful to make an initial general point about the underlying issues. In the utility industries, public policy has in reality to deal with two distinct monopoly positions. The first is monopoly in product markets, which arises from cost conditions in networks: it is generally inefficient to duplicate transmission lines, gas and water pipelines, and so on. The second - and, although it has not been generally appreciated, much the more important - is monopoly in the supply of information. If information were perfect, the regulatory task would be relatively trivial - a point made by Hayek many years ago in his famous debate with Lange on the merits of socialist planning. It is limited information that leads to unfavourable policy trade-offs, and failure to take this Hayekian lesson to heart accounts for several of the difficulties that are beginning to surface in telecommunications and gas supply. If the information available to regulators is poor, in the longer term there will be no way of escaping cost-plus pricing and the weak incentives for internal efficiency that are associated with it. The use of the RPI - X formulae may induce the complacent belief that this problem has been avoided, but after five years, say, the formulae themselves will come up for review; and, unlike in political life and many parts of the financial world, in the ESI five years if very much the short run.

ELECTRICITY DISTRIBUTION

Electricity distribution is a natural monopoly. It follows that there is no way of increasing competition among firms for the business of final consumers without incurring excessively high cost-penalties. That is not to say, however, that all competition is infeasible: it is quite possible to create competition amoung monopolists in areas such as innovation and cost reduction which, in the long haul, are often of much greater significance for consumer welfare than price competition. How can this be done?

The key to promoting competition in electricity distribution lies in preventing the monopolisation of information flows to regulators. If Area Boards are given more independence, regulators will have a greater variety of sources of information on which to base their decisions. In principle, this will enable regulators to reward relatively good performance and penalise relatively bad performance in much the way that a competitive market does. In other words, if the information monopoly does not exist, good regulation can mimic the incentives of a competitive market, even though the firms involved are actually monopolists in their own areas of the country. The jargon term for this effect is 'yardstick competition'.

The introduction of yardstick competition would require the government to be much more explicit as to the criteria that will guide regulatory decisions than it has been in the past: leaving matters to be decided by the Monopolies and Mergers Commission - a body which is, in any case, not well qualified for the purpose - on broadly defined and highly nebulous public interest criteria is simply not a satisfactory option. Similarly, yardstick competition requires the existence of several independent electricity distribution companies. The government should therefore strongly resist any suggestions that the Area Boards should be amalgamated into a single distribution company. This would create an information monopoly and, for the reasons given above, would be damagingly anti-competitive.

If the government does decide both to retain several independent distribution companies and to take the more radical step of basing its regulatory philosophy on yardstick competition, there is a variety of methods of implementing the approach (see Vickers and Yarrow (1988), Chapter 11, for some suggestions). Suffice it to say that relatively simple procedural rules - that would not unduly tax the intellects of even the most obstinate members of the 'keep it simple' school - are readily available.

It is ironic that it is in electricity distribution, where natural monopoly conditions are most widespread, that regulatory problems are the simplest to deal with. The reason is, of course, that the existence of semi-autonomous Area Boards means that the information monopoly is already half broken and pro-competitive (in the broad sense) policy measures need not rely upon substantial restructuring of the industry. Although most discussions of methods to promote competition have focused upon the possibility of restructuring the CEGB, my own view is that this emphasis is somewhat misguided. In many ways it is the future of the Area Boards that is the more important issue. Properly done, privatisation will greatly enhance the role of the Boards and, provided that they receive some protection from the market power of a dominant bulk supplier, will enable them to exert considerable competitive pressures in wholesale markets.

BULK SUPPLY

Because of the difficult trade-off between co-ordination (to overcome externalities) and competition, it would be unwise to rely solely upon structural remedies to promote competition in wholesale markets. Rather, strong regulation of conduct at the wholesale stage is advisable (at least for the medium term), whatever structural option is chosen.

On past precedents, and given political constraints , it is possible that the government will want to avoid a major programme of industrial restructuring at this stage of the privatisation exercise. While some commentators might regard this as unfortunate, it is important to consider what can be done to promote greater competition and more effective regulation in existing structural conditions. Even if electricity generation continues to be dominated by the CEGB's successor company, it will in fact be possible to travel a fair distance in the desired direction if the government can get the details of the regulatory structure right. In this respect the two aims of policy should be, firstly, to weaken the CEGB's information monopoly and secondly, reduce barriers to new entry. Gas privatisation left much to be desired on both counts, but history need not repeat itself.

The CEGB's information monopoly can be reduced by strict disclosure requirements and strong regulatory powers. There is, however, no close substitute for the existence of a competing firm or firms providing independent information as to what is and is not possible and incentives for better performance by the dominant firm for fear of loss of markets and profits. Even if the CEGB is not to be radically restructured, there is still a strong case for a partial divestiture of some of its assets. One or two small competing companies are much better than none at all. Indeed, by a common result of economics and statistical theory, the first pieces of information are likely to be more valuable than the later ones - the 'law' of the diminishing marginal value of information. Provided that regulatory and competition policies protect the smaller firm(s) from anti-competitive behaviour by the market leader, even small rivals could have salutory effects on the CEGB (cf. Mercury in telecommunications).

Regulation of the conduct of a dominant electricity generation company is also vital if entry barriers into the industry are to be lowered. The Energy Act 1983 removed certain statutory obstacles to entry but has largely been ineffective in promoting private production. Like the Oil and Gas (Enterprise) Act 1982, the aims of the legislation were laudable but the technical implementation of the government's intent was flawed.

To prevent entry into the industry being blocked by a dominant generating company, regulators will need to ensure that newcomers have access to the national transmission system (and to any power pooling arrangements) on fair terms, and that the dominant company does not engage in anti-competitive pricing policies. Over the past five years there is little doubt that private producers of electricity could have matched or improved upon the unit cost performance of the CEGB, if only because the latter has been arm-twisted into purchasing coal from the National Coal Board (now British Coal) at prices above market levels. Nevertheless, entry has been viewed as unprofitable because the CEGB has had power to manipulate wholesale tariff structures in a manner that places entrants at a disadvantage.

The CEGB's ability to engage in anti-competitive pricing will continue unless checked by regulatory controls on the structure of wholesale tariffs. That is 'RPI - X+Y' restrictions on the average price level will not be enough: by appropriate manipulations of the service, demand, and energy charges in the Bulk Supply Tariff, a privatised CEGB could, for more or less any reasonable average price level, to rig its tariff structure that Area Boards would find it unprofitable to switch custom to a private producer, even if the latter were more efficient than the CEGB. In the past the Area Boards have been content to go along with the CEGB's strategy but, since such acquiescence would be damaging to their own profits, I do not expect that privatised distribution companies will be quite so passive. Ultimately it would be possible for them to seek redress against tariff rigging by appeals to European competition policy (under Articlee 86 of the Rome Treaty, for example), but it would be far better for the issue to be dealt with by regulatory policy in the UK, not least because of the implications for the domestic coal industry.

Policy towards the coal industry is relevant because

fair competition in bulk supplies requires that generating companies have access to their major input on equal terms. Continued use of a dominant generating company to prop up the domestic coal industry would, as well as being undesirable on allocative-efficiency gounds, quickly lead to a regulatory quagmire in which UK and European policies came into conflict. If it is to remain, therefore, support for the domestic coal industry is best provided by direct financial aid, rather than at the cost of weaker competition and inefficient pricing in the ESI.

My own preferred solution would be something as follows:

(1) RPI - X+Y regulation of average wholesale prices for a fixed initial period, with Y linked to international coal prices and X set to allow, say, a five-year transition from current to internationally competitive prices for coal inputs;

(2) periodic reviews by a specialised regulatory body responsible for both the gas and electricity industries;

(3) review criteria that partially condition decisions in respect of one firm on the performance of other firms;

(4) limitations on the ability of large or dominant generating companies to recover costs by means of fixed charges (i.e. charges unrelated to demand) or other 'lock-in' pricing systems; and

(5) if the grid system is operated by a dominant generating company, a requirement that the dominant firm purchases any supplies offered to it by rivals at prices (net of transmission costs) equivalent to its own charges to distribution companies.

Taken together, suggestions (4) and (5) would substantially reduce the power of a dominant incumbent firm to restrict new entry either through its control of grid operations or through its ability to engage in anti-competitive pricing.

REFERENCES

Vickers, J.S. and G.K. Yarrow (1988) Privatisation: an economic analysis. M.I.T. Press, Cambridge, MA

Part IV

The Lessons

15

The UK Privatisation Model:
Is it Transferable to Developing Countries?

Colin Kirkpatrick*

Britain's experiment in privatising state-owned enterprises has become an international phenomenon. Since the beginning of the 1980s, the concept has been espoused by governments of widely differing ideological persuasion, in both developed and developing countries. In the Third World, a growing number of countries have formulated detailed proposals for privatising significant segments of economic activity, often with the active encouragement of international lending agencies and bilateral aid donors. Privatisation can truly be described as one of the growth industries of the present decade, with the British merchant banking houses prominent in the export of expertise and consultancy services to various parts of the globe. The objective of this chapter is to consider the transferability of the UK privatisation 'model' to less developed countries (LDCs). To what extent are the claims made for the benefits of privatisation likely to be realised in Third World countries?

Lacking a precise definition, the term privatisation has been used to convey the general notion that the role of the market in the economy should be enhanced vis à vis that of the state, that the share of the private sector should increase, with a corresponding reduction in government involvement in the economy. Here, we will distinguish between two main uses of the term. The first refers to a change in the ownership of an enterprise (or part of an

---

* Professor of Development Economics, University of Bradford.
An earlier version of this chapter was presented at the Political Studies Association Annual Conference, University of Aberdeen, April 1987

enterprise) from the public to private sector. Denational-isation or divestiture can proceed in a number of different ways. In the industrial countries where capital markets are well developed, it can be brought about by the sale of all or part of the privatised enterprise's equity to the public. In LDCs, however, where capital markets are rudimentary or non-existent, denationalisation is more likely to involve the sale of the enterprise as a complete entity. Denational-isation may also take the form of joint ventures, which introduce a private sector involvement into the public enterprise. In extreme cases, divestiture may involve the abandonment or formal liquidation of the state-owned enterprise.

A second mode of privatisation involves the liberal-isation, or deregulation, of entry into activities previously restricted to public sector enterprises. The removal of restrictions on market entry is intended to increase the role of competition, and to the extent that private enterprises are successful in entering the hitherto protected markets, a variant of privatisation will have occurred, even though no transfer of ownership of assets has been involved.

The mode of privatisation chosen will be determined in part by the particular objectives which privatisation is intended to meet. The next section therefore examines the motives for, and perceived benefits of, privatisation in LDCs. This is followed by a consideration of the potential impact of privatisation, particularly on enterprise perform-ance. The final section contains some concluding comments.

THE MOTIVES FOR PRIVATISATION

In the UK, the privatisation programme has been driven by both political ideology and pragmatism. When the programme began in 1979, it was largely a reaction to the shortcomings of the public enterprise sector's performance and the failure of previous attempts to exercise effective parliamentary control of their management and operations. By making enterprises accountable to private investors, privatisation was expected to result in increased efficiency and better management. In addition, the proceeds from privatisation met a rising share of the governments's revenue needs, and helped to finance tax cuts. As the programme proceeded, broader political benefits were seen to result from privatisation, through wider share ownership and 'popular capitalism' and employee involvement.

It is not the task of this chapter to evaluate in detail the extent to which these gains have been borne out in practice in the UK. What can be noted, however, is that the claims for privatisation are being subjected to increasingly critical scrutiny. There is growing controversy over the behaviour and performance of the two large privatised utilities, British Gas and British Telecom. Furthermore, it is clear that the impact of privatisation on company performance needs to be seen against the general background of buoyant economic conditions and generally improving performance, thus, making it difficult to disentangle cause-and-effect relations (de Jonqulerès, 1987). Finally, the effect of the recent (Autumn 1987) stock market crash on new shareholders may prove to be a major blow to the spread of popular capitalism, with longer-run political repercussions.

The inclusion of privatisation on the policy agenda in many LDCs reflects a similar confluence of political ideology and pragmatism. Privatisation is one element in a general shift in development policy away from the dirigiste approach that characterised development thinking in the 1950s and 1960s. The perceived failures of development planning and the import substituting industrialisation strategy led to a reorientation towards a market-based view of the development process, in which 'getting the prices right' is seen as the key to more rapid and sustained economic growth.

In the privatisation context, the market-oriented approach to development policy translates into a desire to reduce the share of the public sector in the economy, which is viewed as a constraint on economic expansion:

> It is now widely evident that the public sector is overextended, given the present scarcities of financial resources, skilled manpower, and organis- ational capacity. This has resulted in slower growth than might have been achieved with available resources, and accounts for the present crisis (World Bank, 1981, p. 5).

An ideological commitment to the market can be detected in the policies of the bilateral lending agencies. Commander and Killick (1988) quote from a recent directive given to USAID officials for the orientation of their policy

Is it Transferable to Developing Countries?

discussions with aid recipients:

> Policy dialogue should be used to encourage LDCs
> to follow free market principles for sustained
> economic growth and to move away from govern-
> ment intervention in the economy. This allows the
> market to determine how economic resources are
> most productively allocated and how benefits
> should be distributed.

Where privatisation is seen as one part of a free-market
ideological vision, 'its propositions have become a matter of
belief, so that the testing of claims against the apparent
reality is not regarded as conclusive' (Heald and Thomas,
1986, p. 52). Nevertheless, it is important to note that there
is little empirical support for the general proposition that
the public sector is 'over-extended' in LDCs (Kirkpatrick,
1986; Nunnenkamp, 1986).

The public enterprise sector lies at the heart of the
privatisation debate, and dissatisfaction with the contribution of the state-owned enterprises to the development
process constitutes the single most important motivation for
privatisation in LDCs. Originally established to become
leaders in the LDCs' industrialisation drive and to generate
public savings for investment and growth, the state-owned
enterprise sector is widely perceived to have performed
poorly in fulfilling these objectives.

Perhaps the most common cause of economic inefficiency in the public enterprise sector is political interference. In many LDCs the public enterprise is an important
instrument for political patronage. Senior staff are
frequently political appointments with little industrial
management experience; employment, purchasing and
pricing decisions are subject to political intervention; the
boundaries of government and enterprise control are ill-
defined and continually shifting. The absence of clearly
defined objectives and the limited operational autonomy
given to public enterprises inevitably have an adverse
impact on the efficient internal operations of the public
enterprise sector (Ayub and Hegstad, 1986). There is a
certain amount of evidence on the relationship between
market structure and firm-level performance in LDCs.
Various studies have examined the effect of seller
concentration in the manufacturing sector on price-cost
margins, and have found that in most cases, there is a

positive and statistically significant association between seller concentration and the profitability measure used (Kirkpatrick et al., 1984, Chapter 3). Typically, the relationship is a continuous one, with profit margins being progressively higher in those industries with the higher concentration levels. The evidence from LDCs is therefore consistent with the view that the allocative efficiency of firms - public and private - is improved by a competitive market environment.

While not denying that poor economic performance does occur in the public enterprise sector in LDCs, it is not the case that public enterprises inevitably perform worse than comparable private concerns. Millward's (1988) detailed examination of the available evidence on public and private enterprise performance leads to the conclusion that 'there is no evidence of a statistically satisfactory kind to suggest that public enterprises in LDCs have a lower level of technical efficiency than private firms operating at the same scale of operation'.

The overall financial deficit - defined as the difference between current plus capital expenditure and revenue plus receipts of current transfers and of non-government capital transfers - of public enterprises in LDCs averaged almost 4 per cent of GDP in the mid-1970s, as compared with an average of 1.7 per cent in the industrial countries (Short, 1984).

The financing requirements of the public enterprise sector have a direct effect on macroeconomic performance, and a concern with this impact is reflected in the priority given in the International Monetary Fund's (IMF's) stabilisation programmes to improving public enterprise financial performance. In a survey of 94 Fund-supported adjustment programmes in developing countries during the period 1980-4, it was found that 68 of the programmes included policy recommendations relating to non-financial state enterprises, aimed mainly at improving financial performance (IMF, 1986). Indeed, the current attention given to the financial position of the public enterprise sector in LDCs probably relates more to the macroeconomic consequences of large budget deficits than to a concern with profitability as an indicator of enterprise performance.

Caution needs to be exercised in interpreting financial profitability data, since market structure and regulations can affect the significance of profitabality as an indicator of performance. A monopoly position, with protection from foreign competition, can allow the public enterprise to make financial profits while its economic performance is poor. Price controls can adversely affect the public enterprises financial performance. In addition, public enterprises are often expected to fulfil certain social objectives which may also affect financial performance.

WILL PRIVATISATION WORK IN LDCs?

Privatisation, in the form of a change of ownership, has been advocated on the grounds that it will have a significant impact on economic performance at the enterprise level. It is argued that the change in ownership will impose the discipline of private capital markets on the enterprise, thereby improving productive efficiency. While this argument may be important in industrial countries, it has limited relevance to LDCs, where the capital market is typically underdeveloped and denationalisation will normally involve the sale of the enterprise to individual purchasers, or the introduction of private capital into joint ventures.

A change to partial or complete private ownership can be expected to lessen the scope for political intervention in the operations of the enterprise. The enterprise's objectives will be simplified and the likelihood of arbitrary 'interference' in operating decisions will be lessened, thereby contributing to an improvement in productive efficiency. It may be noted, however, that these changes are not conditional on privatisation: internal reform of the public enterprise is an alternative option for realising the same gains.

It was suggested earlier that allocative efficiency is a function of market structure rather than ownership. Thus, in the absence of competition, denationalisation is unlikely to result in major gains in efficiency performance.

If the principal objective of privatisation is to increase economic performance, the policy priority should be to increase competition, rather than to transfer ownership. However, market competition is often constrained in LDCs: for example, where the public enterprise is a natural monopoly, deregulation may simply permit the monopoly enterprise to engage in anti-competition, predatory activities designed to eliminate competing firms. Market liberalisation often forms one part of the structural adjustment programmes adopted by LDCs on the recommendation of the international development agencies. However, the experience with these programmes in Latin America and elsewhere has highlighted the difficulties of introducing a more competitive market environment (Corbo and de Melo, 1987).

In considering the potential impact of denationalisation it is important to distinguish between the consequences of ownership transfer, and the associated effects on the operations of the privatised enterprise. The immediate effect of asset sales will be a once-and-for-all reduction in the government deficit, but if the sales revenue is used to reduce taxation, the public sector deficit is increased in subsequent years. Where the privatised enterprise is a loss-making concern, the sale to the private sector will involve the government in the payment of a subsidy, which may be implicit or explicit, to the purchaser, and will therefore have little impact on the public finances (Mansoor, 1988). When a public enterprise monopoly is privatised and is granted continued protection from market competition, an improvement in financial performance may simply be a reflection of greater exploitation of market power.

The problems of implementing privatisation in LDCs are increased by the absence of a well-developed capital market. This means that divestiture will have to be made by direct placement with local or foreign interests large enough to handle the transaction. The government may be unwilling, however, to have its assets transferred to certain groups of potential buyers if it results in a further concentration of wealth. In some countries, it will be politically unacceptable to sell enterprises to wealthy racial or minority groups. Similar objections may be raised to increased ownership by foreign interests.

Resistance from interest groups that stand to lose from privatisation is likely to form a powerful political constraint. This opposition will come from the labour force employed in the public enterprises who fear job losses, and from government officials whose area of authority and opportunity for patronage will be reduced. Where liberalisation is threatened, further resistance will come from those groups who currently enjoy the protected economic rents created by the system of regulations and controls. The opposition by various sectional interests that are threatened by privatisation may well be more immediate and more vocally expressed than the anticipated longer-term benefits from greater economic efficiency.

CONCLUSION

The arguments advanced in the preceding section lead to the conclusion that the significance of privatisation as a policy option for LDCs has been exaggerated. Denationalisation is likely to be difficult to achieve, its potential benefits often appear to be limited, and its adoption may involve significant political costs. Deregulation is unlikely to be a sufficient condition for a more competitive market environment.

The current interest in privatisation does reflect a widespread concern with the performance of the public enterprise sector in LDCs, and 'despite the inconclusive nature of the evidence, it is difficult to believe that existing public enterprises are not capable of achieving significant improvements in efficiency' (Hemming and Mansoor, 1987, p. 6). If, as we have argued, the prospects for widespread privatisation in LDCs are more limited than the rhetoric would suggest, then internal restructuring of public enterprise organisation and management and public sector reform are likely to make a more significant, if less newsworthy, contribution to improving public enterprise performance in LDCs.

REFERENCES

Ayub, M.A. and S.O. Hegsted (1986) Public industrial enterprises: determinants of performance. World Bank Research Observer, 2 (1), 79-101

Commander, S. and T. Killick (1988) Privatisation in developing countries: a survey of the issues. In P. Cook and C. Kirkpatrick (eds), Privatisation in less developed countries, Wheatsheaf Books, Brighton

Cook, P. and C. Kirkpatrick (eds) (1988) Privatisation in less developed countries. Wheatsheaf Books, Brighton

Corbo, V. and J. de Melo (1987) Lessons from the Southern Cone policy reforms. World Bank Research Observer, 2 (2), 111-42

Heald, D. (1988) The relevance of UK privatisation for LDCs. In P. Cook and C. Kirkpatrick (eds), Privatisation in less developed countries, Wheatsheaf Books, Brighton
——— and D. Thomas (1986) Privatisation as theology. Public Policy and Administration, 1, 49-66

Hemming, R. and A.M. Mansoor (1987) Privatization and

public enterprises. IMF Working Paper, Fiscal Affairs Department, WP/87/9, 25 February

International Monetary Fund (IMF) (1986) Fund-supported programs, fiscal policy, and income distribution. Occasional Paper 46, Washington, DC

Jonquieres, G. de (1987) UK experience: competition still the issue. Financial Times (London), 16 September

Kirkpatrick, C. (1986) The World Bank's views on state-owned enterprises in less developed countries: a critical comment. Rivista Internazionale di Scienze Economiche e Commerciali, 33 (6-7), 685-96

—— N. Lee and F. Nixson (1984) Industrial structure and policy in less developed countries. George Allen and Unwin, London

Mansoor, A. (1988) The fiscal impact of privatisation. In P. Cook and C. Kirkpatrick (eds), Privatisation in less developed countries, Wheatsheaf Books, Brighton

Millward, R. (1988) Measured sources of inefficiency in the performance of private and public enterprises in LDCs. In P. Cook and C. Kirkpatrick (eds), Privatisation in less developed countries, Wheatsheaf Books, Brighton

Nunnenkamp, P. (1986) State enterprises in developing countries. Intereconomics, July/August, 186-93

Short, R.P. (1984) The role of public enterprises: an international statistical comparison. In R.H. Floyd, C.S. Gray and R.P. Short, Public enterprise in mixed economies, IMF, Washington DC

World Bank (1981) Accelerating development in Sub-Saharan Africa: an agenda for action. World Bank, Washington DC

16

Inferences from the UK Privatisations and the Developing Country Context*

V. V. Ramanadham

This chapter has a dual focus: it contains inferences from the UK experience in privatisation, highlighting the ways in which certain problems have been met and its several unresolved questions; and an attempt is also made to look at the situation of developing countries in the context of each major point of inference.

To begin with, the concept of privatisation has essentially been implemented in the UK through denationalisation or transfer of a public ownership into private hands. Contracting-out has been a distant second, alongside deregulation and promotion of competition (which will be discussed below).

There are at least two reasons why, in developing countries, the concept of privatisation has to be pursued in the sense of a 'continuum' comprised of three options: ownership, organisational and operational changes. Firstly, the numbers involved are large: for example, India has more than 250 public enterprises at the central level and a much greater number at the level of the state governments; and Kenya had 234 public enterprises in 1982.[1] It would be an arduous task to push them through total denationalisation at once.[2] Secondly, several enterprises need to be prepared for denationalisation first, even where that option has been decided upon, such that their viability improves sufficiently for the flotation to be successful.

* This chapter has been prepared with UNDP funding as part of the basic working paper for the Interregional Workshop on Privatisation to be held at Templeton College, 23-27 May 1988.

There are three unique points about the case for privatisation in the UK.

(1)   A close study of the literature on public enterprise and privatisation in the UK suggests that the nationalised industries have not been assigned a significant developmental role (except for such sporadic cases as the National Enterprise Board). The 'commercial' element in their objectives has been predominant.

(2)   Similar is the conclusion in the context of their role as an income-distributional tool.

(3)   The socio-political climate on 'efficiency' has undergone a noticeable change over the last decade or two. Here is an apt, illustrative observation:

> There has been an enormous change in the content of the idea of efficiency. In the post-war era efficiency and growth had a social purpose. Through policies to promote full employment and the welfare state, the benefits of growth were meant to be widely spread. In the late 1980s profitability is the vital measure and purpose of efficiency. Companies are not in business for social purposes, they are not even in business to make products, they are in business to make profits.[3]

These factors have provided a congenial background for the implementation of privatisation in the UK. There is, in addition, the subtle conservative notion that labour in the nationalised industries holds the nation to ransom and that union power should be exorcised.[4] The Prime Minister's observation in the first week of December 1987, on the eve of the postal workers' strike threat, that if they struck, the monopoly of the Post Office would be removed, is an interesting reference in this context.

It is needless to expatiate on the point that the above factors have a different weight in the cross-section of developing countries.

A strong argument has been advanced in the UK that the government's control relationships with public enterprises have been so unsatisfactory - tending on undesirable interferences - that 'the dead hand' of Whitehall (changed into 'the itchy fingers' by R. H. Smethurst)[5] could only be removed through privatisation. The Morrisonian 'arms length' relationships have long proved unworkable[6] and came to be fashioned on lines of exigency and ad hocism from time to time.

The government-public enterprise interface in developing countries is, on the whole, far less satisfactory.[7] Whether that could be an equally powerful reason for the UK version of privatisation is a difficult question. Perhaps there is no single and simple answer. A recent official observation from Thailand has illustrative value at this point: 'Privatisation in Thailand is more about raising efficiency than transfer of ownership.'[8]

The processes of implementation of privatisation in the UK reveal a triangular conflict situation. There have been three related factors among which conflicts arose, namely:

(1) the government's anxiety to make flotation successful per se;

(2) the government's interest in raising sizeable sales proceeds; and

(3) the objective of promoting competition in the sector of operations concerned.

One may broadly categorise these, respectively, as a political objective, the Exchequer objective and the efficiency objective.

The first objective seems largely to have been achieved barring the recent Stock Exchange impacts on the British Petroleum (1987) share offer; and the privatisation wagon rolls on without deceleration. When we come to the second factor, we face problems of analysis. There is some evidence to suggest that the offer prices have been relatively low (vide the comments of the National Audit Office with reference to British Airways,[9] and the comments of the Committee of Public Accounts[10]). One can retort at hindsight; yet to the extent that there is truth in the comments, the interests of the public exchequer, i.e. the taxpayer, have been subordinated to the 'prime objective' - namely, the successful sale to the private sector. In the event 'maximisation of the proceeds of sale, while extremely important, was a secondary consideration'.[11] In addition, the Committee of Public Accounts repeatedly emphasised 'the importance of seeking a satisfactory return to the tax payer by maximising the proceeds from the sale of the company'.[12] The fact that terrific over-subscriptions have been the general rule is of some significance in this context, though it has been argued that they only reflected the high elasticity of demand for shares within a small range of pricing.

It is the third objective that is the least satisfactorily met - a point we shall consider in the next sub-section. Suffice it to note at this stage that the first two factors, along with the objective of providing a wide spread of ownership, stood in the way of an efficiency-oriented transfer of a public enterprise to the private sector.

The lessons for developing countries are as follows:

(1) there has to be clarity as to the importance of improving the marketisation of enterprise behaviour, in any scheme of divestiture; and

(2) extreme care is necessary in fixing the price at which a public enterprise is to be sold to private parties.[13] The absence of well-developed stock exchanges complicates the price-fixing decisions. The different techniques of pricing and offer of shares followed in the UK are worth a close study for adaption to local conditions.

Let us turn to the basic issue of competitive efficiency as a product of privatisation in the UK.

Competition is an extraordinarily efficient mechanism. It ensures that goods and services preferred by the consumer are delivered at the lowest economic cost. It responds constantly to changes in consumer preferences. It does not require politicians or civil servants to make it work.[14]

This observation, not from a textbook, is unexceptional, with one qualification prompted by the UK experience - namely, provided enough competition follows. It has not followed yet,[15] with minor exceptions (in bus transport - and even here, certainly not fully).[16] The broad reasons are as follows:

(1) Privatisation has left the pre-privatisation sizes and monolithic organisations undisturbed - for example, British Telecom, British Gas and British Airways. Even BAA PLC remains just as large as a single 'holding' complex; and attempts are now being made to explore ways of introducing some degree of competition (for example, through Mercury Communications having just won the right to compete with British Telecom in pay-phone business).

(2) The 'innocent barriers' as well as the 'strategic barriers' to competition and entry are proving real, even in bus transport dominated by National Express in many areas.

(3) The major enterprises have been privatised as single entities so as to attract public interest in the flotation of a potential monopoly and also to avoid attitudinal confrontation with the top management of the enterprises who little liked the parcelling out of an empire. The latter factor has attracted the description of being 'the self-interested influence of nationalised industry management.[17]

No wonder public complaints against some of the privatised enterprises have been so loud and frequent that measures at the level of control and regulation are being resorted to - a point to be discussed in the next sub-section.

There are several points of interest for developing countries in this area:

(a) On grounds of economies of scale the intrinsic scope for introducing competition in many sectors of privatisable activity may be more limited than in the UK.

(b) Constraints on entry and exit are likely to be more severe. It is possible that, in extreme cases, there might be a wasteful loss of resources introduced into a sector, with doubtful allocational or productive efficiency.

(c) Technical skills in establishing the logicality of a contemplated break-up of a gigantic enterprise (for example, electricity board or a heavy electricals corporation) are not likely to be sufficiently abundant and conclusive.

However, a basic decision would be necessary as to which goods currently produced by public enterprises could be shifted to the discipline of market forces without a disadvantage.

Since competition, the engine of efficiency, is still to roll off by itself, a progressively growing complement (or surrogate in a partial sense) has been in evidence in the shape of public control of regulation - for example, OFGAS in the case of British Gas, OFTEL for British Telecom, CAA for BAA PLC and the Office of Fair Trading (OFT) and the Monopolies and Mergers Commission (MMC) for all. Its major preoccupation tends to be to devise instruments of control that limit the disadvantages that result from the absence of competition. The November 1987 reference of British Gas by the OFT to the MMC illustrates the issues:

The lack of a clear basis for different contracts and of a clear relationship to changes in the price of alternative fuels or British Gas's own costs;

The wide differences in prices said to be paid by customers with similar requirements;

Contracts were for three months or less, adding to the complaints about the difficulty of estimating costs; and

British Gas's unwillingness to quote a price for interruptible supplies until the customer had installed dual-firing equipment.[18]

As new disadvantages are sighted, the control framework tries to catch up, though with a time-lag and with strong-to-weak results.[19]

The recent initial approval of both the MMC and the government to a merger of British Caledonian with British Airways reflected, broadly, an acquiescense in the reduction of competition that the privatised British Airways may have faced from another UK-based enterprise, though it is true that it continues to experience international competition.

The problems posed by the limits to competition in practice in the privatised industries,[20] prompting a large edifice of eagle-eyed public regulation in the UK, are a serious issue for developing countries to ponder. They will have more sectors to deal with, and perhaps with less experience and technical skills in regulation. (In many countries there are no direct parallels to the British institutions, the OFT and the MMC). It will be long before circumstances of oligopoly give place to real competition in many more areas than in the UK. The fundamental issue is not that privatisation calls for public control, but that the needed protection to the consumer and the desired allocational efficiency in a given sector must be ensured independently of whether an enterprise is in the public or private sector. It is this question that developing countries should begin to tackle at once, without being sanguine about competitive efficiency making its sudden appearance on privatisation in every case - an appearance still awaited in the UK.

The UK privatisations are credited with promoting wide share ownership in the country. Some nine million, out of a population of about 57 million, now hold shares. It is claimed that a capital-owning democracy is evolving, with one in every five adults holding shares., A few comments would be in order.

(a) Whether the numbers will stay on, if not increase, in the course of time, after the loyalty bonus periods run out, is not clear. There have been substantial reductions in the numbers of small shareholders in some cases; for example, in British Aerospace PLC the number fell from 44,062 to 3,279 within a year after flotation, in the 0-99 shares category; from 81,558 to 12,849 in the 100-449 shares category, and so on.[21]

(b) In the aggregate, the small shareholders account for a very small percentage of the equity capital of the privatised enterprises (except for the management buy-outs). Skewness in corporate ownership, therefore, does not seem to have been forced down by privatisation.

(c) It is doubtful if owning a few shares in one or two

obviously profitable, utility-type companies, which the privatised enterprises broadly represent, is a substantial symptom of entrepreneurship on the part of the small shareholder - though, one may argue, it is a beginning.

These issues gather greater significance in developing countries, where share ownership is very highly skewed. It is said of Pakistan that all shares are held by 200 families.[22] In Kenya disenchantment has often been voiced at the reversion back to the Asians of many enterprises taken over by indigenous business men. To take an example from the developed world, Italy, it is feared that 'privatisation could lead to a further concentration of economic power in the hands of a few families'.[23] On the whole, the average small shareholder in most developing countries would be less talented in investment portfolio management, would face far higher transaction costs when selling or buying shares,[24] and might be under more frequent pressures of economic circumstances to dispose of holdings, unless the government were to step in with 'financial public enterprise' continuously to offset these problems.

A further question that developing countries may face concerns the propriety of bonus and low-price incentives on share offers during privatisation. In an economy in which the likely beneficiaries are bound to be an infinitesimal proportion of the population, doubts can arise on the macro equity of such measures.

An allied issue refers to the UK practice of concessional treatment of the workers and pensioners in the allotment of shares. This might be happening in the private sector too. There is an asymmetry, however. In the private sector, the decision for the owners is whether and what kind of benefits to concede to the workers; whereas in the case of a public enterprise it is the taxpayer's equity that is offered on soft terms (or gifted away) to the workers. This point would be of far greater substance in developing countries, where the workers in public enterprise clearly fall in far higher income brackets than the vast majority of the people - the rural, landless agricultural labour, the artisans and the considerable numbers without employment. (Thus, for example, 43 per cent of the people live below the poverty line in Nepal, and a slightly smaller number, in

India.)

Once this issue is out of the way, the UK experiment of involving a majority of the workers of a privatised enterprise as shareholders is worth emulation, though its success as a fully fledged entrepreneurial change will be limited to relatively small enterprises with high labour intensity.

The value of worker ownership of a privatised enterprise needs to be understood properly. In the UK the proportion of the workers' shareholding, on initial allotment, varied only between 0.03 per cent in the case of Enterprise Oil PLC and 4.3 per cent in Associated British Ports PLC out of the company's total equity capital. (In management buy-outs, it is of course far higher.) Their essential interest continues to be in wage benefits which far exceed the dividend on their slender share quantum. 'Against whom will they now strike?' is a rhetorical question. They did strike in British Telecom. Here again is a point to ponder for developing countries, where trade union impacts are far more complex and serious than in the UK.

The UK privatisations emphasise the importance attached to 'marketing techniques' in the sale of the enterprises. This is a wide term which also covers certain elements of substantive value. Firstly, attention has been paid to promote co-operation on the part of the management and the workers of an enterprise slated for privatisation. The National Freight Corporation 'buy-out' transaction illustrates this and emphasises the effectiveness of communication with the workers as a factor contributing to the success of the denationalisation. In almost all cases of major privatisation, the employees were offered several kinds of advantages in the context of the share offer.

Secondly, care has been taken to involve 'small' applicants, though preferential allotments - vide the BAA PLC flotation already cited; where necessary, shares were 'clawed in' from the institutional investors for the sake of 'individual' applicants; the 'loyalty bonus' was offered - a powerful attraction; and graduated payments towards the share price, yet with proportionately high dividend benefits from the beginning, were devised - for example, in the October 1987 BP share offer, and in the earlier British Gas share offer.

Thirdly, different kinds of pricing and selling channels

have been adopted so as to attract a variety of potential applicants, domestic - small and institutional - and foreign. (In the latter case, limits have been fixed in most cases.) In addition, generous underwriting terms have been offered. (The recent BP offer was a special case.)

Fourthly, advice has been taken from a number of merchant banks and the Bank of England as to the techniques of selling, the prices to be fixed, the timing of the share offer and its parcelling among major potential categories of applicants. At times the major adviser and the major underwriter happened to be the same. A potential conflict of interest may have been implicit in such an arrangement.

Finally, media publicity has been well planned and the sheer logistics of applying for shares greatly simplified. One could act easily through many of the bank and building society offices, and even borrow from them most of the money payable on application. An interesting chart covering the steps in privatisation is shown in the Appendix to this chapter.

Developing countries would gain from a close study of all these aspects, once a decision is made to denationalise an enterprise. The preparation of the prospectus is a tricky job, for it has to induce the potential applicant. It has to present facts in an atractive manner - for instance, the historic-cost data have often been used in the UK prospectuses; and it has to project prospects of good profit (in the UK, it appears that several substantive decisions have been subordinated to this interest, as argued earlier).

A major question on which the smoothness of divestitures in developing countries depends relates to the extent of foreign capital to be admitted as equity holder. Different countries seem to be adopting different stances in this regard; for example, Ivory Coast and Senegal are relatively permissive, while Mexico is relatively hesitant.[25]

Many of the privatisations in the UK seem to have been preceded by some kind of preparation. Firstly, there have been government control measures for a long time, which drove the enterprises under the rigorous impacts of market surrogates like targets, performance aims and, most prominently, external financing limits. These have, of course, not been meant as a step in the privatisation programme. Likewise, labour redundancies have been consistently reduced in enterprises marked by excessive labour - for example, British Airways; and the process has been going on in the British Steel Corporation, British Rail, and so on.

Several enterprises have been financially restructured. Capital write-offs and fresh cash injections - for example, in the case of Leyland - took place. The balance sheets thus took an attractive garb. In addition, certain ad hoc measures calculated to improve the prospect of success of privatisation have been taken. Thus, for example, in the case of British Aerospace PLC,

> the Government had been advised very strongly by its merchant bank advisers that a reduction in distributable reserves would reduce the attractiveness to the market of the company which was to be floated; it therefore decided not to require the £55m to be paid.[26]

This was the sum due to the government from that company.

Another instance is the government's offer of £47m towards the pension fund liability of the National Freight Consortium, which reduced the net cash incomes to the public exchequer from a possible £53.5m to just £6.5m: this made the 'management buy-out' straightforward.

With privatisation around the corner, the general direction of public enterprises has been towards accelerating organisational and operational changes that pushed them nearer to the market-place - a smooth path towards eventual privatisation. The Jaguar case aptly illustrates this phenomenon.[27] What happens in British Rail is also interesting. Easily separable, non-core activities like hotels and Sealink have been hived off; and many inputs are acquired across the market if in-house supply proves more expensive.[28] For about two years prior to privatisation, BAA PLC was engaged in internal changes that decentralised operating behaviour and introduced the element of least-cost acquisition of inputs. And so on. It should also be noted that the government has refrained from using the public enterprises as tools of social policy.

There are several lessons here for developing countries. Their public enterprise portfolio is so heterogeneous, in point of technical efficiency, profit efficiency, accumulated losses and employee motivation that far-reaching restructuring would be necessary in most cases. This would be advisable, irrespective of a decision on divestiture; and it would amount to the implementation of the non-ownership modalities of privatisation.

The privatisation programme is likely to take a long time in developing countries which have hundreds of public enterprises; and in several cases the non-ownership options would remain the more practicable ones in the immediate context. Recent changes in the organisational structures in Argentina[29] and actual additions to public enterprise investments in Brazil[30] 'with private sector investment remaining sluggish' evidence the point.

Pre-divestiture preparation would confer on developing countries a visible shield against the loose suspicion that a sale price has been not only a distress price but one that was deliberately manipulated to suit a potential buyer. Unlike in the UK, where many of the major privatisations related to enterprises making profits, especially since 1980, large numbers in developing countries have an unenviable financial record and can easily attract the suspicion.

It would be purposeful for developing countries to infer from the UK experience that several substantive changes, which matter on grounds of efficiency improvement and have been brought about after privatisation, did not in fact need privatisation as a pre-condition: for example, the alteration of the monolithic BAA into a holding-company structure, the introduction of 'market versus in-house' decisions on input acquisition and the involvement in foreign business transactions. With minor changes in the Act in some cases and none in others, these could have been achieved in the pre-privatisation regime. The lesson is, therefore, that a developing country does not have to assume that certain desirable marketising changes are only possible through divestiture and need not wait for divestiture before introducing such changes. In converse, it is not automatic that privatisation will bring about all desirable marketing changes, as the UK experience again suggests.

Brief reference needs to be made to the unique price control technique that the UK privatisations have adopted. An 'RPI minus X' formula has been preferred to a system of profit control (through which prices may be assumed to be under control). Briefly, it takes the given price structure for granted and permits of changes in line with the retail price index, but to a smaller extent as set by the 'X factor'. The 'X factor' implies that improved productivity or cost economy should keep the price rise below the RPI trend. This attractive formula has several qualifications, into which we do not propose to go at this point.[31]

In view of its wide use in the UK and claims of superiority over the 'fair rate of return' approach in America, it is worthwhile for developing countries to look deeply into the formula for its applicability to their conditions. Firstly, a fundamental asymmetry in the situation arises from the fact that the pre-privatisation price level in the UK has been the product of years of target setting and financial restructuring exercises. Neither of these has been extensively, or at all, undertaken in developing countries. Secondly, the price-and-output conditions of nationalised industries in the UK have, for about a decade now, been under MMC investigations, the like of which have been lacking in developing countries. Thirdly, developing countries have far less knowledge than the UK on the order of investments that each of the many privatisable enterprises will need in the near future. The permissible price level, it may be appreciated, has eventually to be a function of the permissible investment returns.

The major privatisation measures in the UK, involving public enterprises, called for the initial legal step of conversion into the company form with an equity structure. The flotation then followed; and where a special regulatory apparatus was felt necessary, provision was made for it in the privatising legislation. Several matters, including the 'Special Share' were left to the articles of association, with which Parliament would not be concerned while passing the Act.

In so far as the public corporations in developing countries are concerned, the legal step, first of all, would have to be similar, so as to fit a public enterprise into the private sector corporate format and free it from the specific provisions for government control contained in the Corporation Act. However, many of their public enterprises are already in the company form. What may, therefore, be necessary in their case will be to pass an overall Act, dealing with cross-sectional questions like:

(a) the extent of shareholding that a single shareholder is permitted to hold;

(b) the extent of any government shareholding;

(c) any version of the UK's 'Special Share';

(d) the limits of foreign ownership;

(e) any special forms of accountability to the consumer or the public either over a transitory period or all along - for example, in the case of electricity supply; and

(f) any deviations from the provisions of the Companies Act, for a transitory period or for a far longer period. Ideally, these should be minimised.

The Act may have schedules (differently under these different heads), listing the companies to which a provision applies; and the minister may be allowed to make changes from time to time and lay a statement before Parliament. In this way issues that tend to be of a policy nature in developing countries would rightly attract Parliament's attention.

In conclusion, what lessons does the UK experience offer developing countries with reference to the concept of comparative advantage as the basic guideline on privatisation? In the UK the nationalised industries have been seen as organisations meant predominantly for commercial or profit efficiency; and on this ground conclusions on their prior image have been so popular that detailed appraisals of their comparative advantage did not appear necessary. Such a view naturally gained strength from the Conservative Party's conviction that private enterprise is more efficient.

The decisional process cannot be equally simple in developing countries - let alone those countries whose socio-political system necessitates the continuance of a major part of the economy remaining in the public sector. Even for the other, more flexible mixed economies, there will be a need to apply the concept of 'comparative advantage' before deciding on divestiture or denationalisation. The reasons may be presented in the following terms. Firstly, many of the public enterprises have a 'public' element in them;[32] and their efficiency has to be judged in socio-economic terms.

Developing Country Context

The comparative advantage lost or retained by a given enterprise is to be understood as the 'social' comparative advantage.

Secondly, this has to be judged after allowing for the organisational and operational measures of marketisation which are possible in a country's circumstances. In other words, the present state of losses of an enterprise cannot invariably be taken as reflecting its intrinsic loss of comparative advantage.

Thirdly, the numbers involved are so large that even a divestiture decision has to be worked out within a time-frame which may extend over a long period in many countries - perhaps 20 years. The timetable itself calls for the identification of the priorities of candidature for denation-alisation. Once again the determining factor should be the extent of loss of comparative advantage.

Finally, unlike in the UK, the nature of success of private enterprise and its managerial culture is not conclusively established in several countries, especially the least developed, new entrants into industry. Another basic issue that complicates judgements in this respect is: how genuinely 'domestic' or indigenous is the management of large-scale industry and business in the private sector? Where value is attached to this question, the decisional weights to be introduced in evaluating the comparative advantage or otherwise of a public enterprise will be correspondingly influenced.

To conclude: the UK experience in privatisation is rich. The experiments have been interesting and some techniques somewhat ingenious. Privatisation has been a governmental commitment and the pace both swift and determined. The logistics have been articulated so as to make privatisation a success per se. However, it is not clear that the right answers to ensure the substantive efficiency of the privatised industries have yet been found.

A discerning study of the UK experience would be rewarding to developing countries - not on what to denationalise or for concluding that denationalisation is the only modality of privatisation - but in understanding what may be done while implementing a divestiture decision and, in some respects, what not to do, consistent with their own social ethos. In particular, it would be useful to grasp the nature of preparation that preceded a prospectus or share offer.

The UK experience suggests that, particularly in

258

developing countries, privatisation is a much harder exercise than nationalisation itself and calls for more difficult decisions than in the UK.

NOTES

1. Working Party on Government Expenditures (Nairobi, 1982).
2. For instance, The Economist Intelligence Unit observes that 'of the 150 state enterprises which have been earmarked for privatisation hardly any have commenced production under private ownership': Country Report (London), no. 4 (1987).
3. Charles Leadbeater, The policies of prosperity (Fabian Society, no. 523, London, 1987).
4. For instance, 'Public sector trade unions have been extraordinarily successful in gaining advantages for themselves in the pay hierarchy by exploiting their monopoly collective bargaining position. Herbert Morrison's dreams of employee responsibility are a caricature of the true position.' - John Moore, 'Why privatise?' (in J. Kay, C. Mayer and D. Thompson (eds), Privatisation and regulation - the U.K. experience (Clarendon Press, Oxford, 1986).
5. See John B. Heath, 'Privatisation: the case of BAA PLC' (Chapter 11, this volume); John Hatch, 'Privatisation and the consumer' (Chapter 4, this volume); and R.H. Smethurst, 'Privatisation and regulation' - all papers presented at the Seminar on Privatisation held at Templeton College, Oxford, September-December 1987.
6. See the National Economic Development Office, A study of UK nationalised industries: their role in the economy and control in the future (HMSO, London, 1976).
7. Recent evidence comes from a government-commissioned policy paper in India, which speaks of 'too many back-seat drivers' and concludes that 'greater freedom' for the public enterprises is central to reform ('Survey on India', Financial Times (London), 25 November 1987, p. xiv).
8. 'Survey on Thailand', Financial Times (London), 2 December 1987, p. 17.
9. British Airways 'may have been under-valued and under-priced when it was floated for just under £900m'. 'The opening premium of 44 pence on the partly paid price of 65 pence and 55 pence on the fully paid share of 125 pence was worth an extra £300m.' - as cited in The Times (London), 22

July 1987.

10. 'The price was over cautious. It ... seems likely that the tax payer could have benefited further from the sale.': Third Report from the Committee of Public Accounts, Session 1985-8, Sale of Government shareholding in British Telecommunications PLC (35, HMSO, London, 1985), p. xii.

11. Seventeenth Report from the Committee of Public Accounts, Session 1983-4, Sale of Government shareholdings in publicly-owned companies (443, HMSO, London, 1984), p. vi.

12. Thirty-first Report from the Committee of Public Accounts, Session 1984-5, Incorporation of Royal Ordnance Factories (417, HMSO, London, 1985), p. vii.

13. The Economist Intelligence Unit has some interesting comments on the selling and sale prices of public enterprise with reference to Guinea: 'The process within the government appears to be moving very slowly ... and offers considerable scope for corruption. The task of determining the sell-off price for these enterprises is notoriously difficult, and easily susceptible to manipulation by vested interests, both Guinean and foreign' - Country Report (London), no. 4 (1987).

14. Moore, 'Why Privatise' (1983). Speech reproduced in Kay, Mayer and Thomson 'Privatisation and Regulation in the UK Experience' (Clarendon Press, Oxford, 1986).

15. 'When the test comes, it is far from clear that the Government's free-enterprise instincts are anything like as committed to competition as they are to private enterprise.' - David Heald, 'Will the privatisation of public enterprises solve the problem of control?', Public Administration, vol. 63, no. 1.

16. See David Thompson, 'Privatisation: introducing competition opportunities and constraints', Seminar on Privatisation, Templeton College, Oxford, September-December 1987.

17. The Times (London), 22 May 1987.

18. As reported in the Financial Times (London), 26 November 1987, p. 1.

19. With reference to British Gas, it has been observed that 'the regulatory framework hardly seems adequate to control such a powerful and dominant industry': Katherine Price, 'Privatising British Gas: is the regulatory framework adequate?', Public Money, vol. 6, no. 1 (June 1986), p. 19.

20. George Gardiner, MP, observed at the Conservative Party Conference at Blackpool that 'The experience of

British Telecom and British Gas tells us never again to turn public monopolies into private ones'. - The Times (London), 7 October 1987.

21. Tenth Report of Public Accounts, Session 1981-2, Sale of shares in British Aerospace; sales of Government shareholdings in other publicly owned companies and in British Petroleum Ltd; postponement of payments (189, HMSO, London, 1982), p. 15.

22. Overseas Development Institute, Briefing Paper, September 1986.

23. 'Privatisation, Italian style', Financial Times (London), 28 September 1987.

24. Even in the UK 'private investors ... will continue facing difficulty in finding a reasonably-priced broker to carry out smaller equity transactions'. The 'minimum dealing charges' may be £20.00 - 'expensive if you have only a few hundred pounds worth of shares' - Teresa Hunter, the Guardian (London), 5 December 1987, p. 25.

25. The Economist Intelligence Unit, Country Report, Mexico (London), no. 4 (1987), p. 9.

26. Tenth Report of Public Accounts, Sale of shares in British Aerospace, p. vi.

27. David Chambers, 'Managing operations and the relevance of privatisation', Chapter 9, this volume.

28. Since the adoption of competitive tendering for example, orders for locomotives and coaches worth some £420m have been placed and the private sector has won over £200m worth of them. In addition, privately owned wagons are about 30 per cent of all wagons running on the BR system: British Railways Board, Annual Report and Accounts, 1986-7 (London, 1987), p. 9.

29. The organisational changes include the establishment of a state holding-company, which is to agree with the executive (via the Interministerial Committee) production and investment targets: The Economist Intelligence Unit, Country Report, Argentina (London), no. 1 (1987), pp. 13-14.

30. The Economist Intelligence Unit, Quarterly Economic Review of Brazil, no. 1 (1986), pp. 11-12.

31. Sre Dieteur Helm, 'RPI minus X and the newly privatised industries: a deceptively simple regulatory rule', Public Money, vol. 7, no. 1 (June 1987).

32. See V.V. Ramanandham, The nature of public enterprise (London, 1984), Part I, for a full discussion of the 'public' and the 'enterprise' elements in the concept of public enterprise.

APPENDIX: Outline of typical steps to privatisation

**Outline of Typical Steps
to Privatisation**
(Illustrative example *not* based
on a particular case)

PUBLIC CORPORATION
Governed by statute
Loan financed
Public sector style
administration
Some monopoly business

FEASIBILITY STUDY
Study undertaken by
civil servants, merchant
banks or management
consultants

BACKGROUND & OPTIONS
Report to Ministers on
possibility, options and
prerequisites of any sale

MINISTERIAL DECISION
Decision in principle to
proceed, choice of option
to be pursued.
In this example sale of the
business as one unit by
share flotation

STAGE 1

* With acknowledgements to HM Treasury

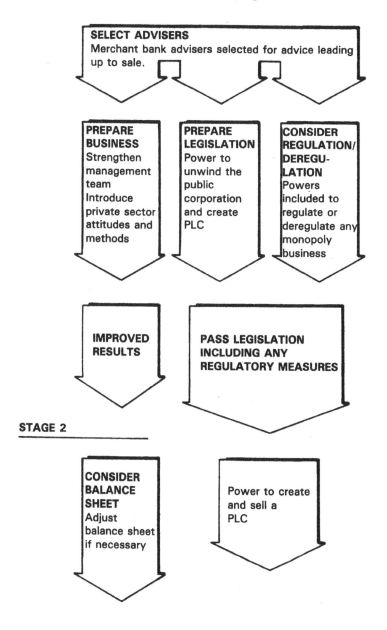

SELECT ADVISERS
Merchant bank advisers selected for advice leading up to sale.

PREPARE BUSINESS
Strengthen management team
Introduce private sector attitudes and methods

PREPARE LEGISLATION
Power to unwind the public corporation and create PLC

CONSIDER REGULATION/ DEREGU- LATION
Powers included to regulate or deregulate any monopoly business

IMPROVED RESULTS

PASS LEGISLATION INCLUDING ANY REGULATORY MEASURES

STAGE 2

CONSIDER BALANCE SHEET
Adjust balance sheet if necessary

Power to create and sell a PLC

Developing Country Context

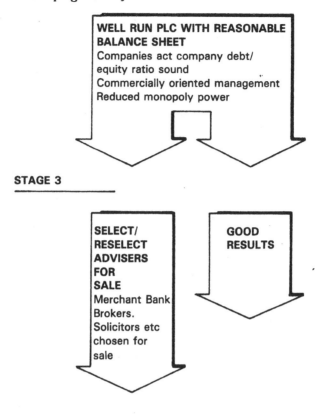

WELL RUN PLC WITH REASONABLE
BALANCE SHEET
Companies act company debt/
equity ratio sound
Commercially oriented management
Reduced monopoly power

STAGE 3

SELECT/
RESELECT
ADVISERS
FOR
SALE
Merchant Bank
Brokers.
Solicitors etc
chosen for
sale

GOOD
RESULTS

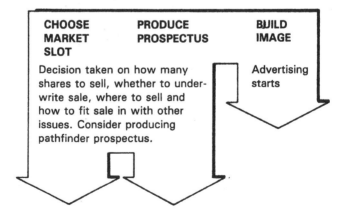

CHOOSE
MARKET
SLOT

PRODUCE
PROSPECTUS

BUILD
IMAGE

Decision taken on how many
shares to sell, whether to underwrite sale, where to sell and
how to fit sale in with other
issues. Consider producing
pathfinder prospectus.

Advertising
starts

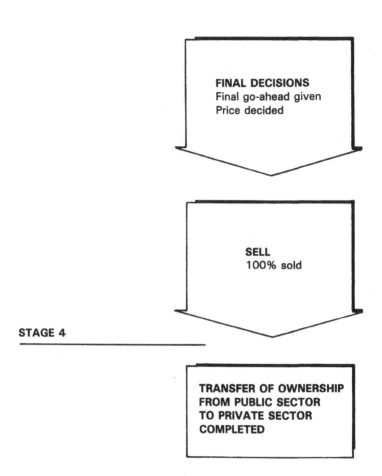

STAGE 4

Source: John Moor, <u>Privatisation in the United Kingdom,</u>
pp. 18-21.

Part V

Concluding Review

17

A Concluding Review

V.V. Ramanadham

The papers included in this volume were presented at the Seminar on Privatisation conducted at Templeton College, Oxford, September-December 1987. The objectives of the Seminar were, firstly, to bring out the analytical and empirical aspects of privatisation with extensive reference to the UK experience; Secondly, to speculate on the new problems, including those of regulation, which privatisation may raise; and thirdly to draw relevant lessons for developing countries on privatisation. The contributors, along with the discussants, constituted a purposeful mix of academics, government officials and enterprise executives. Many of them have been directly involved in the actual implementation of privatisation measures in the UK. David Thompson's observation that 'the lively discussions ... provided more thoughtful feedback than any other seminar presentation which I have given on this topic' is perhaps illustrative of the nature of the discussions that the seminar promoted.

Though all the papers drew on the UK experience, some focused on issues such as the concept and rationale of privatisation, the interests of the consumer and the employee, the managerial culture, competitive efficiency, and regulation. Some covered in cross-sectional terms, the financial and legal processes of privatisation and certain developments consistent with the broad concepts of the privatisation model; some related to specified sectors like BAA, transport, water, electricity and gas; and two papers were inferential in theme, seeking to comment on the relevance of the UK experience to developing countries.

This concluding review tries to avoid repetition of the material contained in the papers, except for unavoidable references.

A Concluding Review

THE CONCEPT OF AND RATIONALE FOR PRIVATISATION

The discussions on the concept of privatisation brought out the large variety of ideas that it conveyed and emphasised that the essence of privatisation lay in the 're-marketisation' of operations, the functional theme emphasised by Ramanadham. On this criterion doubts were raised as to how far every ownership change implemented in the UK was accompanied by freedom or perfection in capital markets, labour markets and product markets. The one thing that was certain was that the profits would go to the private investors, and that within the constraints of public regulation, managerial behaviour would align itself to the owners' profit motivations.

Discussion on the 'continuum' concept of privatisation developed in Ramanadham's paper showed the relevance of major operational reforms such as pricing in relation to cost and cost disaggregations by major product lines, or the granting of permission to a production division to buy an input from the open market rather than be tied to internal supply, or the planning of production on grounds of cost at the margin in a multi-plant situation. Where such reforms are hard to come by through internal action, the government may have to intervene by enunciating criteria that press the enterprise into management behaviour of the market-disciplined kind. Some recent OECD surveys provide illustrations of governmental action in Portugal, for the first time, in favour of programme contracts between the government and the enterprise, target setting, management contracts for profit sharing, and so on[1] and in Spain, in favour of reconstruction or restructuring in the case of an identified group of INI enterprises.[2]

Whether the re-marketing surrogates should be external in origin is not really the important aspect of the continuum concept of privatisation. In practice, however, the major surrogates, such as decentralised organisation, the establishment of profit centres, the determination of disaggregated profit targets, closure of plants, redundancy policies, direct resort to capital markets, and liquidations, often call for either formal or informal attention, if not approval, of the government. In many countries even less major surrogates like the determination of productivity norms, the introduction of an incentive bonus for the employees and the purchase of certain inputs through the tender system, can only materialise with the acquiescence, if not clear approval, of the government.

By design, the seminar did not enter into explicit consideration of the political motivations underlying privatisation in the UK. The very concept of 'failure' of public enterprise attracted analytical attention. Perhaps in terms of profit some public enterprises may have failed but in accepting such a conclusion one overlooks the fact that there have been conscious injections of social policies into their operations. Several questions arise here. Firstly, are the policies by themselves wrong? Secondly, should public enterprise be singled out for implementing them? Thirdly, should the financial results of an enterprise exposed to the impacts of such policies be taken as an index of its failure? These questions seem to have received far too limited attention as the general conclusion that the government's relationships with public enterprises have been so unsatis-factory that privatisation would be the obvious solution gained in popularity.

The criticism that public enterprise has failed is on more valid ground in those cases in which the intended social returns themselves have not materialised, as desired, and where the trade-off between the social returns realised and the financial returns foregone is unfavourable. What is needed, then, is a reversal of government impositions which are realised to be of questionable value, not merely in terms of financial returns but in terms of social returns too. There is a slow move in this direction the world over, even if under the pressures of the IMF agreements.

Let us pursue the point. If a public enterprise is privatised, what happens to the government's pursuit of social policies relevant to its operations? They have to be implemented through the budget, unless it is decided that the social policies be abandoned. Alternatively, they should be imposed on a whole range of privatised enterprises - for example, by making an industrial licence conditional on the production of a merit good of a given size or in a specified location, or on the adoption of an input policy that favours small-scale or ancillary industrial units.

Where the government's inverventions have a deleter-ious effect on the finances of the enterprise and are not justified on social grounds, either, and the government nevertheless persists with the interventions, we may construe that there has been a severe loss of the comparative advantage of the enterprise remaining in the

271

public sector. The case for privatisation may be rationalised in this way. The seminar repeatedly brought out the point that many top executives of the nationalised industries saw in privatisation a means of freeing themselves from the 'dead hand' of Whitehall.

It looked as if some seeds of failure were sown by the very acts of nationalisation. Maurice Garner referred to the way in which extremely large and monolithic public enterprises were created in the UK and entrusted almost to the same managers as those who had been in charge beforehand. Exceptions apart, the managers of the much smaller former companies, some of whom could be considered as 'failures', were not the best-fitted to take charge of the new giants.

Furthermore, the managerial culture of most of the single-product nationalised industries has been over-biased towards the engineering aspects and adequate market orientation has been wanting. Thus, for example, not to have a 'brown-out' was a more powerful incentive for the electricity managers than to keep the excess capacity low. This partly resulted from the lack of clarity in their goal options.

The point was also made that the entrepreneurial competence of public enterprise executives had been greatly conditioned by the many market insulations they enjoyed. Privatisation could improve the situation. However, that by itself would not be a 'sufficient' answer to the problems. Market forces ought to play an effective role in the privatised sector; and in their absence the right kind of regulatory framework had to be evolved.

THE CONSUMER, THE EMPLOYEE AND THE MANAGER

The seminar considered the results of privatisation from the angle of the consumer, the employee and the managerial culture.

The discussions that followed several of the present-ations emphasised that the benefits of privatisation to the consumer lay essentially in the competition that it introduced - for competition would offer the fruits of efficiency in operations, provide choice of product, stimulate a downward push in costs, and lead to price reductions.

'Everybody is a sudden believer in competition',

observed John Hatch; and he went on to draw a logical picture of how competition could not be very meaningful in electricity distribution, nor in the generation activity, though it was possible to introduce it in the construction of generating stations. Even here the disintegration of the Central Electricity Generating Board (CEGB) into some five regional units might, initially, have to reckon with imperfections in the high-skilled managerial market. If, however, a device were found whereby the capital costs of generating stations could be kept low for a planned size of output, the benefit to the consumer would be considerable, considering that this is a highly capital-intensive industry.

One might contend that, had competition prevailed in the field of generation, the situation of CEGB's excess capacity created in the 1960s could have been avoided. This point calls for further analysis. It is in the nature of public enterprise in an infra-structural field to 'err' on the side of excess capacity so as not to limit the conditions for economic development which significantly depends on it. On the other hand, by and large, private enterprise continuously limits itself to creating capacity that has a reasonable chance of being nearly fully utilised. This might condition economic development that calls for a plentiful supply of power. In either case there is a cost to the consumer. What is essential is an accurate demand forecasting, followed by the necessary investments, such that neither costs of excess capacity nor costs of under-supply would harm the consumer's interests. If privatisation ensures this condition more certainly than public enterprise, it would clearly be to the consumer's advantage. Whether it will depends on how effective competition can be in practice in the field of generation.

The uneconomical but job-creating advanced gas-cooled reactor technology of the CEGB suggests that the interests of the workers clashed with those of the consumers; and the latter suffered because of the monopoly characteristics of the organisation. The lesson emerges, again, that to the extent that a privatised organisation does not find itself exposed to effective competition, a similar shift of benefits from the consumer to the worker can repeat itself.

Another instance of adversity to consumer interest was cited with reference to the heavy subsidy that the electricity-supply industry offered to the National Coal Board.

It is difficult to say whether privatisation immediately

relieves the consumer of this burden, unless the government then prefers to bear it as a direct charge on the budget or unless coal imports at lower prices are permitted and take place continuously. If national interests or any other factors limit the imports, market forces will keep British coal prices correspondingly high and the electricity consumer will have to treat them as an unavoidable input cost.

In the course of the discussions on consumer interest with specific reference to electricity prices, two issues came up for special notice. Firstly, how high could self-financing be permitted to be on the part of the electricity supply enterprise(s)? The higher this quantum, even if in the name of the long-run marginal cost, the heavier the current burdens on the consumer. The problem is basically the same whether the enterprise is in the public or in the private sector, except that in the former case the consumer's disadvantage turns out to benefit the taxpayer, whereas in the latter it helps the private shareholder.

Secondly, how far do the benefits of improved productivity realised from time to time reach the consumer? There can be a tendency for their disproportion-ate shift to the workers and/or the shareholders. It is true that the 'RPI minus X' formula obliges the enterprise to offer some benefit of improved productivity to the consumer. However, non-rising prices can produce the deceptive impression that the consumer's interest is not endangered; whereas in reality, the situation might be one in which the costs are lowered but the prices are not. The situation will change in favour of the consumer if effective competition prevails.

The limited experience that privatised telecommunic-ations and gas enterprises provided encouraged the discussants to argue that the consumer should be 'compens-ated' properly for poor service at the hands of a privatised enterprise. 'Rebates' in bills or 'presents' should be mandatory in proven cases of consumer hardship in terms of quality of output or service in its manifold senses.

There is a basic aspect of the privatisation modalities in the UK, which has an in-built disadvantage to the consumer. The emphasis on making the sale of an enterprise successful seems to have had an influence in keeping large monopolies from being broken into potentially competitive units. Moreover, public monopolies have become private monopolies - a thought for the consumer to ponder.

There is an issue of long-term relevance to the

consumer. In the UK, in healthy contrast to many other economies with large public enterprise sectors, some progress has been made in the direction of formulating performance indicators and publishing them in the annual reports of the enterprises. Whether interest continues in improving that technique, it is rather too early to say. There might be some contraction in the availability of such information on the grounds that it is 'sensitive'.

As regards the employee interest under privatisation, the seminar recognised that labour in privatised industries experienced a somewhat different scenario from what used to obtain in the public enterprise regime. It is far from clear, however, that the changes are entirely due to the mere fact of privatisation. Even in the enterprises not privatised, labour has been having a tough time in the UK. The general climate for negotiations with management has fundamentally changed; and redundancies have been tackled rigorously in the interest of improving the productivity and the commercial results of the enterprises. In fact, treatment of redundancies has been a long process in the nationalised industries sector.

While it is true that the statutory strength behind union negotiations in the case of a public corporation has disappeared after privatisation, the tendency to roll back trade unionism as such is perceptible in such nationalised industries as British Rail. The 'single channel communication', emphasised at one time, has been giving way to decentralised dealings with labour. The concept of 'participation' is shifting from union participation to labour participation outside of the trade unions. These changes should be traced more to overall changes in the labour markets than to the phenomenon of privatisation. To cite an example, the British Transport Hotels' attitude to trade unions is not so much a product of the privatisation of the hotels hived off from British Rail as a characteristic of how the hotel industry in the country behaves.

On the role of the worker as a shareholder - a feature of most privatisations - discussions suggested that:

(1) the capital holding is extremely small - except in a stray National Freight Consortium;

(2) the continued interest of the worker in holding on to the shares in his or her own company can only be judged after the period of the loyalty bonus; and

(3) when a conflict arises between the wage interest

and the dividend prospect, the former would be his or her dominant concern. The 1987 strike in British Telecom evidenced a strike by shareholder-workers.

From the angle of theory, what seems to cause a decline in the privileged position of the worker is not privatisation as such, but the competition which accompanies privatisation. Where it does not, as in the case of British Gas, the decline may not be significant, and the interests of the investor and the worker might be in gentle collusion, as against the consumer.

The seminar brought out several interesting points concerning managers and managerial culture in the context of privatisation. Nick Woodward's presentation provided a useful scenario on the 'cultural' implications of privatisation. Over the long run the managerial culture in a privatised enterprise may level with that in the cross-section of private enterprise. However, there is likely to be a learning time, which depends on many factors.

One of these relates to the monopoly characteristics that continue to be retained by a privatised enterprise. It might be long before spectacular differences in its managerial behaviour present themselves, either in terms of intra-enterprise relationships - i.e., manager-worker and personnel relationships, or in terms of the enterprise-consumer interface. Ceteris paribus, the absence of effective competition, even if some token competition seems to exist, helps dampen and delay the emergence of new trends in the way in which managers are impelled to behave; for by hypothesis, market forces tend to be too weak in triggering drastic changes in managerial culture. In this connection, it is of interest to note that where the pressures of competition, in whatever way, are real, even the industries that remain nationalised are already presenting features of evolution of a new managerial culture.

The same logic suggests postulating that, if limits to consumer's choice continue to prevail, they correspondingly help to maintain whatever mutual relations existed as between the managers, whose thrust for improved productivity and cost reductions might be work, and the workers who would seek to enjoy the benefits of monopoly. It is where competition becomes virile - as perhaps only in bus transport privatisation so far in the UK - that the attitudes of labour and the strategy of managerial behaviour will undergo a perceptible change. Even managerial decentral-isation would depend on how far the chief executive and the other top managers would wish to permit a weakening of the erstwhile 'empire' culture.

Freedom from the 'dead hand of Whitehall', came up again in the present context. This was clearly a major point of appeal that the idea of privatisation provided to many public enterprise managers. It is difficult to speculate on what precise changes the newly won freedom brings about in managerial culture. The top managers' behaviour will no doubt reshape itself into one of far greater autonomy than before; and their attitudes to the workers and to middle levels in the managerial ladder are likely to be more relaxed in the absence of inhibitions on the pursuit of commercial strategies. At the same time the 'loose hand' of regulation established under privatising legislation, along with the jurisdiction of the Monopolies and Mergers Commission, can create new problems for the enterprise, with an unpredict-able import for the enterprise culture. Will it develop an environment of battle of wits, will unco-ordinated control measures confuse the commercial environment for manager-ial behaviour, or will the enterprise develop somewhat of a defensive attitude on questions of efficiency, cost and consumer satisfaction? In other words, great relevance attaches to the question of how exactly the enterprise's relationships with regulatory agencies differ from its erstwhile interface with the government departments.

During discussions, considerable stress was laid on the related aspect of information availability for the public and the consumers. It is generally believed that most public enterprises in the UK have been persuaded, if not required, as per the White Paper (Cmnd 7131) of 1978, to publish useful performance indicators, to research into improving the indicators, and to provide everyone with the opportunity of comparing performance with aims or expectations. At the minimum, they could be a starting-point for exploring how far they represented a state of efficiency, at least in physical terms. True, the indicators have not been perfect and would merit the criticism that Woodward offered; yet they did evolve in the enterprise management an attitude of not only having to inform the public but appearing to be on the improvement-track from year to year in respect of their operations and in improving the usefulness of the indicators technique. Such an attitude subsumes elements of consumer orientation. Will this be in jeopardy on privatisation? In broader terms, the issue relates to how consumer-oriented privatised managers tend to behave under their particular conditions of organisation and exposure to competition.

An issue that received little attention during the discussions was how significantly privatisation would improve professional managerial culture. It is generally assumed that in developed countries public enterprises are under professional managers; and privatisation does not therefore add much to the professionalising of managerial behaviour. (Exceptions do exist: for example, the tripartite board constitutions in French public enterprises endow Civil Servants with a significant role in management; and the Austrian system of political representations on public enterprise boards could also introduce a non-professional dimension in the board behaviour.) In the public enterprises of most developing countries a significant number of board members as well as top executives - for example, chairmen-cum-managing directors - are drawn from non-professional sources and tend to behave differently from professional managers. Even if numerically they constitute a small proportion in the managerial structure, their impact potential is severe. In such a situation privatisation can help remove the weight of non-professional influences on managerial behaviour and induce the development of a managerial culture in which commercial strategy and logistics play a dominant role.

There is a special situation that merits notice. Some (major) public enterprises like post and telecommunications (in the UK) and irrigation, electricity and railways (in many countries) had departmental beginnings; and when they assumed an autonomous status the departmental culture took a long time to change. The managerial behaviour generally had an engineering and technical bias; and marketing, general management and consumer-orientation have been feeble - vide John Hatch's references to the Central Electricity Generating Board. If privatisation touches an enterprise in such a situation, it will have a long way to go before further improvements in consumer-oriented management style establish themselves indelibly. Where it is doubtful that effective competition accompanies privatisation, it would be wise for governments to look seriously into the management culture, style and structure of a potential candidate for privatisation and prepare it for certain healthy changes. Replacing an 'incompatible' (executive) chairman is one example.

Finally, there is a qualification to the initial observation that the managerial culture of a privatised enterprise will eventually reach the level of the private corporate sector. Just how eventually, we do not know: it depends on whether and how far a given privatised industry differs from the generality of private enterprises in its industry or market characteristics. Public utilities are an obvious category that distinguishes itself. In such cases the managers will be under the glare of special structures of public vigilance and regulation and, therefore, constrained to keep in mind the continuing compulsions of public accountability. In a sense the need to qualify their commercial strategies with certain elements of the 'public interest' will continue to exist, if for no other reason than to ward off public demands for de-privatisation.

EFFICIENCY AND REGULATION

Questions relating to competition in a privatised sector repeatedly attracted the attention of the seminar; and doubts were expressed on whether privatisations in the UK have so far been accompanied by effective competition in the sectors concerned.

From the efficiency point of view, the benefits of privatisation are proportional to the real strength of competition in the product and other markets. Can public policy help create it? Yes, to some extent, if the enterprise is restructured into smaller but economical units before or during privatisation. In this way an important cause of 'innocent barriers' to competition or entry can be controlled. Where such a measure is not taken or is ineffective in practice, even as David Thompson's comments on the 'National Express' case suggest, the only option available for public policy is to exercise control in such a way as to limit the impacts of the 'strategic barriers' to entry practised by the incumbent. In this way the benefits of deregulation can unfold themselves. Where entry is too difficult in practice, and the argument of contestable markets proves rather theoretical, what we need, eventually, is monopoly regulation.

Restructuring an enterprise before or at the point of privatisation is, therefore, of major importance. Apart from the unpalatability of such a measure in the context of making a success of the flotation, it is not very easy to decide on the sizes of units into which the enterprise may be broken without loss of technical economies. The concept of 'network' economies cannot be totally ignored either. The debate on the nature of the break-up of the CEGB illustrates the point. Proper decision-making in this respect can take time; and it may be jeopardised if the government is anxious to rush into privatisation. British Gas and British Airways illustrate the complexity of the problem of creating competition even as privatisation takes place.

An interesting aspect of hiving off the competitive non-core activities of a public enterprise into the private sector came out during the discussions. While this process provides the consumer with certain advantages, there can be an incidental consequence for the remainder of the public enterprise. The managers would lose the benefit of feedback that the competitive operations were offering in developing a market-oriented style of management.

Three questions assumed prominence in the discussions on public regulation. The first concerned the agencies of regulation. Each privatised industry has its own specialist regulatory framework like OFTEL, OFGAS and CAA. There is the Monopolies and Mergers Commission (MMC) to which references can be made by the Minister. There is also the National Audit Office which has a freelance go at the industries. The problem of a co-ordinated approach to regulation might gradually prove difficult under these conditions. The second related to the degree of expertise and influence that the MMC possessed in practice. The terms of reference are as per the Minister's determination; several issues are almost outside its purview, such as the pricing policy and the relations between the sponsoring department and the industry; and final decision on a recommendation remains a ministerial prerogative. The MMC is a small body, with relatively limited resources and is only now beginning to establish its regulatory role, the National Audit Office being a powerful 'rival'. An interesting aside also came up: whom would the MMC 'expose' - a nationalised industry in which the sponsoring department has been intervening, or a privatised industry whose merits have now been the refrain of the government's policies for eight years? Public examinations are also 'one off' exercises.

Thirdly, the claims of superiority of the 'RPI minus X' formula of price control over the profit control technique (or the American 'fair rate' basis) are question-begging. This formula offers some guidance on how prices may move, despite difficulties of being perfect about the value of 'X'; but there is the fundamental problem of how (well) the initial price level (or structure) is arrived at. It does have to have a relationship with the return on capital employed, in whatever manner it is considered as an item recoverable from the price. The permissible quantum of self-financing has also to be built into it, in whatever manner, and perhaps differently from industry to industry. Major structural changes that overtake an industry from time to time call for a review of the capital used and necessary under the circumstances of technology and markets encountered. The accumulated needs of investment, as in the water sector, also call for special attention while deciding on the price structures and, implicitly, on the issue of returns on capital employed. On all these considerations, it is too simplistic to be sanguine about the 'RPI minus X' formula as the last word. Its chief merit lies in emphasising productivity improvement as a qualification to price increases.

The thought lingered in the minds of many discussants that privatisation, which has brought about an ownership change, did not put an end to public involvement in regulating the conduct of the privatised industries.

THE PROCESSES OF PRIVATISATION

The aim of making a financial success of a privatisation measure appeared to be dominant in the UK. If the government or the taxpayer wishes to derive the maximum financial gain from the transaction, the appeal of the share offer might turn out to be limited. If adequate subscription for the share offer were to be ensured, there could be a tendency towards compromising with a desired and publicised goal of privatisation - namely, the promotion of competition. The view was widely held among the discussants that the organisational structure and the monopoly characteristics of the enterprises were not sufficiently altered to ensure the best interest of the consumer.

Another conflict was implicit in the privatisation process. An assurance of full sale of shares almost required large allotments to bulk holders (namely, institutions like pension funds and investment houses), compromising with the ideal of promoting very wide ownership by individuals.

281

A Concluding Review

(Management buy-outs such as the National Freight Consortium constituted an exception.) The question was raised as to how far the buying of an equity by 'small' holders, who might have preferred a risk-free loan, would turn out to be in their eventual interest. Fortunately, most of the major privatisation shares - for example, British Telecom, British Gas and BAA PLC - belong to the utility category, and enjoy a reasonable degree of stability of demand, have been profitable, continue to maintain their monopoly structures, and have been sold at relatively low prices, considering their asset values and earning power. The real test for the small shareholder comes with enterprises that widely differ from this scenario - a highly realistic prospect in many countries.

The recent experience with the British Petroleum share offer (in October 1987) prompted the view that the intrinsic problems of pricing in a 'secondary' sale called for a clearer understanding than has been permitted by the overwhelming circumstance of the Stock Exchange crash in mid-October 1987. The latter may have rendered inactive the potential stock market reactions of the then existing shares to the very favourable terms attached to the secondary issue, which in their turn might have produced the effect of restrained interest in the issue on the part of the potential subscribers. Does this line of thinking place a premium on the advisability of effecting privatisation through a one-offer technique; or does it recommend a more restrained generosity in the terms of a 'secondary' offer?

On the whole, the seminar looked at privatisation sales essentially from the angle of pricing techniques and making a success of privatisation, but did not extend to a consideration of the relative interests of the parties concerned from the angle of income and wealth distribution - most importantly, the question of selling off 'the family silver'. At one stage Gerry Grimstone threw in a brief hint that the sale of the profitable nationalised industries in the UK was in fact to the long term advantage of the public Exchequer itself; but the discussants did not have the requisite data to pursue the point.

Referring to the company structure of a privatised enterprise, the seminar thought that it was too early to speculate on how the relative spheres of influence on the part of the shareholders and the managers would work themselves out in the course of time. The shareholders are the owners and the ultimate arbiters under the law, but if the powerful top managers slowed down healthy changes in the managerial culture, the boasted millions of shareholders might find themselves in a relatively weak position. Restrictions on block holding, for example, beyond 15 per cent of total equity, are good in one sense but make concerted shareholder control correspondingly feeble. To whom would the managers be really accountable - of course, to shareholders in formal terms.

The discussions on the financial aspects of privatisation brought into debate certain interesting propositions which seemed obvious on the surface, for instance, that the introduction of 'debt' capital in British Gas would create an incentive for efficiency. The incentive might not be of particular significance in the case of an enterprise whose profitability was almost certain to be so high that meeting the interest (or debt-servicing) obligation posed no problem at all. Another proposition is that what matters in the case of a public enterprise is the rate of return, whereas it is the market valuation that matters in the case of a privatised enterprise. The latter, it is assumed, looks at the future earning capacity of the enterprise, whereas the former is a historical fact. While it is true that market valuation is not important for a public enterprise totally owned by the government, the rate of return is not without relevance for market valuation, for it reflects the track record of the enterprise and its management and ordinarily constitutes a backdrop for potential investors.

A variety of views were expressed on the notion of accountability of a privatised enterprise to shareholders. The very fact that the management has to face a large 'crowd', as against the single shareholder of a public enterprise, is of some importance in this context. In substance, do the shareholders have a short-term interest, namely, in current dividends, or the long-term interest of the enterprise ranging over consumer satisfaction and the 'public interest'? These latter interests are more explicitly vested in regulatory agencies and in the 'special share', if any, in the case of a privatised enterprise.

An interesting aspect of the price-profit area came up for oblique reference. If a privatised enterprise adopted accounting policies that understated profits, the 'RPI minus X' formula does not raise one's eyebrows by itself, though the real fact is that behind an apparently reasonable price structure, there occurs a little-noticed accumulation of profit and capital appreciation. Perhaps such matters would be considered in the quinquennial investigations by the MMC. The point remains, however, that the price formula cannot be neutral to the concept of the permissible profit level.

An interesting presentation of the success story of Jaguar raised several points of relevance to privatisation. Three causes of improvement in its financial results were obvious: firstly, a dynamic management drive, secondly, the government's unique interface with the enterprise; and thirdly, the swinging 'banner' of privatisation round the corner.

The last factor was in the nature of an accelerator. The second was of crucial importance, in that it consisted not only of the government refraining from the kind of interferences earlier practised (in the name of macro objectives) but of positive action which took at least three major forms - namely, the financial restructuring including capital write-offs, the injections of cash (£100 million as cited in David Chamber's chapter), and the disintegration of the Jaguar unit from the Leyland giant. The first factor was, of course, what facilitated commercial progress, given the environment of the other two factors.

In broader perspective, the question arises as to whether the second factor, without reference to the third or in total absence of the likelihood of privatisation in a given case, would be enough to produce the improved results, given the first - namely, a dynamic management. If competition or contestability were a real possibility to reckon with, perhaps it would. In fact, that should be the essence of the privatisation measure itself.

The concept of 'potential market value', emphasised by David Chambers, appears to coincide with a definitive denationalisation option. However, where privatisation takes other versions - and there can be real need for them in several countries - the concept can well be the old and familiar 'profitability', which, in fact, is an important element in the market evaluation of the enterprise. Where the shares are not quoted on the stock exchange or where there is no share capital in the case of an enterprise, insistence on profitability, through targets or whatever other tool, has to be a genuine goal. Proper provision should be made for any constraining social objectives.

An indisputable value of the Jaguar case is that it not only emphasises the relevance of preparing an enterprise for privatisation but indicates certain crucial logistics of doing so.

THE SECTORS

The seminar specifically covered a few sectors of activity - BAA, bus transport, and gas, already privatised; and water and electricity, which still remain in the public sector.

BAA PLC

Among the points worth highlighting from the BAA privatisation experience, both for a full understanding of it and for drawing generalised inferences, the foremost seemed to be the elaborate preparation that went into the measure. It included the White Paper on airline competition policy and the massive report by Inspector Graham Eyres on Heathrow and Stansted in 1984, the 1985 White Paper on airports policy, the extensive preparations on the side of BAA itself, and the meticulous, though apparently slow, legislative process that culminated in an Act double the size of the original Bill.

It was clear from the discussion that despite the preparations, valid questions of substance remain. John Heath's references to the importance of the political factor and of the person at the helm of BAA merit appreciation while analysing the question. The questions that the Heath paper stimulated belonged to three categories. Firstly, what are the changes in BAA's organisational approach and operations that did not really require privatisation as practised? Trimming the head office, for example, would not have been impossible on BAA's own volition. The market forces introduced into the input choices of the airports through the formation of British Airport Services Ltd out of the earlier 'Group Services' could have been ensured through internal organisational reforms.

As for the claim that diversification of activities has been made possible by privatisation, there is no reason to assume that the non-airport activities 'from which the BAA as a nationalised industry has been excluded' (the 1985 White Paper, p. 44) could not have been brought within BAA's purview by an amendment to the Act. Overseas business activities which, though unsuccessfully, were carried out through British Airports International, also illustrate the point. These activity extensions were not, strictly speaking, conditional on privatisation in the sense of total ownership divestment by the government, though privatisation certainly triggered them. However, they called for financial resources which the PSBR might have rendered difficult; and more importantly, 'public enterprise culture' might have stood in the way of looking out for new risks, which could be considered by critics as involving the utilisation of scarce resources for non-airport or non-domestic purposes.

The second category of questions concerned the elements of substance that probably did not undergo a significant change consequent on privatisation. A major structural change did take place - namely, the conversion of each of the seven airports into an independent company. While there is no reason why this could not have been effected without ownership privatisation, elements of natural monopoly continue to exist, and the contemplated measures of public regulation imply a regard for the concept of the continuing benefits of a large seven-airport unification, which, for example, eliminates 'undesirable rigidity' in the 'administration of Government policy for route licensing and traffic distribution, and for airport development' (ibid., p. 45). Furthermore, the White Paper suggests that for 'efficiency gains' not to be jeopardised the four individual Scottish airports needed to be tied into a sub-holding level below BAA PLC.

The next category of question is, in a sense, a logical extension of the previous one and is more fundamental: how far do privatisation as adopted and the organisational structure of BAA PLC contain elements of cross-subsidisation? Is cross-subsidy 'inhibited' by the technique of separate companies within BAA PLC, as claimed in the 1985 White Paper?

To start with, there is cross-subsidisation at the very level of capitalisation and ownership. The private investor has brought the shares on the strength of the apex BAA PLC's aggregate earning capacity; and the capitalisation attributed to individual airport companies in their accounts does not reflect any evaluation by the capital market. (The 96-page prospectus of BAA PLC does not include the financial statements - for example, the opening balance sheets - of the subsidiary companies. They were obviously considered unnecessary while raising capital.) Appreciation in share values, benefits of any bonus share issues and the prospects of raising capital for the purposes of a given airport in the future, will all depend on the aggregate situation of BAA PLC's finances, though one can argue that every investment decision will be characterised by very rigorous 'internal' processes of review. (Were these absent in the pre-privatisation era?)

There is then the problem of cross-subsidisation at the level of annual earnings. The effects of losses as well as relatively low profits will pass upwards on the holding-company ladder, although one can argue that each airport management will be under internal pressures to do better. Clearly, there will be transparency in the cross-subsidisation. What is not clear is whether BAA PLC is designed by public policy to be an instrument of such cross-subsidisation, or how far changes in airport prices calculated to remedy the cross-subsidisation will be considered an acceptable managerial action, as distinct from being impediments to public policy as regards traffic distribution among airports and the maintenance of a given airport at a preferred level of capacity and within a preferred range of airport prices. It is also not clear how far the contemplated 'RPI minus X' basis of price control treats a whole structure of prices at an airport such as Stansted or Prestwick, which accentuate cross-subsidisations within the BAA PLC system; and more basically, how the level of prices charged by an airport represents an excessive use of its monopoly power. The (quinquennial) reviews by the MMC might alone be the answer to these questions.

The discussions dealt extensively with the positive role that the management played in the successful passage of a public enterprise to a privatised status, as well as the managerial decentralisation that has been progressively introduced. Where does the consumer stand however? Does the privatised monopoly improve the consumer's position in respect of prices and quality of services and in respect of cross-subsidisations?

Bus transport

The session that focused on privatisation of bus transport brought out some of its rather unique features. In the first place, the National Bus Company (NBC) has been under privatisation, not through the usual method of selling a whole enterprise as a single undertaking - for example, as with British Telecom, British Gas, and the British Airports Authority - but through its disintegration into many, smaller-sized companies. Analytically this is in conformity with the economics of the bus transport industry. It is amenable to small-fleet organisations, without serious loss of scale economies; it is not capital-intensive; and technical inter-relations in the supply of services are not fundamental.

Secondly, this is perhaps the first industry-wide privatisation that has done justice to the concept of introducing competition in an area of operations dominated by a monolithic enterprise - namely, the NBC. The ease of entry, thanks to the relatively limited capital investments needed within a minimal regulatory framework, can ensure the influence of market forces on the supply of the services and on the fares.

Thirdly, bus transport privatisation was preceded by deregulation; and as John Rickard emphasised, when it came it could in fact be interpreted as a step, albeit major in size, in the direction of effectuating deregulation. Here is a significant contrast with several other (and earlier) privatisations, which have promoted a search, after the event, for the most appropriate means of introducing competition.

Fourthly, bus transport privatisation gave scope for the technique of management buy-outs (with limited discounts) - a technique that the labour-intensive industry characteristics made possible. (Here, the wage-costs could account for 'as much as two-thirds of total costs' - <u>Buses</u>, Cmnd 9300, p. 36).

A point of broader interest could be drawn from a careful understanding of the Rickard paper and discussions. Here was a privatisation (of bus transport), whose justification totally rested on the concept of comparative advantage as the most defensible basis of privatisation, as against cash in-flows to the public Exchequer or the bare fact of losses. (This point was emphasised in Ramanadham's paper with which the seminar started - see Chapter 1.) Some statistical evidence on the comparative advantage of private operations can be found in ibid.

In a proper approach to the application of the comparative advantage concept, one has to treat the contractual payment that the operators receive from local authorities for certain services as a transparent public subsidy. Even here there are two favourable points:

(1) Tender-bidding by operators for the subsidised services can ensure that the subsidy-payers' (local authorities') costs are the lowest possible; and

(2)   competitive innovations in the supply of services -
for example, minibuses with clever routing - may
elevate certain services (or routes) now in need of
revenue subsidies above the related cost level.

The other issue relates to the degree of relevance of
the UK experience in bus transport privatisation to
developing countries. Several contrasts suggest themselves.
Traffic dependence on the public bus service is far higher
than the 8 per cent of total passenger transport in the UK
(ibid., p. 26). This suggests that government policies
regarding public enterprise versus privatisation cannot take
easy risks. The needs of opening up new areas and
maintaining 'some' services on sparsely trafficked routes
would be far heavier than in the UK where only 15 per cent
of the bus-using population and 10 per cent of the total bus
passenger kilometres are rural. The extent of public
subsidies analogous to the UK features of 'revenue support',
'concessionary fare' subsidies, 'special innovation grants' and
'transitional grants for rural services', is likely to constitute
far higher proportions of the operators' total revenues than
the 38 per cent in Great Britain in 1983/84 (under the first
two heads). Herein lies potential administrative concern
regarding the transfer of funds from the Exchequer to the
operators. Most importantly, it is not certain if in many
developing countries market forces are sophisticated enough
to tilt the comparative advantage criterion in favour of
total privatisation: for history might repeat itself, in that
operators would flock to a few good routes, while leaving
the rest unserved; and what is worse, fare freedom might be
so exercised as to leave many operators, whose accounting
knowledge and business acumen are too inadequate,
bankrupt. All this would introduce instability into the bus
transport industry, apart from a wasteful use of resources
and some incidental damage to the orderly growth of small-
scale entrepreneurship.

Gas

The seminar spent some time discussing the 'RPI minus X'
formula. As noted in certain other sessions, the formula
works with some ease, once the starting-point of price is
agreed. In such cases as gas there has been a general feeling
that the profits have been relatively high; and by deduction,

the prices should be considered to have been high too. From now on the movement of gas prices will, no doubt, be linked with the RPI, insisting, however, that a part of the cost rise implicit in the movement of the RPI must be absorbed by productivity improvements, as per the 'X' factor. In the case of gas there is also the '+Y factor' which deals with the movements of actual cost of gas purchased by British Gas from other sources. This has been necessary because of the large volume of gas purchasing by British Gas; that in fact accounted for more than half of the enterprise's costs.

If future investments will not be such as to raise the unit cost, or if they will cause a decline in the unit cost, that would be noted while determining the 'X' factor from time to time. Where the future investments raise the average cost and such an increase is not adequately reflected in the RPI, a revision of the formula will become necessary. Moreover, where the trend of gas costs, independently of the future investments factors, varies widely from that in the RPI, there will be a need to make adjustments to the formula. One possibility mentioned at the seminar was that the MMC might look into this aspect once every five years.

Water

The water sector is not yet privatised in the UK, though there has been enough material, including government documents, on which to base the discussions on the leads provided in W.R. Harper's chapter. A major question that almost puzzled the seminar was: what precisely were the benefits of privatisation that could not be derived today with the same kind of public regulation as is proposed to follow privatisation? An interesting aspect of the question related to why the framework of regulations realised to be of great relevance to the water industry had not been thought of to date: for even while in the public sector, the industry intrinsically presents features that call for public regulation.

The view was expressed that, on the whole, the advantage of privatisation in this sector might at best be marginal, giving full weight to arguments relating to the day-to-day interferences from the government and the PSBR constraint. Neither of these considerations can be considered as intrinsic to public enterprise relations with governments; and several exceptions do exist in both developed and developing countries. In addition, as Harper's chapter clearly indicates, the chances of competition in the water industry are so few and the compulsions of public regulation so heavy that the marginality of benefit consequent on what will amount to a mere change in ownership calls for clear recognition.

The absence of a unified structure in the water industry seems to be a matter of some significance in the context of privatisation: for, unlike in the case of the BAA or British Telecom, the transfer of public assets to private hands will be in several bits, and not as one total enterprise. This by itself may entail problems in fixing the share prices and inviting meticulous inter-authority comparisons. That will not be all: the relative financial conditions of the different authorities vary, partly on grounds of environment, demography and the original or inherited debt position; and their needs of future investments will also be quite unequal, partly because of the varying needs of asset replacement and environment-oriented action. The prices of water will be dissimilar in different regions served by different companies and the relationship that the price bears to cost will also be quite diverse. Not that these will be new facts; but such facts will trigger far sharper criticism from the consumers than has so far been noticeable. This will substantially add to the problems of the regulatory framework which will be set up under privatisation. Incidentally, another serious question lands in the court of regulatory agencies - namely, the equity of cross-subsidisations among consumer groups in a privatised situation which does not adequately uphold market forces.

Hence, the scope for public determination of guidelines on the pricing issues will remain quite large.

Electricity

In the context of privatising the electricity supply industry the discussions emphasised that the two issues - namely, the structural changes in the industry and the nature of the regulatory framework - should be considered together ex ante.

Referring to the contractual systems canvassed as a sequel to heroic measures of vertical disintegration of generation and transmission and of a break-up of the CEGB into a few units, the seminar felt that they would throw up serious problems of technical co-ordination, which were usually dealt with efficaciously within a single organisation. The costs of such problems need to be identified and quantified and then a comparison should be made with the expected economies of competition of the generation level. If the comparison suggests a net cost economy, the consumer will benefit. Enough work has not been done on this issue nor on the possibilities of cartellisation or collusion among the few units into which the CEGB may be broken.

The superiority of the 'RPI minus X' formula over a profit control device again came in for discussion. In preferring the formula some make the easy assumption that the profit regulation approach gives an incentive for over-capitalisation. What could happen in the latter case is that capital expenditures are incurred without sticking to adequate criteria of investment meant to meet a competently made demand forecast, based on the best technology available - for, so it is assumed, any investment will be rewarded. However, 'capital necessary' concept, as against the 'capital used', takes care of this snag, assuming that it could be established with reasonable certainty. It is in the absence of such a precaution and of a machinery for probing cost efficiency that the 'fair return' principle can degenerate into an objectionable 'cost plus' formula.

An interesting point came up in the course of the discussions. As our experience with British Telecom and British Gas has already shown, the arm of regulation is extending into several micro issues - for example, the price structure as against the mere price level with which the 'RPI minus X' formula is expected to deal. The range of regulation is tending to be quite elastic; and future governments could wield it unpredictably. Would this be inhibitive of investment by a privatised industry in capital-intensive long-term projects?

Looking at the problems presented by George Yarrow, one wondered whether the best course would not be 'incremental' privatisation, for example, through insisting on 'bids' in respect of new stations from the CEGB and any others. In other words, a well-designed public interface with the electricity supply industry, capable of producing substantial economies in the operations, would be superior to a mere denationalisation with ineffective or complex regulatory structures.

LESSONS FOR DEVELOPING COUNTRIES

At several points in the discussions, references were made to the significance of the UK experience to developing countries. There was generally clear agreement on the relevance of the 'continuum' concept of privatisation enunciated by Ramanadham in the opening session (Chapter 1).

Colin Kirkpatrick's presentation of the broad range of issues concerning the most appropriate way in which privatisation could be understood in the context of developing countries served to reiterate that idea. It appeared that emphasis on the idea of reforms in the public enterprise sector, alongside liberalisation, would be purposeful as against mere insistence on denationalisation and changes in ownership.

Several arguments generally advanced in favour of privatisation came in for intensive scrutiny: for instance, how far is the poor performance of public enterprise in financial terms an acceptable plea for privatisation in the sense of an ownership change into private hands? Given the constraints on the size of output, structure of output and operations, location of investments, gestation characteristics and social preferences in the areas of prices and employment - all of which are inherent in the development strategies of most developing countries, an enterprise transferred from the public to the private sector is likely to represent about the same record of financial performance. Moreover, its burdens on the Exchequer will continue to remain, though in the open form of subsidies which will have to be offered to private entrepreneurs in compensation for the financial adversity of their operations. The prospect of a decline in costs through managerial or operational efficiency exists, no doubt, and the burdens on the Exchequer can be correspondingly lower than before; provided the theoretical assumptions underlying the efficiency of privatised enterprises in developing countries are realised. These could be so realised, if adequate competition were possible. Whether it will exist is doubtful in several Third World countries.

Public enterprise deficits in several cases have been the result of severe goal conflicts in developing countries and not necessarily a reflection of inefficiency in raising surpluses. The issue would really be not that deficits occur; but whether the government genuinely desires that deficits

293

should not occur. On grounds of budget stringency most governments do wish public enterprise deficits to be minimal, if not eliminated; yet at the same time they cannot openly give up policy preferences that stand in the way of realising such a result. To look at privatisation as a deficit-removing device is, therefore, an over-simplification of the developing-country situation.

Besides, little is known about the managerial culture of private enterprises in developing countries; and there is wide suspicion that many of them - except in a few industries like textiles - raise a profit more surely out of varying degrees of monopoly than out of efficiency in terms of technology, high productivity, resource conservation and consumer-orientation. The track record of private enterprise in technology development is itself not encouraging.

The discussants emphasised however, that non-ownership changes which gradually but surely introduced some surrogates for market forces were urgently called for; and felt that an undue emphasis on privatisation in terms of denationalisation might be counter-productive in many cases. It might even produce an unhealthy reaction.

It was noted that the term 'privatisation' was not yet the right slogan in certain developing countries, if it just meant denationalisation. There has, however, been a clear trend in thinking towards ensuring better performance in the public enterprise sector. 'Unbundling' the aggregate of operations on the part of many an enterprise through contracting-out would be a desirable means to explore, as would be the introduction of radical organisational changes in large monolithic enterprises. Such would be helpful market-oriented and 're-marketising' devices which take public enterprises on the path of the private-sector model.

Some attention was paid by the seminar to the few sporadic examples of privatisation given publicly in certain international documents. It was not clear as to how many of them might be in the nature of treating the symptoms rather than the root causes. Furthermore, one has to look at what role foreign capital has been conceded in achieving certain of these privatisations, and whether the socio-economic policies of many developing countries will permit the admission of foreign capital ownership on the large scale that privatisations, to be rapidly successful, might involve.

Applied to developing countries, the option of privatisation in ownership terms is as yet largely a Trojan horse. However, the experience of the UK, where large-scale privatisations have been undertaken with vigour, is worth serious study. A genuine appreciation of the contrasts between the UK conditions and the circumstances of developing countries is likely to shorten their learning time in pursuing the most plausible programmes of privatisation in the most feasible time-frame. The epitome on the contrasts presented by Ramanadham in Chapter 16 is purposeful from this point of view.

NOTES

1. OECD Economic Surveys, Portugal (1985/1986), pp. 26-7.
2. OECD Economic Surveys, Spain (1985/1986), p. 35.

Index

Printed in the United States
by Baker & Taylor Publisher Services